THE
KRAUS
PROJECT

THE KRAUS PROJECT

ESSAYS BY

KARL KRAUS

TRANSLATED AND ANNOTATED BY

JONATHAN FRANZEN

WITH ASSISTANCE

AND ADDITIONAL NOTES FROM

PAUL REITTER AND DANIEL KEHLMANN

A BILINGUAL EDITION

FOURTH ESTATE • *London*

Fourth Estate
An imprint of HarperCollins*Publishers*
77–85 Fulham Palace Road,
Hammersmith, London W6 8JB
www.4thestate.co.uk

First published in Great Britain by Fourth Estate in 2013

Simultaneously published in the US by Farrar, Straus and Giroux in 2013

1

The original essays and afterwords in this volume are from Karl Kraus's
collection *Untergang der Welt durch schwarze Magie*, ed. Christoph Wagenknecht
(Frankfurt am Main: Suhrkamp, 1989). "Man frage nicht . . ." appeared in
Die Fackel no. 888, October 1933.

A catalogue record for this book
is available from the British Library

ISBN HB 978-0-00-751743-5
ISBN TPB 978-0-00-751824-1

Designed by Abby Kagan
Hand-lettering and illustrations by Matt Buck

Printed and bound in Great Britain by
Clays Ltd, St Ives plc

MIX
Paper from
responsible sources
FSC™ C007454

TO

DORIS AVERY

AND IN MEMORY OF

GEORGE AVERY

Contents

THE KRAUS PROJECT

Heine und die Folgen

HEINE
AND THE
CONSEQUENCES[1]

1. Along with Goethe, Heinrich Heine (1797–1856) was the most famous German literary figure of the nineteenth century. He was known
not for his novels (he didn't write any) or his drama (his plays were
never much produced) or his thinking (it was deliberately unsystem-
atic) but for his lyric poetry and for the characteristic wit and irony of

his reportage and travel writing and polemics. His countrymen could all quote his witticisms (e.g., "The more I get to know people, the more I like dogs") and recite his poems (an extraordinary number of them were set to music), and his style and attitudes made him an attractive figure internationally. Although he had some of Norman Mailer's pugnacity and political ambition and talent for self-advertisement, and some of Mark Twain's quotability, his posthumous reputation probably bears better comparison with a figure like Bob Dylan than with that of any writer. To his many admirers, especially in France, Heine's flight in 1831 from German repression to Parisian "exile" was a moment of iconic significance akin to Dylan's switch to electric guitar at the Newport Folk Festival in 1965. Like Dylan, Heine was a Jew who converted to Christianity (for Heine, it was an early and humiliating career exigency), but in the eyes of his readers he remained distinctively a Jew, and the reader of this essay should keep in mind that Karl Kraus's attempted demolition of Heine's reputation was not simply an assault on a pop hero of Dylanesque stature but a salvo in the cultural wars of antisemitism and Zionism that were raging in Germany and Austria at the beginning of the twentieth century.

The non-German-speaking reader may want to know that "Heine" rhymes with "mynah."

Karl Kraus (1874–1936) was an Austrian satirist and a central figure in fin de siècle Vienna's famously rich life of the mind. From 1899 until his death, Kraus edited and published the influential magazine *Die Fackel* (*The Torch*); from 1911 onward, he was also the magazine's sole author. Although Kraus would probably have hated blogs, *Die Fackel* was like a blog that pretty much everybody who mattered in the German-speaking world, from Freud to Kafka to Walter Benjamin, found it necessary to read and have an attitude toward. In Kraus's many aphorisms, he was no less quotable than Heine—"To be sure, a dog is loyal. But why should that make it an example for us? It's loyal to man, not to other dogs."—and at the height of his popularity he drew thousands to his public readings.

In later footnotes I'll recount how I fell under Kraus's spell and undertook to translate the essay/polemic/satire/manifesto "Heine and

the Consequences," which appeared as a pamphlet in 1910 and in *Die Fackel* in 1911 and which, like much of Kraus's best work, has hitherto frightened off English translators. For now, let me just make a small plea for patience with Kraus's prose. He's hard to read in German, too—deliberately hard. He was the scourge of throwaway journalism and a stickler for the interpenetration of form and content, and to his followers (he had a cultlike following) his dense and intricately coded style formed an agreeable barrier to entry; it kept the uninitiated out. Kraus himself remarked of the critic and playwright Hermann Bahr, whom he'll be attacking here, "If he understands one sentence of the essay, I'll retract the entire thing." When I first read Kraus, I was baffled by a lot of his sentences. But as I reread him and began to figure out what he was up to, the sentences suddenly popped into clear focus, one after another, until eventually I could understand almost all of them; it was like learning a foreign language.

And Kraus *is* foreign, more so than his better-known contemporaries, because his work was so particularly tied to his own time and place—to long-forgotten controversies, to rivals now obscure, to newspapers and literary works that only scholars read anymore. And yet, paradoxically, Kraus has more to say to us in our own media-saturated, technology-crazed, apocalypse-haunted historical moment than his more accessible contemporaries now do. He himself was well aware of the paradox: he was a farseeing prophet whose work was always focused on what was right in front of him. He was, very consciously, speaking to *us*; but to be able to hear him we have to know what he was talking about. I've therefore mustered a large corps of footnotes to elucidate his topical and literary references, to offer some shortcuts to deciphering his sentences, to give an account of the angry young person I was when I first read him, and to suggest some ways in which his work might matter to the world we live in now.

Zwei Richtungen geistiger Unkultur: die Wehrlosigkeit vor dem Stoff und die Wehrlosigkeit vor der Form. Die eine erlebt in der Kunst nur das Stoffliche. Sie ist deutscher Herkunft. Die andere erlebt schon im Stoff das Künstlerische. Sie ist romanischer Herkunft. Der einen ist die Kunst ein Instrument; der andern ist das Leben ein Ornament. In welcher Hölle will der Künstler gebraten sein? Er möchte doch wohl unter den Deutschen wohnen. Denn obgleich sie die Kunst in das Patentprokrustesbett ihres Betriebs gespannt haben, so haben sie doch auch das Leben ernüchtert, und das ist ein Segen: Phantasie gewinnt, und in die öden Fensterhöhlen stelle jeder sein eigenes Licht. Nur

Two strains of intellectual vulgarity: defenselessness against content and defenselessness against form. The one experiences only the material side of art. It is of German origin. The other experiences even the rawest of materials artistically. It is of Romance origin. To the one, art is an instrument; to the other, life is an ornament. In which hell would the artist prefer to fry? He'd surely still rather live among the Germans. For although they've strapped art into the Procrustean Folding Bed of their commerce, they've also made life sober, and this is a blessing: fantasy thrives, and every man can put his own light in the barren window frames.[2] Just spare me the pretty ribbons! Spare me this

2. In the dichotomy of "Romance" versus "German," which runs throughout this essay, "Romance" refers to "Romance language" or "Latin," particularly French or Italian.

Paul Reitter, the distinguished Kraus scholar and the author of the more learned of these footnotes, points out that the line about the "barren window frames" is taken from Schiller's poem "The Song of the Bell" ("Das Lied von der Glocke"). Kraus is constantly, and without attribution, quoting and echoing texts that would have been familiar to his audience but are mostly not familiar to foreign readers a century later.

keine Girlanden! Nicht dieser gute Geschmack, der dort drüben und dort unten das Auge erfreut und die Vorstellung belästigt. Nicht diese Melodie des Lebens, die meine Musik stört, welche sich in dem Gebrause des deutschen Werktags erst zu sich selbst

good taste that over there and down there delights the eye and irritates the imagination. Spare me this melody of life that disturbs my own music, which comes into its own only in the roaring of the German workday.[3] Spare me this universal higher level

3. Kraus's suspicion of the "melody of life" in France and Italy still has merit. His contention here—that walking down a street in Paris or Rome is an aesthetic experience in itself—is confirmed by the ongoing popularity of France and Italy as vacation destinations and by the "envy me" tone of American Francophiles and Italophiles announcing their travel plans. If you say you're taking a trip to Germany, you'd better be able to explain what specifically you're planning to do there, or else people will wonder why you're not going someplace where life is beautiful. Even now, Germany insists on content over form. If the concept of coolness had existed in Kraus's time, he might have said that Germany is uncool.

This suggests a more contemporary version of Kraus's dichotomy: Mac versus PC. Isn't the essence of the Apple product that you achieve coolness simply by virtue of owning it? It doesn't even matter what you're creating on your MacBook Air. Simply using a MacBook Air, experiencing the elegant design of its hardware and software, is a pleasure in itself, like walking down a street in Paris. Whereas, when you're working on some clunky, utilitarian PC, the only thing to enjoy is the quality of your work itself. As Kraus says of Germanic life, the PC "sobers" what you're doing; it allows you to see it unadorned. This was especially true in the years of DOS operating systems and early Windows.

One of the developments that Kraus will decry—the dolling-up of German language and culture with decorative elements imported from Romance language and culture—has a correlative in more recent editions of Windows, which borrow ever more features from Apple but still can't conceal their essential uncool Windowsness. Worse yet, in chasing after Apple elegance, they betray the old austere beauty of PC functionality. They still don't work as well as Macs do, and they're ugly by both cool and utilitarian standards.

erhebt. Nicht dieses allgemeine höhere Niveau, auf dem es so leicht ist zu beobachten, daß der Camelot in Paris mehr Grazie hat als der preußische Verleger. Glaubt mir, ihr Farbenfrohen, in Kulturen, in denen jeder Trottel Individualität besitzt, vertrotteln die Individualitäten. Und nicht diese mediokre Spitzbüberei der eigenen Dummheit vorgezogen! Und nicht das malerische Gewimmel auf einer alten Rinde Gorgonzola der verläßlichen Monotonie des weißen Sahnenkäses! Schwer verdaulich ist das Leben da und dort. Aber die romanische Diät verschönert den

---

And yet, to echo Kraus, I'd still rather live among PCs. Any chance that I might have switched to Apple was negated by the famous and long-running series of Apple ads aimed at persuading people like me to switch. The argument—that Macs are pretty, easy to use, free of bugs, unsusceptible to viruses, etc.—was eminently reasonable, but it was delivered by a personified Mac (played by the actor Justin Long) of such insufferable smugness that he made the miseries of Windows attractive by comparison. You wouldn't want to read a novel about the Mac: what would there be to say except that everything is groovy? Characters in novels need to have actual desires; and the character in the Apple ads who had desires was the PC, played by John Hodgman. His attempts to defend himself and to pass himself off as cool were funny, and he suffered, like a human being. To return to Kraus's dichotomy, I could easily imagine the PC being played by a German actor and the Mac by a Frenchman, never the other way around.

I'd be remiss if I didn't add that the concept of "cool" has been so fully coopted by the tech industries that some adjacent word like "hip" is needed to describe those online voices who proceeded to hate on Justin Long and deem John Hodgman to be the cool one. The restlessness of who or what is considered hip nowadays may be an artifact of what Marx famously identified as the "restless" nature of capitalism. One of the worst things about the Internet is that it tempts everyone to be a sophisticate—to take positions on what is hip and to consider, under

of refinement from which it's so easy to observe that the news-paper seller in Paris has more charm than the Prussian publisher. Believe me, you color-happy people, in cultures where every blockhead has individuality, individuality becomes a thing for blockheads.[4] And spare me this mediocre chicanery in place of one's own stupidity! Spare me the picturesque moil on the rind of an old Gorgonzola in place of the dependable white monotony of cream cheese! Life is hard to digest both here and there. But the Romance diet beautifies the spoilage; you swallow the

---

pain of being considered unhip, the positions that everyone else is tak-ing. Kraus may not have cared about hipness per se, but he certainly reveled in taking positions and was keenly attuned to the positions of others. He was a sophisticate, and this is one reason *Die Fackel* has a bloglike feel. Kraus spent a lot of time reading stuff he hated, so as to be able to hate it with authority.

4. You're not allowed to say things like this in America nowadays, no matter how much the billion (or is it two billion now?) "individualized" Facebook pages may make you want to say them. Kraus was known, in his day, to his many enemies, as the Great Hater. By most accounts he was a tender and generous man in his private life, with many loyal friends. But once he starts winding the stem of his polemical rhetoric, it carries him into extremely harsh registers.

("Harsh," incidentally, is a fun word to say with a slacker inflection. To be harsh is to be uncool; and in the world of coolness and uncool-ness—the high-school-cafeteria social scene of Gawker takedowns and Twitter popularity contests—the highest register that cultural crit-icism can safely reach is snark. Snark, indeed, is cool's twin sibling.)

As the essay will make clear, the individualized "blockheads" that Kraus has in mind here aren't hoi polloi. Although Kraus could sound like an elitist, and although he considered the right-wing antisemites idiotic, he wasn't in the business of denigrating the masses or lowbrow culture; the calculated difficulty of his writing wasn't a barricade against

Ekel: da beißt man an und geht drauf. Die deutsche Lebensordnung verekelt die Schönheit, und stellt uns auf die Probe: wie schaffen wir uns die Schönheit wieder? Die romanische Kultur macht jedermann zum Dichter. Da ist die Kunst keine Kunst. Und der Himmel eine Hölle.

the barbarians. It was aimed, instead, at bright and well-educated cultural authorities who embraced a phony kind of individuality—people Kraus believed ought to have known better.

It's not clear that Kraus's shrill, ex cathedra denunciations were the most effective way to change hearts and minds. But I confess to feeling some version of his disappointment when a novelist who I believe ought to have known better, Salman Rushdie, succumbs to Twitter. Or when a politically committed print magazine that I respect, *n+1*, denigrates print magazines as terminally "male," celebrates the Internet as "female," and somehow neglects to consider the Internet's accelerating pauperization of freelance writers. Or when good lefty professors who once resisted alienation—who criticized capitalism for its restless assault on every tradition and every community that gets in its way—start calling the corporatized Internet "revolutionary," happily embrace Apple computers, and persist in gushing about their virtues.

bait and go belly-up. The German regimen spoils beauty and puts us to the test: how do we re-create it? Romance culture makes every man a poet. Art's a piece of cake there. And Heaven a hell.[5]

5. Submerged in this paragraph is the implication that Vienna, which was Kraus's great subject, was an in-between case. Its language and orientation were German, but it was the co-capital of the Austro-Hungarian Empire, which was Roman Catholic and reached far into southern Europe, and it was in love with its own notion of its special, charming Viennese spirit and lifestyle. ("The streets of Vienna are paved with culture," goes one of Kraus's aphorisms. "The streets of other cities with asphalt.") To Kraus, the supposed cultural charm of Vienna amounted to a tissue of hypocrisies stretched over profound and soon-to-be-catastrophic contradictions, which he was bent on unmasking with his satire. The essay's opening paragraph may come down harder on Latin culture than on German, but Kraus was actually fond of vacationing in Italy and had some of his most romantic experiences there. For him, the place with the really dangerous disconnect between content and form was Austria, which was rapidly modernizing and industrializing while retaining early-nineteenth-century political and social models. Kraus, being a newsman manqué, was obsessed with the role of modern newspapers in papering over the contradictions. Like the Hearst papers in America, the bourgeois Viennese press had immense political and financial influence and was demonstrably corrupt. (Kraus devoted much of his early career to exposing its corruption, gleefully naming names.) Although, unlike Hearst, who created the Spanish-American War in 1898, the Viennese press never succeeded in directly starting a conflict, it profited greatly from the First World War and was instrumental in sustaining charming Viennese myths like the "hero's death" through years of mechanized slaughter. The Great War was precisely the Austrian apocalypse that Kraus had been prophesying, and he relentlessly satirized the press's complicity in it.

Vienna in 1910 was, thus, a special case. And yet you could argue that America in 2013 is a similarly special case: another weakened em-

Heinrich Heine aber hat den Deutschen die Botschaft dieses Himmels gebracht, nach dem es ihr Gemüt mit einer Sehnsucht zieht, die sich irgendwo reimen muß und die in unterirdischen Gängen direkt vom Kontor zur blauen Grotte führt. Und auf einem Seitenweg, den deutsche Männer meiden: von der Gansleber zur blauen Blume. Es mußte geschehen, daß die einen mit ihrer Sehnsucht, die andern mit ihren Sehnsüchten Heinrich Heine für den Erfüller hielten. Von einer Kultur gestimmt, die im Lebensstoff schon alle Kunst erlebt, spielt er einer Kultur auf, die von der Kunst nur den stofflichen Reiz empfängt. Seine Dichtung wirkt aus dem romanischen Lebensgefühl in die deutsche Kunstanschauung. Und in dieser Bildung bietet sie das utile

pire telling itself stories of its exceptionalism while it drifts toward apocalypse of some sort, fiscal or epidemiological, climatic-environmental or thermonuclear. Our Far Left may hate religion and think we coddle Israel, our Far Right may hate illegal immigrants and think we coddle black people, and nobody may know how the economy is supposed to work now that our manufacturing jobs have gone overseas, but the actual substance of our daily lives is total electronic distraction. We can't face the real problems; we spent a trillion dollars not really solving a problem in Iraq that wasn't really a problem; we can't even agree on how to keep health-care costs from devouring the GNP. What we can all agree to do instead is to deliver ourselves to the cool new media and technologies, to Steve Jobs and Mark Zuckerberg and Jeff Bezos, and to let them profit at our expense. Our situation looks quite a bit like Vienna's in 1910, except that newspaper technology (telephone, telegraph, the high-speed printing press) has been replaced by digital technology and Viennese charm by American coolness.

Heinrich Heine, however, has brought the Germans tidings of this Heaven, to which their heart is drawn with a longing that has to rhyme someplace and that leads in subterranean passages directly from the countinghouse to the Blue Grotto. And, on a byway that German men avoid: from chopped liver to the blue flower.[6] It was inevitable that the one with their longing and the other with their longings would consider Heinrich Heine the Fulfiller. Tuned by a culture for which the mere material of daily life suffices as a complete artistic experience, Heine provides mood music for a culture whose experience of art begins and ends with the attractions of its content.[7] His writing works from the Romance feel for life into the German conception of art.[8] In

6. From Jewry to Romanticism, is what Kraus appears to be suggesting with the final phrase. The blue flower is the mysterious central symbol of the unfinished novel *Heinrich von Ofterdingen*, by the German Romantic poet Novalis. (It's also the title of Penelope Fitzgerald's wonderful novel about Novalis.) Chopped liver is—chopped liver. We'll get into the question of Kraus's antisemitism by and by. He was Jewish himself.

7. Paul Reitter comments: "The German word rendered here variously as 'material,' 'content,' and 'subject matter' is '*Stoff*,' which looks unassuming but poses the same translation challenge as that storied source of frustration, '*Geist*.' For just as '*Geist*' can signify not simply 'spirit' or 'mind' but also a combination of those two ideas, '*Stoff*' brings together the notions 'content' and 'material' and 'subject matter,' and this means that, much of the time, none of the terms will feel quite adequate."

8. "In the spring of 1831 Heine moved from Hamburg to Paris, where he would spend nearly half his life—he died at fifty-eight, in 1856. Clearly, Heine loved the place. He loved the food; he loved the women; he loved being in an environment that was less restrictive than the one he had left. And in various ways, the city embraced Heine back: it was in Paris, not Prussia, that Heine became a celebrity. As he once quipped to a friend, if a fish were asked how it felt to be a fish in water, it would

dulci, ornamentiert sie den deutschen Zweck mit dem französischen Geist. So, in diesem übersichtlichen Nebeneinander von Form und Inhalt, worin es keinen Zwist gibt und keine Einheit, wird sie die große Erbschaft, von der der Journalismus bis zum heutigen Tage lebt, zwischen Kunst und Leben ein gefährlicher Vermittler, Parasit an beiden, Sänger, wo er nur Bote zu sein hat, meldend, wo zu singen wäre, den Zweck im Auge, wo eine Farbe brennt, zweckblind aus Freude am Malerischen, Fluch der literarischen Utilität, Geist der Utiliteratur. Das Instrument zum Ornament geworden, und so entartet, daß mit dem kunstgewerblichen Fortschritt in der täglichen Presse kaum noch jene Dekorationswut wetteifern kann, die sich an den Gebrauchsgegenständen betätigt; denn wir haben wenigstens noch nicht gehört, daß die Einbruchsinstrumente in der Wiener Werkstätte

---

surely answer, 'like Heine in Paris!' But if Heine and Paris had a kind of chemistry, his Francophilia also had its programmatic side. Through his writings as a foreign correspondent for German newspapers, as well as through such works as *The Romantic School* and *On the History of Religion and Philosophy in Germany* (both of which first appeared in French translation), Heine tried to act as a cultural mediator. What he was hoping for—and going for, too—was a synthesis of opposites: of the life-affirming 'sensualism' he associated with the French and the intellectually rigorous culture of German 'spiritualism.' Needless to say, 'Heine and the Consequences' mocks Heine's project while retaining elements of its logic." —PR

this configuration it offers the *utile dulci*, it ornaments German functionality with French spirit.[9] And so, in this easy-to-read juxtaposition of form and content, in which there is no discord and no unity, it becomes the great legacy from which journalism continues to live to this very day, a dangerous mediator between art and life, a parasite on both, a singer where it should only be a messenger, filing reports where a song would be in order, its eye too fixed on its goal to see the burning color, blinded to all goals by its pleasure in the picturesque, the bane of literary utility, the spirit of utiliterature.[10] Instrument made into ornament, and so badly degenerated that even the current mania for decorating consumer goods can scarcely keep up with the progress of applied art in the daily press; because at least we have yet to hear that the Wiener Werkstätte is manufacturing burglary tools.[11]

9. "A phrase from Horace (*Ars Poetica*), '*utile dulci*' signifies 'the practical along with the enjoyable' or 'usefulness along with pleasure.'" —PR

10. This was probably not a sentence that Kraus had to worry about Hermann Bahr understanding. It's a pure distillation of Kraus's hatred of the liberal press, and the import of its paradoxes is easier to grasp once you've read the entire paragraph.

11. "The Wiener Werkstätte—literally 'Viennese Workshop'—was an artists' association set up around an actual workshop, which was highly color-coordinated: everything in the metal department was painted red, everything in the bookbinding studio gray, everything in the carpentry shop blue, etc. Founded in 1903 by the architect Josef Hoffmann and the painter Kolo Moser, the association aimed to act on the ideals of the English workshop movement. Hoffmann and Moser wanted to produce beautiful handicrafts that people could use in their daily lives. Accordingly, the Wiener Werkstätte turned away from elaborate *Jugendstil* ornamentation and promoted instead an ethos of 'objectivity.' As Hoffmann put it, not so stirringly, at the end of the Werkstätte's manifesto, 'We stand with both feet in the real world and

erzeugt werden. Und selbst im Stil der modernsten Impressions-
journalistik verleugnet sich das Heinesche Modell nicht. Ohne
Heine kein Feuilleton. Das ist die Franzosenkrankheit, die er uns

---

need commissions.' These came in spades. The Sanatorium Purkersdorf, constructed in 1904–5, established the WW as a new force in the
world of Viennese design. Critics marveled at how the building's flat
roof and concrete and iron structure departed from the prevailing Viennese styles, and the WW soon attracted new talents to its stable—
including, for a time, Egon Schiele and Oskar Kokoschka. The latter
was one of Kraus's few allies among Viennese artists; he made his mark
by designing some of the WW's signature postcards. For Kraus,
though, the WW's program of creating art objects that were simultaneously use objects was irredeemably wrongheaded.

"I think, by the way, that a lot of Germans would accept Kraus's
opposition of uncool Germanic solidity vs. cool Romance frivolity. It's
a live value (and stereotype) in German culture, especially these days.
The debt crisis in southern Europe—along with Germany's role as the
voice of fiscal responsibility—has given the dualism a new immediacy.
Der Spiegel (the *Time* magazine of Germany) recently declared that the
"old biases" about Greeks and Italians "have returned." But even back
when the expense of rehabbing and detoxifying the former GDR was
the big economic complaint, the dualism was palpable. During my student years in Heidelberg, in the early 1990s, it was all around me. Simply to be an American was to invite people to define Germanness; and
if their pronouncements didn't turn on a point about beer consumption, or weren't of the soul-searching, Holocaust-related kind, they almost always contained elements of Kraus's opposition. Fellow students
wanted me to recognize that French theory hadn't caught on in Germany because French theorists preferred showmanship to the rigor
demanded by the German intellectual tradition. My boss at the Foot-
locker where I worked wanted me to appreciate the 'typical' functionality of the unfashionable German athletic gear that our foreign
customers hardly ever bought (this was before the rebirth of Puma and

And even in the style of the most up-to-the-minute impressionistic journalism the Heinean model does not disqualify itself.
Without Heine, no feuilleton.[12] This is the French disease he

---

Adidas as hipster attire). The dentist I went to proudly informed me:
'German fillings aren't pretty, but they hold up. That's how we do things
here.'

"It's in a similar spirit that Germans have called for more uncool-
ness. Some of them did in 2006, for example, when the German national soccer team broke with its World Cup traditions by putting hip
coaches on the sidelines and playing with plenty of finesse. The team
was fun to watch, and it did well and won applause in the German media. But for a lot of German soccer fans it just didn't seem German
enough. Of course, many Germans worship coolness, and many Germans, such as Walter Benjamin and Joachim Löw (the current German
national soccer coach), look cool even to the non-German world. As
we all know, moreover, Germans make cool things. A genealogy of successfully stylized appliances might even trace the Mac's heritage to a
German culture of design—or rather, to the very fin de siècle culture of
design whose advent Kraus is bemoaning in 'Heine and the Consequences.' For the fusing of art objects and use objects in Germany and
Austria didn't simply lead to ornamented use objects; it also resulted in
sleek, practical, proto-Jobsian coffeemakers and candleholders (go
from a Wiener Werkstätte exhibition to an Apple store, and you'll see
what I mean). Nevertheless, German history poses a challenge for
Germans who want to be cool. The lingering sense that uncoolness is a
national characteristic, and that other people (African Americans, Italians, etc.) are the naturally cool ones, makes for a self-defeating, self-
reinforcing desperation in the pursuit of coolness. Trying too hard to
be cool is, after all, very uncool." —PR
12. "The feuilleton is, as its name suggests, of French provenance. Or,
more precisely, the French journalist Julien Louis Geoffroy is the father
of the form. On January 18, 1800, Geoffroy, an editor at the Paris-
based newspaper the *Journal des Débats*, started using the space left

eingeschleppt hat. Wie leicht wird man krank in Paris! Wie lockert sich die Moral des deutschen Sprachgefühls! Die französische gibt sich jedem Filou hin. Vor der deutschen Sprache muß einer schon ein ganzer Kerl sein, um sie herumzukriegen, und dann macht sie ihm erst die Hölle heiß. Bei der französischen aber geht es glatt, mit jenem vollkommenen Mangel an Hemmung, der die Vollkommenheit einer Frau und der Mangel einer Sprache ist. Und die Himmelsleiter, die zu ihr führt, ist eine Klimax, die du im deutschen Wörterbuch findest: Geschmeichel,

over on the paper's advertising insert for his own cultural commentary: 'feuilleton' literally means 'small sheet.' The name stuck, and it continued to stick even after newspapers had begun to make the feuilleton part of their main body. Today, most major German-language newspapers still offer a feuilleton section, where, as was the case in Kraus's time, one finds reviews, essays on culture, short fiction, and travel reports, among other things."—PR

smuggled in to us.[13] How easy it is to get sick in Paris! How lax the morality of the German feel for language becomes! The French language lets every *filou* have his way with her. You have to prove yourself a man in full before the German language will give you the time of day, and that's only the beginning of the trouble you're in for. With French, though, everything goes smoothly, with that perfect lack of inhibition which is perfection in a woman and a lack in a language. And the Jacob's ladder that leads to her is a climax you'll find in the German dictionary:

13. "In 1848 Heine suffered a physical breakdown from which he never recovered. He spent the last eight years of his life in bed—his 'mattress grave,' as he called it. Although no medical evidence has ever indicated as much, Heine's condition was once thought to have resulted from syphilis. With the word *Franzosenkrankheit*, a popular term for syphilis, Kraus is alluding to—basically invoking—that idea." —PR

A good analogue here might be the "disease" of French theory that became epidemic in American English departments after 1980 and engendered several decades of jargon-choked academic criticism. Good French literary theory did for mediocre American scholars exactly what Kraus claims that Heine's breezy, neologism-coining, Frenchified German did for the latter-day journalistic hacks of Vienna: it allowed you to feel and sound smart and au courant without actually having to think for yourself. You simply turned the crank, and out came the conclusion that Western culture is imperialistic and barren. French theory was, as Kraus would have said, the most agreeable of excuses for avoiding literature itself. Mastering the theoretical jargon required some upfront effort, but applying it to defenseless literary texts was *easy*; and *easy*, with its connotation of sexual looseness, is what Kraus here is accusing the French language of being.

This is not to slight the insights of Saussure, Barthes, Foucault, Derrida, or Bourdieu, which can be powerful tools of cultural analysis, nor to deny that when I packed my suitcases for Berlin, in the fall of 1981, the books I took along were, with the exception of *Gravity's*

Geschmeide, Geschmeidig, Geschmeiß. Jeder hat bei ihr das Glück des Feuilletons. Sie ist ein Faulenzer der Gedanken. Der ebenste Kopf ist nicht einfallsicher, wenn er es mit ihr zu tun hat. Von den Sprachen bekommt man alles, denn alles ist in ihnen, was Gedanke werden kann. Die Sprache regt an und auf, wie das Weib, gibt die Lust und mit ihr den Gedanken. Aber die deutsche Sprache ist eine Gefährtin, die nur für den dichtet und denkt, der ihr Kinder machen kann. Mit keiner deutschen Hausfrau möchte man so verheiratet sein. Doch die Pariserin braucht nichts zu sagen als im entscheidenden Augenblick très joli, und man glaubt ihr alles. Sie hat den Geist im Gesicht. Und hätte ihr Partner dazu die Schönheit im Gehirn, das romanische Leben wäre nicht bloß très joli, sondern fruchtbar, nicht von

---

Rainbow, all theory. I had a dense volume of Lacan and another of Derrida, along with various Marxists and French-influenced American theorists. The world needed criticizing, and literary theory was one of the ways I intended to do it. My fiancée and I, separated by the Atlantic Ocean, proceeded to devote many pages of our early letters to practicing our theoryspeak. These pages were fun to write and all but impossible to read. What people used to say of Chinese takeout—that you were hungry again an hour after eating it—soon came to be true, for me, of literary theory. Of the dozen books I schlepped over to Berlin, *Gravity's Rainbow* was the only one I finished. By the time my fiancée was planning her midwinter visit, I was giving her a long list of novels to bring along for me.

Geschmeichel, Geschmeide, Geschmeidig, Geschmeiß.[14] Anybody and everybody can procure her services for the feuilleton. She's a lazy Susan of the mind. The most well-grounded head isn't safe from flashes of inspiration when it deals with her. We get everything from languages, because they contain everything that can become thought. Language arouses and stimulates, like a woman, brings joy and, with it, thought.[15] The German language, however, is a companion who will think and make poetry only for the man who can give her children. You wouldn't want to be married like this to any German housewife. And yet the woman of Paris need say nothing except, at the crucial moment, *très jolie*, and you'll believe anything of her. Her mind is in her face. And if her partner had beauty in his brain as well, Romance life would not

14. Flattery, trinkets, pliant, rabble: in German these are consecutive dictionary entries, and the German reader experiences a spasm of pleasure in the aptness of the sequence as Kraus here applies it. Kraus loved linguistic accidents like this and was wont to ascribe deep significance to them. When I was twenty-two, I did, too. Nowadays they seem to me a little cheap.

15. Many of Kraus's generalizations about women sound unattractive today. In the years before the First World War, he consistently portrayed men as the intellectual achievers, women as the repositories of the human capacity for sensual pleasure. About all that can be said in defense of this view is that Kraus's style depended on extreme, pithy contrasts—"A woman's sexual pleasure compares to a man's like an epic to an epigram" is one his famous aphorisms—and that he meant it nicely. Kraus liked and admired women, and his circle of friends included female intellectual achievers, the poet Else Lasker-Schüler among them, but for a long time his amorous experience was mainly with actresses. His tone changed after he fell in love with the aristocrat Sidonie Nádherný, in 1913.

Niedlichkeiten und Nippes umstellt, sondern von Taten und Monumenten.

Wenn man einem deutschen Autor nachsagt, er müsse bei den Franzosen in die Schule gegangen sein, so ist es erst dann das höchste Lob, wenn es nicht wahr ist. Denn es will besagen: er verdankt der deutschen Sprache, was die französische jedem gibt. Hier ist man noch sprachschöpferisch, wenn man dort schon mit den Kindern spielt, die hereingeschneit kamen, man weiß nicht wie. Aber seit Heinrich Heine den Trick importiert hat, ist es eine pure Fleißaufgabe, wenn deutsche Feuilletonisten nach Paris gehen, um sich Talent zu holen. Wenn einer heute wirklich nach Rhodus fährt, weil man dort besser tanzen kann,

be merely *très jolie* but fecund, ringed not by bibelots and dainties, but by deeds and monuments.[16]

If they say of a German author that he must have learned a lot from the French, this is the highest praise only if it isn't true. For it means: he's indebted to the German language for what the French gives to everybody. People here are still being linguistically creative when people over there are already playing with the children, who came blowing in, nobody knows how. But ever since Heinrich Heine imported the trick, it's been purely an exercise in diligence if a German feuilletonist goes to Paris to fetch himself some talent.[17] If somebody nowadays actually goes to Rhodes because people dance better there, he is truly an excessively

16. The German deeds and monuments Kraus has in mind are cultural—Goethe, Kant, Schopenhauer, Beethoven—and in 1910 it was fair to say that the Germans had outdone the French in lyric poetry, philosophy, and classical music. If Kraus slights France's superior novelistic achievement, ignoring Balzac and Stendhal and Flaubert (not to mention Proust, who was embarking on his grand project around this time), it's because he didn't care about novels. Literature for Kraus was poetry and drama and epigram, not epic. His favorite writers were Shakespeare and Goethe.

17. "Heine began producing literary travel reportage—that is, feuilletonistic writing—about a decade before he relocated to Paris: his *Letters from Berlin* appeared in 1822. Kraus and his earliest readers would have been aware of this fact—almost everyone who read Kraus had read Heine—and it would have prompted at least some of Kraus's readers to wonder about the status of his genealogy. Is Kraus really trying to tell the story of how the feuilleton got to Germany? Or is he doing something else?"—PR

Taking the bait of Prof. Reitter's two pedagogically flavored questions, I'll venture to say that Kraus is doing something else. The seeming weakness of the essay—a weakness advertised in its very title—is Kraus's failure to "prove" that Heine is the *cause* of bad journalistic writ-

so ist er wahrlich ein übertrieben gewissenhafter Schwindler. Das war zu Heines Zeit notwendig. Man war in Rhodus gewesen, und da glaubten sie einem den Hopser. Heute glauben sie einem Lahmen, der in Wien bleibt, den Cancan, und mancher spielt jetzt die Bratsche, dem einst kein Finger war heil. Der produktive Anteil der Entfernung vom Leser ist ja noch immer nicht zu unterschätzen, und nach wie vor ist es das fremde Milieu, was sie für Kunst halten. In den Dschungeln hat man viel Talent, und das Talent beginnt im Osten etwa bei Bukarest. Der Autor, der fremde Kostüme ausklopft, kommt dem stofflichen

---

ing in Kraus's Vienna. I think Reitter is right to suggest that at least some of Kraus's readers recognized the title as an absurd claim, deliberately exaggerated for comic effect. What Kraus seems really to be doing is combining his agon with Heine with his critique of his journalistic competitors and manufacturing a make-believe genealogy: because there's a *kinship* between the bad writing of Heine and that of his feuilletonistic successors, let's make believe that there's a direct *inheritance*. I'm put in mind of a rock-and-roll lyric by my beloved Mekons: "Call it intuition, call it luck / But we're right in all that we distrust." A satirist has to believe this in order to write with any force. Kraus distrusts Heine, he distrusts the feuilletonists, and his trust in his gut sweeps aside the need for fact-based literary-historical argument.

Reitter adds: "Kraus's genealogy is also designed to provoke. It bears an egregious resemblance to a highly influential antisemitic narrative spread by Richard Wagner, among many others: Jewish journalists ruin German *Kultur* by importing into it decadent, fraudulent foreign models."

conscientious swindler. That was still necessary in Heine's day. You'd been to Rhodes, and back here people believed that you could dance.[18] Today they'll believe that a cripple who has never left Vienna can dance the cancan, and many a person who never had a single good finger now plays the viola.[19] The profitable return on distance from the reader should never be underestimated, and foreign milieus continue to be what gets taken for art. People are very talented in the jungle, and talent begins in the East around the time you reach Bucharest.[20] The writer who knocks the dust off foreign costumes is getting at the fascination of the

18. "Kraus is playing with a proverb that was better known in his day, '*hic Rhodus, hic salta*'—here is Rhodes, here you should leap. This comes from an Aesop's fable and has to do with an athlete who purports to have executed a mighty jump on Rhodes. But since Heine himself had played with the same proverb in his poem "Plateniden," Kraus is also playing on a quotation, which he'll cite more directly later in the essay. The poem's title is a mocking reference to Count von Platen, whose feud with Heine Kraus (and these footnotes) will also take up later." —PR

19. "A lightly reworked line from one of Heine's ballads, 'The Pilgrimage to Kevlaar' ('Die Wallfahrt nach Kevlaar'). The original reads 'many a person who otherwise didn't have a single healthy finger can now play the viola.'" —PR

20. This sentence is very funny in German. I can't translate it any better, and so I have to resort, dismally, to trying to explain the humor. Kraus is again going after *easiness*—here, the ease with which foreign travel lends spice to writing. The joke is, approximately, that the jungle is fascinating to us non–jungle dwellers, and that we mistake this fascination for talent on the writer's part. Thus: people are very talented in the jungle. Kraus ridicules this phenomenon by way of contrasting himself with Heine, whose best-known prose was his travel writing and his dispatches from Paris. Although Kraus vacationed abroad and spent parts of the First World War in Switzerland, his life's work was focused ex-

Interesse von der denkbar bequemsten Seite bei. Der geistige Leser hat deshalb das denkbar stärkste Mißtrauen gegen jene Erzähler, die sich in exotischen Milieus herumtreiben. Der günstigste Fall ist noch, daß sie nicht dort waren; aber die meisten sind leider doch so geartet, daß sie wirklich eine Reise tun müssen, um etwas zu erzählen. Freilich, zwei Jahre in Paris gewesen zu sein, ist nicht nur der Vorteil solcher Habakuks, sondern ihre Bedingung. Den Flugsand der französischen Sprache, der jedem Tropf in die Hand weht, streuen sie dem deutschen Leser in die Augen. Und ihnen gelte die Umkehrung eines Wortes Nestroys,

---

clusively on Vienna, and it obviously galled him to hear foreign-traveling writers praised for their "talent." It galled him so much that he turned against the word "talent" itself; later in the essay he'll use it directly against Heine, connecting it with an absence of "character" (as Heine's rival Ludwig Börne famously had). But here I think his venom is directed more at admirers of jungle writing than at its producers. The former are perpetrating bad literary values, the latter merely making the most of such talent as they have. There is, after all, a long tradition of writers venturing overseas for material. The funniest fictional example may be the young man Otto, who, in William Gaddis's *The Recognitions*, goes to Central America in quest of the character he natively lacks, but the inverse relationship between travel and character is found in real life, too. I'm thinking of Hemingway, whose style was as strong as his range of theme was narrow (would he actually have had anything to say if he'd been forced to stay at home?), and of Faulkner, a writer of real character whose best work began after he gave up his soldier dreams and his New Orleans flaneurship and returned to Mississippi. You can't really fault Hemingway for being aware of his own limitations, but you can (and Kraus would) fault the culture for making him the face of twentieth-century American literature.

Hemingway's star seems to have faded a little, so a takedown of him now wouldn't be as incendiary as Kraus's takedown of Heine, but he's an interestingly parallel case, not only in the general outlines (both he

material in the most convenient way imaginable. And so a reader with a brain has the strongest distrust imaginable of storytellers who knock about in foreign milieus. The best-case scenario continues to be that they weren't there; but most of them are unfortunately so constituted that they actually have to take a trip in order to tell a story. Of course, to have spent two years in Paris isn't merely the advantage of such Habakkuks, it's their definition.[21] They strew the drifting sand of French, which finds its way into the pockets of every dolt, into the eyes of German readers. And let the inverse of an epigram of Nestroy,[22] this true

---

and Heine were expats in Paris, obsessed with their literary reputations, and famously nasty to writers they perceived as rivals) but in their literary methods. Kraus's critique of Heine's writing—that it was fundamentally hack journalism, dressed up in an innovative and easily copied style—could apply to a lot of Hemingway's work as well.

21. "Many of the Austrian feuilletonists whom Kraus detested spent part of their career in Paris. For example, Theodor Herzl did a stint as the Paris correspondent for Vienna's paper of record (the *Neue Freie Presse*). And the hated Hermann Bahr had two formative years of work in Paris.

"The more direct reference is to a comedy by the Viennese author Ferdinand Raimund (*The Alp King and the Misanthrope*, 1828), in which there's a servant named Habakuk who likes to mention that he spent two years in Paris, because, as he puts it, doing so gets him 'a lot more respect.'

"The German version of 'Heine and the Consequences' in *Schriften zur Literatur* (1986), annotated by Christian Wagenknecht, helped me identify this and many other references. Wagenknecht's annotations to 'Nestroy and Posterity,' in the same volume, proved to be as vital a resource. Wagenknecht has done a lot for Kraus readers, and it's a pleasure to acknowledge my debt to his work."—PR

22. "Johann Nestroy (1801–1862) was one of the few Austrian authors Kraus admired. Kraus explains just how Nestroy speaks to him in the

dieses wahren satirischen Denkers: ja von Paris bis St. Pölten gehts noch, aber von da bis Wien zieht sich der Weg! (Wenn nicht auf dieser Strecke wieder die Heimatsschwindler ihr Glück machen.) Mit Paris nun hatte man nicht bloß den Stoff, sondern auch die Form gewonnen. Aber die Form, diese Form, die nur eine Enveloppe des Inhalts, nicht er selbst, die nur das Kleid zum Leib ist und nicht das Fleisch zum Geist, diese Form mußte nur einmal entdeckt werden, um für allemal da zu sein. Das hat Heinrich Heine besorgt, und dank ihm müssen sich die Herren nicht mehr selbst nach Paris bemühen. Man kann heute Feuilletons schreiben, ohne zu den Champs Elysées mit der eigenen Nase gerochen zu haben. Der große sprachschwindlerische Trick, der sich in Deutschland viel besser lohnt als die größte sprach-schöpferische Leistung, wirkt fort durch die Zeitungsgeschlechter und schafft aller Welt, welcher Lektüre ein Zeitvertreib

---

essay 'Nestroy and Posterity' (1912), whose title marks it as the companion piece to 'Heine and the Consequences.' Kraus applauds Nestroy for sending up some of the very populist ideals that Heine advanced; and Kraus salutes, as well, the 'verbal barricades' Nestroy put in the way of the process that Heine supposedly did so much to promote: the trivialization of culture. Above all, Kraus underscores the value of Nestroy's satirical techniques. Where Heine 'loosened the corsets of the German language,' Nestroy realized its deepest linguistic possibilities. Kraus's compliment to Nestroy is that his is the first German satire in which 'language forms thoughts about things.' So, for Kraus, where Heine had consequences, his less famous and less celebrated contemporary Nestroy has relevance." —PR

My translation of "Nestroy and Posterity" begins on page 135.

satirical thinker, apply to them: things go well enough from Paris to St. Pölten, but from there to Vienna the road gets very long![23] (If the local swindlers don't make a killing of their own along this stretch.)[24] Now, with Paris, not only the content was acquired but the form as well. The form, though—this form that is only an envelope for the content, not the content itself; that is merely dress for the body, not flesh to the spirit—this form only had to be discovered once for it to be there for all time. Heinrich Heine took care of that, and thanks to him our gentlemen no longer need betake themselves to Paris. You can write feuilletons today without having personally sniffed your way to the Champs Élysées. The great trick of linguistic fraud, which in Germany pays far better than the greatest achievement of linguistic creativity, keeps working in generation after generation of newspapers, furnishing casual readers everywhere with the most agreeable of

23. "'The going is good up to Stockerau, but from there on the journey is long.' Nestroy is supposed to have said this about traveling from Vienna to America, and a version of the saying occurs in his play *Der alte Mann mit der jungen Frau* (*The Old Man with the Young Woman*, 1849). Later users of the epigram swapped out Stockerau and America for other place names, including the ones featured in Kraus's reworking of it: St. Pölten—like Stockerau, an old town, just north of Vienna—and Paris. Kraus's meaning appears to be that with the flair they've acquired in Paris, Austrian journalists can effortlessly dazzle readers in the provinces; however, once those journalists get close to Vienna, where feuilletonism is already rampant, the road to success becomes harder."—PR
24. "With 'local swindlers' (*Heimatsschwindler*), Kraus is alluding to the regional writers (*Heimatdichter*) whose critical success he viewed as the culmination of acts of fraud. Much to his chagrin, one of them, Karl Schönherr, had just been decorated with the prestigious Bauernfeld Prize. Kraus's suggestion, in any case, is that instead of trying to make it as feuilletonists in Vienna, some of the returning authors cash in along the way, becoming regional writers who manage to couple

ist, den angenehmsten Vorwand, der Literatur auszuweichen. Das Talent flattert schwerpunktlos in der Welt und gibt dem Haß des Philisters gegen das Genie süße Nahrung. Ein Feuilleton schreiben heißt auf einer Glatze Locken drehen; aber diese Locken gefallen dem Publikum besser als eine Löwenmähne der Gedanken. Esprit und Grazie, die gewiß dazu gehört haben, auf den Trick zu kommen und ihn zu handhaben, gibt er selbsttätig weiter. Mit leichter Hand hat Heine das Tor dieser furchtbaren Entwicklung aufgestoßen, und der Zauberer, der der Unbegabung zum Talent verhalf, steht gewiß nicht allzuhoch über der Entwicklung.

---

their Parisian confections with provincial flavors. The neologism *Heimatsschwindler* carries an echo of coupling driven by venality, because it's also a play on the term *Heiratsschwindler*, or 'marriage swindler.' And since duplicitous marriage figures in Nestroy's farce *Liebesgeschichten und Heiratssachen* (*Love Stories and Marriage Matters*, 1843), *Heimatsschwindler* serves as well to thicken the web of references to Nestroy's work in this passage." —PR

excuses for avoiding literature.[25] Talent flutters aimlessly in the world and gives sweet nourishment to the philistine's hatred of genius. Writing feuilletons means twining curls on a bald head; but these curls please the public better than a lion's mane of thoughts. Esprit and charm, which presumably were necessary in developing the trick and becoming adept at it, are now passed on by it automatically. With an easy hand, Heine pushed open the door to this dreadful development, and the magician who brought talent within reach of the unendowed surely himself doesn't stand all that far above the development.[26]

25. Who has time to read literature when there are so many blogs to keep up with, so many food fights to follow on Twitter?
26. "Kraus was hardly alone with his contempt for the feuilleton. Here, in fact, he's creating a mash-up of two distinctive, if not always dissimilar, patterns of opposition to the form. One we might call a high modernist critique. For such figures as Robert Musil, Hugo von Hofmannsthal, Walter Benjamin, Theodor Adorno, and, above all, Kraus, the key problem with the feuilleton is that it objectifies what should be most subjective. With its air of intimacy, its emphasis on evoking the mood of its author, and its abundance of clever observations, the classic fin de siècle feuilleton seems like nothing other than a highly subjective response to the world. But read feuilletons closely, and you'll see that they are the opposite of personal. Feuilletons are mass-produced, fast-moving, seriously addictive commodities that are overrunning the space in which actual literature is read, and undermining the ability of newspaper readers to develop their own imaginative responses to the news—or to anything else, for that matter. Thus, more or less, this thinking went. At the same time, the feuilleton was a favorite target among antisemitic propagandists, who tended to portray it as a debauched and debauching un-German genre that Jews—especially Heine—had managed to bring into German culture. Take the essay 'The Sovereign Feuilleton,' which was first published around 1890 and whose author, Heinrich von Treitschke, was an important figure in the

Der Trick wirkt fort. Der Verschweinung des praktischen Lebens durch das Ornament, wie sie der gute Amerikaner Adolf Loos nachweist, entspricht die Durchsetzung des Journalismus mit Geistelementen, die aber zu einer noch katastrophaleren Verwirrung führen mußte. Anstatt die Presse geistig trocken zu legen und die Säfte, die aus der Literatur „gepreßt", ihr erpreßt wurden, wieder der Literatur zuzuführen, betreibt die fortschrittliche Welt immer aufs neue die Renovierung des geistigen Zierats. Das literarische Ornament wird nicht zerstampft, sondern in den Wiener Werkstätten des Geistes modernisiert. Feuilleton,

early days of Germany's antisemitic movement. Having elsewhere claimed that Heine 'shows Germans just what separates them from the Jews,' Treitschke sketches Heine imbibing the feuilletonistic spirit by sucking down 'the foam of the French passion drink' in a state of high 'arousal.' Treitschke then accuses Heine and the feuilleton of dislodging *the* core value of German letters: the prizing of content over form. Hence Theodor Lessing's remark, in a feuilleton of 1929, that 'the word feuilletonist' is 'the nastiest insult in the German language.' Hence, too, the attempts by certain scholars to read 'Heine and the Consequences' as a 'symptom' of 'Jewish self-hatred' on Kraus's part." —PR

The trick keeps working. Paralleling the kitschification of practical life via ornament, as traced by the good American Adolf Loos, is an interlarding of journalism with intellectual elements, but here the resulting confusion is even more catastrophic.[27] Instead of draining the press intellectually and restoring to literature the juices that were "extracted" from it—extorted from it— the progressive world proceeds ever afresh with the renovation of its intellectual decorations. The literary ornament doesn't get demolished, it gets modernized in the Wiener Werkstätten of the mind. Feuilleton, mood reporting, fluff pieces—the motto

27. "Adolf Loos (1870–1933) was many things—for example, a polemicist, a music critic, and the cofounder of the short-lived culture magazine *The Other*. But he achieved much more success—and notoriety—in his actual métier: architecture. Finished in 1910, his starkly unornamented 'Haus am Michaelerplatz,' which stands opposite the Hofburg, repelled some members of the royal family so much that they avoided the doors that opened onto it. Loos was also known for being one of Kraus's closest friends and for leading a complicated personal life: he contracted syphilis as a young man, married a series of much-younger women, wound up at the center of a pederasty scandal, and died a pauper. What Loos wasn't was 'American.' However, he did spend a few formative years in the United States during the 1890s, and for the rest of his life he was quick to convey his enthusiasm for American culture, and especially for Anglo-American fashion trends. This is why Kraus describes Loos as he does. It's hard to imagine, though, that Kraus means to frame Loos's aesthetic outlook as somehow being American. Kraus himself felt quite differently about the United States, and yet, as he stresses, he shared Loos's stance on the conflating of art objects and use objects. As Kraus puts it in an aphorism, 'Adolf Loos and I—he literally and I verbally—have done nothing other than demonstrate that there's a difference between an urn and a chamber pot, and that culture gets the space it needs to live from this difference.'"—PR

Stimmungsbericht, Schmucknotiz – dem Pöbel bringt die Devise „Schmücke dein Heim" auch die poetischen Schnörkel ins Haus. Und nichts ist dem Journalismus wichtiger, als die Glasur der Korruption immer wieder auf den Glanz herzurichten. In dem Maße, als er den Wucher an dem geistigen und materiellen Wohlstand steigert, wächst auch sein Bedürfnis, die Hülle der schlechten Absicht gefällig zu machen. Dazu hilft der Geist selbst, der sich opfert, und der Geist, der dem Geist erstohlen ward. Der Fischzug einer Sonntagsauflage kann nicht mehr ohne den Köder der höchsten literarischen Werte sich vollziehen, der „Volkswirt" läßt sich auf keinen Raub mehr ein, ohne daß die überlebenden Vertreter der Kultur die Hehler machen. Aber weit schändlicher als diese Aufführung der Literatur im Triumph dieses Raubzugs, weit gefährlicher als dies Attachement geistiger Autorität an die Schurkerei, ist deren Durchsetzung, deren Verbrämung mit dem Geist, den sie der Literatur abgezapft hat und den sie durch die lokalen Teile und alle andern Aborte der öffentlichen Meinung schleift. Die Presse als eine soziale Einrichtung, weils denn einmal unvermeidlich ist, daß die Phantasiearmut mit Tatsachen geschoppt wird, hätte in der fortschrittlichen Ordnung ihren Platz. Was aber hat die Meldung,

"Feather Thy Nest"[28] brings the poetic flourish, too, into the homes of the masses. And nothing is more important to journalism than restoring the gloss, again and again, to the glaze of corruption. The more it adds to the profiteer's intellectual and material wealth, the greater its need to cloak its ill intentions pleasingly. In this, the Mind itself lends a hand, sacrificing itself, as does the spirit that was stolen from the Mind. A Sunday edition's catch can no longer take place without dangling the highest of literary values as bait, the *Economist* no longer goes in for robbery unless the surviving representatives of culture act as lookouts.[29] But far more disgraceful than literature's marching in the triumph of this pillage, far more dangerous than this *attachement* of intellectual authority to the villainy, is the villainy's interlarding, its gilding, with the Mind, which it has siphoned off from literature and which it drags along through the local pages and all the other latrines of public opinion. The press as a social institution—since it's simply unavoidable that the dearth of imagination get filled up with facts—would have its place in the progressive order. But what does the news that it rained in Hong Kong have to do with

28. "A popular advertising slogan used to sell home furnishings and decor. Kraus lampooned it more than once."—PR
29. "Kraus may well be naming a title here, in which case he would have in mind *Der österreichische Volkswirt* [The Austrian Economist], a newspaper that was founded in 1908 and that focused on economics and politics—its contributors would include such heavyweights as Josef Schumpeter and Friedrich von Hayek. Kraus could be implying that even newspapers without literary pretentions are afflicted by feuilletonism. Or he could simply be referencing the heading of the business insert in many Austrian papers: the 'Volkswirt.'"—PR

daß es in Hongkong geregnet hat, mit dem Geist zu schaffen? Und warum erfordert eine arrangierte Börsenkatastrophe oder eine kleine Erpressung oder gar nur die unbezahlte Verschweigung einer Tatsache den ganzen großen Apparat, an dem mitzuwirken Akademiker sich nicht scheuen und selbst Ästheten den Schweiß ihrer Füße sich kosten lassen? Daß Bahnhöfe oder Anstandsorte, Werke des Nutzens und der Notwendigkeit, mit Kinkerlitzchen dekoriert werden, ist erträglich. Aber warum werden Räuberhöhlen von Van de Velde eingerichtet? Nur deshalb, weil sonst ihr Zweck auf den ersten Blick kenntlich wäre und die Passanten sich nicht willig täglich zweimal die Taschen umkehren ließen. Die Neugierde ist immer größer als die Vorsicht, und darum schmückt sich die Lumperei mit Troddeln und Tressen.

the Mind? And why does an arranged stock-market catastrophe or a small extortion or even just the unpaid suppression of a fact demand the entire grand apparatus, in which academics don't shy from collaborating and for which even aesthetes offer a taste of the sweat of their feet? That train stations or public toilets, works of utility and necessity, are cluttered up with decorative junk is tolerable. But why are thieves' dens fitted out by van de Velde?[30] Only because their purpose would otherwise be obvious at a glance, and passersby would not willingly have their pockets turned inside out twice a day.[31] Curiosity is always stronger than caution, and so the chicanery dolls itself up in tassels and lace.

30. "Henry van de Velde (1863–1957), a Belgian artist and theorist, was treated by the members of the Wiener Werkstätte as a source of inspiration. Some of the Werkstätte's champions found him inspiring, too. I'm thinking, in particular, of Kraus's nemesis Hermann Bahr, who once called van de Velde 'the greatest master of interior design working today.' Loos, by contrast, proposed that prisons looking to institute harsh new forms of punishment should simply hire van de Velde to decorate their cells. This was something van de Velde would be happy to do, Loos intimated with some justification. In the 1890s, van de Velde repeatedly enjoined artists to enter into the world of crafts and design, and 'impress beauty on every aspect of our lives.'" —PR
31. I.e., presumably, by buying a morning and an evening paper. It's worth keeping in mind that Kraus isn't speaking metaphorically of "thieves." Newspapers such as the *Neue Freie Presse* really were engaged in stock-market manipulation, smear campaigns, real-estate speculation, advertisements masquerading as editorial content, and Hearst-like (Fox News–like!) political machinations, all of it under a gauze of Viennese aestheticism.

"The founder of *Die Presse*, an important Viennese daily, was once quoted as saying that his goal was to own a paper in which every single line was paid for—i.e., bought by someone with the means and will to manipulate the news." —PR

Ihren besten Vorteil dankt sie jenem Heinrich Heine, der der deutschen Sprache so sehr das Mieder gelockert hat, daß heute alle Kommis an ihren Brüsten fingern können. Das Gräßliche an dem Schauspiel ist die Identität dieser Talente, die einander wie ein faules Ei dem andern gleichen. Die impressionistischen Laufburschen melden heute keinen Beinbruch mehr ohne Stimmung und keine Feuersbrunst ohne die allen gemeinsame persönliche Note. Wenn der eine den deutschen Kaiser beschreibt, beschreibt er ihn genau so, wie der andere den Wiener Bürgermeister, und von den Ringkämpfern weiß der andere nichts anderes zu sagen, als der eine von einem Flußbad. Immer paßt alles zu allem, und die Unfähigkeit, alte Worte zu finden, ist eine Subtilität, wenn

It owes its best advantage to that Heinrich Heine who so loosened the corset on the German language that today every salesclerk can finger her breasts. What's ghastly about the spectacle is the sameness of these talents, which are all as alike as rotten eggs. Today's impressionistic errand boys no longer report the breaking of a leg without the mood and no burning of a building without the personal note that they all have in common. When the one describes the German kaiser, he does it exactly the same way the other describes the mayor of Vienna, and the other can't think of anything to say about wrestlers except what the one has to say about swimming in a river. Everything suits everything always,[32] and the inability to find old words counts as

32. Kraus is making fun of the prevailing style of prewar Viennese impressionistic journalism, heavy on adjectives and larded with "deep thoughts," but his line "Everything suits everything always" will ring true to any contemporary America Online subscriber who has suffered through the recent tabloidization of AOL's home page, with its revolving lazy Susan of news items and of advertisements masquerading as news items. What's great about these items, in a horrible way (or horrible in a great way), is that their format is rigidly fixed, regardless of their content. Thus we might find, consecutively,

New Missing Girl Clues Point to Horror

Sierra LaMar, 15, was last seen a month ago leaving her Northern California home to attend high school. She never made it.

Discovery suggests "worst case" scenario

and

Eyebrow-Raising Way She Lures Men

Actress Jennifer Love Hewitt says that she keeps a kitchen item stashed in her purse—and apparently, it's a proven love potion.

Strange thing she dabs all over her body

If Kraus were alive today, he might reprint these two items side by side in *Die Fackel*, perhaps with a one-line gloss suggesting that the final hot link of the first be exchanged with that of the second, since the prurience of the two items is identical.

You could object that Kraus, whose favorvite targets were middlebrow, wouldn't have bothered to satirize a tabloidized website. But today's middlebrow American papers, like *The New York Times* and *The Washington Post*, are the products of a mid-twentieth-century ideal of journalistic objectivity. The best examples of the earnest triviality and subjective grandstanding that characterized Vienna's liberal press are now found on cable TV and the Internet. And many of AOL's hyperlinks lead to respectable news services; the grotesqueries are in the headlines, reflecting the commercial Internet's number one imperative, which is to generate clicks. Considering how many respectable writers and newspapers (including the *Times*) are big fans of the Internet these days, it seems fair to take a Krausian look at the asininities that the click-imperative engenders—to imagine the fun Kraus might have had with AOL's self-deconstructing juxtaposition of

Do You Know When Suri Was Born?

Tom and Katie's fashionable tot was born at a time of year that signals "new beginnings"—and she isn't the only famous offspring who was.

What she shares with Mariah Carey's twins

with

Are You Too Obsessed with Celebs?

Sure, a juicy headline about pregnancy or divorce tends to spark the interests of many—but experts say it could be damaging.

Think you're addicted? Click here

Where to begin with the glossing of this one? The tin-eared deployment of the word "tot"? The elegant one-line self-satirization of the commercial Internet? (Think you're addicted? Click here!) The reverent

invocation of "experts"? And obsessed is okay? Just don't be "too" obsessed to function as a consumer? I suspect that Kraus, who believed that linguistic mistakes are never accidental—that bad morals and bad faith reveal themselves in bad usage—would have seized on the deliciously wrong word "interests," which, being plural, can only mean "advantages" in this context. He might have supplied the missing word "corporate" before it, or suggested that "many" be replaced by "the privileged" or "the few."

In the same spirit that inclined me to sympathize with the personified PC and hate the personified Mac, I remained loyal to AOL for thirteen years. But I finally read one too many items like:

Grandpa Found Guilty of Bizarre Abuse

An Indiana man forced his three grandsons on grueling hikes in the Grand Canyon, withheld water and choked and kicked them.

What he did with broccoli is vile

What is vile is for AOL to use the word "vile": to invade my privacy by presuming that I would use the same word to describe what the grandfather did. And so I've quit AOL and signed on with hegemonic Gmail. Which at least, in messages to me like "It's pretty quiet here. Time to expand your circles? Try one of these links," is up-front about the fact that it's invading my privacy. Up-front, too, about the norm by which it is deeming my circle of contacts insufficient.

Paul Reitter believes that AOL might indeed have interested Kraus. "This will sound a bit glib," he says, "but for Kraus the one thing scarier than people reading the *Neue Freie Presse* may have been people not reading it. In 1904 he wrote that 'next to the Jewish press, the antisemitic press has a lower degree of dangerousness, and thus doesn't require such sharp monitoring, because of its greater degree of talentlessness.' But the first real, illustrated, tabloidlike Viennese newspaper, the *Illustrirtes Wiener Extrablatt*, was also a recurring target in *Die Fackel*. Furthermore, when Vienna got an even more sensationalistic and, from our perspective, modern-seeming tabloid in 1923 (*Die Stunde*), Kraus paid a lot of attention to it, describing its new formula as

schon die neuen zu allem passen. Dieser Typus ist entweder ein Beobachter, der in schwelgerischen Adjektiven reichlich einbringt, was ihm die Natur an Hauptwörtern versagt hat, oder ein Ästhet, der durch Liebe zur Farbe und durch Sinn für die Nuance hervorsticht und an den Dingen der Erscheinungswelt noch so viel wahrnimmt, als Schwarz unter den Fingernagel geht. Dabei haben sie einen Entdeckerton, der eine Welt voraussetzt, die eben erst erschaffen wurde, als Gott das Sonntagsfeuilleton

---

'murder, sports, crossword puzzles.' Its journalism was less duplicitous, but its greater rapacity and inanity were alarming. Kraus eventually went after that inanity and got into a feud with the paper's publisher, Imre Békessy, who used vicious means against him, including retouched photographs on the front page of the paper. (Kraus in turn managed to dig up dirt on Békessy and drive him back to his native Hungary.) Kraus was always interested in how the news was disseminated, and the Internet would surely have commanded his attention, because that's where the news is disseminated these days. And if *Die Fackel* can feel bloglike, the feuilleton resembles the blog even more closely. Indeed, with the intermingling of blogs and non-blog journalism in the most respected places (the online *New Yorker*, the online *Times*), we're experiencing a reemergence of one of the problems that Kraus was fixated with: the ascendance of an impressionistic journalistic form that has institutional cachet but is of questionable quality as both reportage and self-expression."

subtlety when the new words already suit everything. This type is either an observer who in opulent adjectives amply compensates for what Nature denied him in nouns, or an aesthete who makes himself conspicuous with his love of color and his sense of nuance and still manages to perceive things in the world around him as deeply as dirt goes under a fingernail.[33] And they all have a tone of discovery, as if the world had only just now been created, when God made the Sunday feuilleton and saw that it was

33. Reitter has kindly supplied a pair of examples of the sameness of the adjective-loving journalistic talents of Kraus's time. The translations are mine:

> General Fitschew is a stocky, medium-tall man whose face is round and full and whose skin has a rosiness to it and seems transparently delicate. Only a few white strands are mixed into his dark mustache, and his small eyes are lightning-quick in their animation, roving restlessly back and forth, as if trying to deny their own rootedness, as if wanting to look simultaneously both outward and inward.

> One has to have seen this pale, fine-featured face with its dull gray eyes and its drooping, reddish-blond mustache, one has to have heard this tired and unspeakably mild man speaking, to arrive at an exact appreciation of his value. He sits there, impassive and indifferent, his face resigned, his entire figure sunk into itself, every feature suggesting the sufferer, the unfortunate—then suddenly he is gripped by a chance word—and now he stretches his head upward, life returns to the motionless organism, his hands go to work, his eyes flash, and out of his mouth spring short, wild sentences full of deep, lively wisdom.

This kind of writing is uniquely awful, but is it really that different from what you can find in the *Times* today? Consider the lede of a front-page Arts and Leisure piece from May 13, 2012:

erschuf und sahe, daß es gut war. Diese jungen Leute gehen zum erstenmal in ein Bad, wenn sie als Berichterstatter hineingeschickt werden. Das mag ein Erlebnis sein. Aber sie verallgemeinern es. Freilich kommt die Methode, einen Livingston in der dunkelsten Leopoldstadt zu zeigen, der Wiener Phantasiearmut zu Hilfe. Denn die kann sich einen Beinbruch nicht vorstellen, wenn man ihr nicht das Bein beschreibt. In Berlin steht es trotz üblem Ehrgeiz noch nicht so schlimm. Wenn dort ein Straßenbahnunfall geschehen ist, so beschreiben die Berliner Reporter den Unfall.

If anyone has a right to feel on top of the world, it's Howard Stern—especially inside his elegant, cumulus-high apartment on the West Side of Manhattan, dominated by a solariumlike living room with views on one side extending far up the Hudson and the other encompassing the entire bucolic breadth of Central Park.

Here, too, the tell is in the adjectives.

good.[34] The first time these young people go to a public bath is when they're sent in as reporters. This may be an experience. But they generalize it. The method for depicting a Livingston in darkest Leopoldstadt[35] is obviously of great help to the impoverished Viennese imagination. For it cannot imagine the breaking of a leg unless the leg is described to it. In Berlin, despite foul ambitions, the situation is not so grave. If a streetcar accident occurs there, the Berlin reporters describe the accident. They

34. This is one of my favorite lines. It applies beautifully to today's cable-TV news anchors, who bring the identical tone of urgent wonderment to whatever story they happen to be following, whether it's a tornado in Texas, a new weight-loss drug, another actress having another baby, or an assassination in the Middle East. The tone can be found on AOL, too, with an additional garbled note of condescension:

Old People Are Miserable

OK so that's not really true. In fact, it's a major misconception about getting older—and that's not the only thing we're getting wrong.

What you don't know about aging

Here again, with the confusion of "you" and "we," I feel my privacy being invaded.

35. "Leopoldstadt was the Lower East Side of fin de siècle Vienna. It was the location of Vienna's 'Jewish section' and thus had an air of the exotic. Playing on this, as well as on the similarity between its name and 'Leopoldville,' the city in the Congo that H. M. Stanley (of Stanley and Livingston fame) founded in 1881, Kraus is associating Leopoldstadt with Stanley's report about searching for and finding Livingston in what is now Tanzania: the report was published in German under the title *Im dunkelsten Afrika* (*In Darkest Africa,* 1890)."—PR

Sie greifen das Besondere dieses Straßenbahnunfalls heraus und ersparen dem Leser das allen Straßenbahnunfällen Gemeinsame. Wenn in Wien ein Straßenbahnunglück geschieht, so schreiben die Herren über das Wesen der Straßenbahn, über das Wesen des Straßenbahnunglücks und über das Wesen des Unglücks überhaupt, mit der Perspektive: Was ist der Mensch? . . . Über die Zahl der Toten, die uns etwa noch interessieren würde, gehen die Meinungen auseinander, wenn sich nicht eine Korrespondenz ins Mittel legt. Aber die Stimmung, die Stimmung treffen sie alle; und der Reporter, der als Kehrichtsammler der Tatsachenwelt sich nützlich machen könnte, kommt immer mit einem Fetzen Poesie gelaufen, den er irgendwo im Gedränge an sich gerissen hat. Der eine sieht grün, der andere sieht gelb – Farben sehen sie alle.

Schließlich ist und war alle Verquickung des Geistigen mit dem Informatorischen, dieses Element des Journalismus, dieser Vorwand seiner Pläne, diese Ausrede seiner Gefahren, durch

single out what is exceptional about this streetcar accident and spare the reader what is common to all streetcar accidents. If a streetcar mishap occurs in Vienna, the gentlemen write about the nature of streetcars, about the nature of streetcar mishaps, and about the nature of mishaps in general, with the perspective: *What is man?* . . . As to the number killed, which might possibly still interest us, opinions differ unless a news agency settles the question. But the mood—all of them capture the mood; and the reporter, who could make himself useful as a rubbish collector for the world of facts, always comes running with a shred of poesy that he grabbed somewhere in the crowd. This one sees green, that one sees yellow—every one of them sees color.[36]

Ultimately, all amalgamation of the intellectual with the informational, this axiom of journalism, this pretext for its plans, this excuse for its dangers, is and was thoroughly Heinean—be it

36. "In his acclaimed study *Fin-de-Siècle Vienna*, Carl Schorske observes that 'in the feuilleton writer's style, the adjectives engulfed the nouns, the personal tint virtually obliterated the object of discourse.' On the causes and true nature of this style, however, Kraus and Schorske differ. Schorske's theory is that the culture of Vienna in 1900 was, in a way, a function of politics. Or, rather, of political failure. Disaffected by the collapse of the liberal governments their fathers had labored to build up, quite a few energetic Viennese 'sons' turned inward to psychological discovery and radical self-reflection. While this trend produced a variety of cultural innovations, it also led, Schorske contends, to some not-so-salutary developments. And the adjective-happy, very 'subjective' response of the critic or reporter that we find in the feuilleton is one of them." —PR

At the risk of overstating the parallels with our own time, I might point out that despair about national politics has likewise led a lot of American sons (and daughters) to retreat into subjectivity, which is the essence of the blog.

und durch heineisch – möge sie auch jetzt dank den neueren Franzosen und der freundlichen Vermittlung des Herrn Bahr ein wenig psychologisch gewendet und mit noch etwas mehr „Nachdenklichkeit" staffiert sein. Nur einmal trat in diese Entwicklung eine Pause – die hieß Ludwig Speidel. In ihm war die Sprachkunst ein Gast auf den Schmieren des Geistes. Das Leben Speidels mag die Presse als einen Zwischenfall empfinden, der störend in das von Heine begonnene Spiel trat. Schien er es doch mit dem

now also, thanks to the more recent Frenchmen and to the friendly agency of Herr Bahr, somewhat psychologically inclined and garnished with yet a bit more "meditativeness."[37] Only once was there a pause in this development—its name was Ludwig Speidel.[38] In him, the art of language was a guest at the greasiest dives of the Mind. The press may feel that Speidel's life was an episode that cut disruptively into the game begun by Heine. And yet he seemed to side with the incarnate spirit of language,

37. "In the mid-1890s Bahr (1863–1934) established himself as a leader within Vienna's emerging culture of modernism, thanks in large part to his theoretical essays. It was Bahr who gave the German term '*Moderne*,' which had simply meant 'modernity,' the added connotation of 'modernism.' But Bahr also achieved a leadership role by working the coffeehouse scene. Older than most of the writers associated with the 'Young Vienna' movement, and outfitted with flowing locks, a big beard, and great connections, Bahr fashioned himself as the avuncular guru of those writers, whom he encouraged to gather around his table at the Café Griensteidl. So when Kraus decided to distance himself from the Griensteidl authors—on the grounds that they were morbidly, and faddishly, obsessed with the condition of their nerves—he made Bahr his point of attack. This was in 1896; and thus began a feud that would stretch into the 1930s. Its duration is easy enough to understand. For one thing, Bahr successfully brought a defamation suit against Kraus in 1900, and Kraus wasn't the kind of person who could get over such a defeat. For another, Bahr continued to align himself with all the wrong causes, as Kraus saw it, e.g., expressionism. And Bahr's cultural reportage strikes just the feuilletonistic tone that Kraus found so formulaic and so insufferable." —PR
38. "Here is another puzzling aspect of Kraus's genealogy of the feuilleton. When Heine died, he was one of Europe's most widely read authors. According to some accounts, in fact, Heine is the very first writer who could amply support himself through book sales. Yet in Kraus's essay, the predominance of Heine's journalistic 'model' is a fin de siècle

leibhaftigen Sprachgeist zu halten und lud ihn an Feiertagen auf die Stätte der schmutzigsten Unterhaltung, damit er sehe, wie sie's treiben. Nie war ein Kollege bedenklicher als dieser. Wohl konnte man mit dem Lebenden Parade machen. Aber wie lange wehrte man sich, dem Toten die Ehre des Buches zu geben! Wie fühlte man, hier könnte eine Gesamtausgabe jene Demütigung bringen, die man einst eßlöffelweise als Stolz einnahm. Als man sich endlich entschloß, den „Mitarbeiter" in die Literatur zu lassen, erdreistete sich Herr Schmock, die Begleitung zu übernehmen, und die Hand des Herausgebers, verniedlichend und verstofflichend, rettete für den Wiener Standpunkt, was durch eine Gruppierung Speidelscher Prosa um den Wiener Standpunkt zu

---

problem, a problem that seems to both contribute to and arise from the cultural moment of the Wiener Werkstätte. In lionizing Ludwig Speidel, Kraus doesn't make the chronological picture any clearer. If Speidel, a Viennese feuilletonist born in 1830, was an exceptional case, what about the rule from which Speidel deviated? How far did Speidel's colleagues get in institutionalizing Heine's style? Complaining about the generation of feuilletonists between Heine and Hermann Bahr, Nietzsche spoke of the 'repulsive stamp of our aesthetic journalism.' But in 'Heine and the Consequences' Kraus has nothing more to say about them." —PR

Point taken. But, again, Kraus isn't even pretending to write a conventional history. I confess I haven't read Speidel, but I like to imagine that his writing was striking for the same kind of freshness, humor, and authenticity that Russell Baker's old columns in the *Times* had.

To which, Reitter again: "An apt comparison, though Baker is a lot funnier than Speidel. To come back to Kraus, I agree and would like to take the claim one step further: Kraus couldn't have written a conventional history even if he'd wanted to. His mind just didn't work that way. Furthermore, there were principles behind this avoidance. In one aphorism, Kraus uses the same brush to tar both conventional his-

summoning it on holidays to the filthiest entertainment places, so that it could see the goings-on. Never was a colleague more dubious than this one. They could parade the living man around, all right. But how long they resisted giving the dead man the honor of a book! How they sensed that a complete edition here could bring that humiliation which they once imbibed by the spoonful as pride. When they finally decided to let the "associate" into literature, Herr Schmock had the cheek to undertake the commentary, and the hand of the editor, making things cute and topical, saved for the Viennese viewpoint as much as could be saved by a grouping of Speidelian prose around the Viennese view-point.[39] An artist wrote these feuilletons, a feuilletonist compiled

---

tory writing and conventional journalism: 'Historians are often just backward-turned journalists.' In another, he makes historians out to be even less appealing: 'Journalism has sullied the world with talent; his-toricism has done the same thing without it.' It's striking, nevertheless, how little interested Kraus is in how the feuilleton actually entrenched itself in the decades after Heine's death. Since Kraus sees this develop-ment as hugely important, you'd think that, somewhere in his essay, he'd say something that would make the biggest gaps in his story a little smaller. But he doesn't."

39. "Schmock is the name of a disreputable Jewish journalist in Gustav Freytag's drama of 1854, *The Journalists*. Freytag himself, by contrast, commanded a lot of respect. He even functioned as a sort of arbiter of good sense in late-nineteenth-century Germany, among both Ger-mans and German Jews. Indeed, Freytag's novel *Credit and Debit* (1855), which features another scurrilous Jewish figure (Feitel Itzig), was often given as a bar mitzvah gift, presumably because the givers thought the book had didactic value for young German Jews. The term 'Schmock,' in any case, could be used the way we use 'Lothario'— i.e., to indicate that someone has the same qualities as the literary character. This is what Kraus is doing with it in 'Heine and the

retten war. Ein Künstler hat diese Feuilletons geschrieben, ein Feuilletonist hat diese Kunstwerke gesammelt – so wird die Distanz von Geist und Presse doppelt fühlbar werden. Die Journalisten hatten Recht, so lange zu zögern. Sie waren in all der Zeit nicht müßig. Man verlangte nach Speidels Büchern – sie beriefen sich auf seine Bescheidenheit und gaben uns ihre eigenen Bücher. Denn es ist das böse Zeichen dieser Krise: der Journalismus, der die Geister in seinen Stall treibt, erobert indessen ihre Weide. Er hat die Literatur ausgeraubt – er ist nobel und schenkt ihr seine Literatur. Es erscheinen Feuilletonsammlungen, an denen man nichts so sehr bestaunt, also daß dem Buchbinder die Arbeit nicht in der Hand zerfallen ist. Brot wird aus Brosamen gebacken. Was ist es, das ihnen Hoffnung auf die Fortdauer macht? Das fortdauernde Interesse an dem Stoff, den sie „sich wählen". Wenn einer über die Ewigkeit plaudert, sollte er da nicht gehört werden, solange die Ewigkeit dauert? Von diesem Trugschluß lebt der Journalismus. Er hat immer die größten Themen und unter seinen Händen kann die Ewigkeit aktuell werden; aber sie muß ihm auch ebenso leicht wieder veralten. Der Künstler gestaltet den Tag, die Stunde, die Minute. Sein Anlaß mag zeitlich und lokal noch so begrenzt und bedingt sein, sein Werk wächst umso grenzenloser und freier, je weiter es dem Anlaß entrückt wird. Es veralte getrost im Augenblick: es verjüngt sich in Jahr-

Consequences.' He's insulting the journalist Hugo Wittmann and, above all, Moriz Benedikt, the all-powerful editor of the *Neue Freie Presse*, whose obituary for Speidel was appended to the essay by Wittmann that introduces Speidel's collected works, which were published in 1910. A little later, Kraus saw fit to stress that being a 'Schmock' generally meant having a Jewish background. 'Nothing is more convoluted,' he wrote, 'than a non-Jewish Schmock.'"—PR

these works of art—the distance between Mind and press becomes doubly appreciable thereby. The journalists were right to hesitate so long. They weren't idle in the meantime. People yearned for Speidel's books—the journalists invoked his modesty and gave us their own books.[40] For it is the evil mark of this crisis: journalism, which drives great minds into its stable, is meanwhile overrunning their pasture. It has plundered literature—it is generous and gives its own literature to literature. There appear feuilleton collections about which there's nothing so remarkable as that the work hasn't fallen apart in the bookbinder's hands. Bread is being made out of bread crumbs. What is it that continues to give them hope? The continuing interest in the subjects they select. If one of them chatters about eternity, shouldn't he be heard for as long as eternity lasts? Journalism lives on this fallacy. It always has the grandest themes, and in its hands eternity can become timely; but it gets old just as easily. The artist gives form to the day, the hour, the minute. No matter how limited and conditional in time and location his inspiration may have been, his work grows the more limitlessly and freely the further it's removed from its inspiration. It goes confidently out of date in a heartbeat: it grows fresh again over decades.

40. "Speidel was indeed too modest to issue a collection of his works, while other journalists eagerly published their own collections. And not long before the edition of Speidel's works finally appeared, the journalist Ludwig Hevesi wrote a book-length 'biographical appreciation' of Speidel. Hevesi, who sometimes wrote under the odd pseudonym Onkel Tom (Uncle Tom), was known for coining the phrase inscribed over the entrance to Josef Olbrich's Secession building: 'To each age its own art, to art its freedom.' Kraus mocked the slogan, along with the movement that adopted it, and he thought poorly of Hevesi. Which is another reason why Kraus felt that Speidel needed to be rescued from his commemorators."—PR

zehnten. Was vom Stoff lebt, stirbt vor dem Stoffe. Was in der Sprache lebt, lebt mit der Sprache. Wie leicht lasen wir das Geplauder am Sonntag, und nun, da wirs aus der Leihbibliothek beziehen können, vermögen wir uns kaum durchzuwinden. Wie schwer lasen wir die Sätze der „Fackel", selbst wenn uns das Ereignis half, an das sie knüpften. Nein, weil es uns half! Je weiter wir davon entfernt sind, desto verständlicher wird uns, was davon gesagt war. Wie geschieht das? Der Fall war nah und die Perspektive war weit. Es war alles vorausgeschrieben. Es war verschleiert, damit ihm der neugierige Tag nichts anhabe. Nun heben sich die Schleier . . .

What lives on material dies before it does. What lives in language lives on with it.[41] How easy it was to read the chitchat every Sunday, and now that we can check it out of the library we can barely get through it. How hard it was to read the sentences in *Die Fackel*, even when we were helped by the incident they referred to.[42] No, *because* we were helped by it! The further we're removed from the incident, the better we understand what was said about it. How does this happen? The incident was close and the perspective was broad. It was all forewritten. It was veiled so that the inquisitive day couldn't get at it. Now the veils are rising . . .[43]

41. I am happy to be confirming the truth of this line by translating Kraus rather than feuilletons from the *Neue Freie Presse*.

42. "Kraus founded *Die Fackel*, his satirical not-quite weekly, in 1899. The first issue appeared, not by chance, on April Fools' Day, and the magazine ran for 922 numbers. It was, again, in 1911 that Kraus stopped publishing contributions from other authors. Despite the difficulty of its sentences, *Die Fackel* had a fairly large circulation—about thirty thousand readers at its peak—and they included many important minds: Arnold Schönberg, Alban Berg, Bertolt Brecht, Franz Kafka, Ludwig Wittgenstein, Thomas Mann, Theodor Adorno, Walter Benjamin, W. H. Auden, and Gershom Scholem, among others. Kraus's topics ranged widely, covering everything from preposition usage to the employment of poison gas in the First World War, but the thematic nub of *Die Fackel* was always Kraus's critique of the Viennese press. This, too, gives Kraus's magazine a bloglike feel. He would often start with a press clipping that he would reproduce and dissect, which is the method of a lot of blogs today: cut, paste, and conquer. *Die Fackel* is available online at http://corpus1.aac.ac.at/fackel."—PR

43. "Kraus thought that people failed to appreciate what he himself saw as the essential paradox of his journalism, which, therefore, he kept on reformulating: 'My readers believe that I write for the day because I

Heinrich Heine aber – von ihm wissen selbst die Ästheten, die seine Unsterblichkeit in einen Inselverlag retten (die zweckerhabenen Geister, deren Hirnwindungen im Ornament verlaufen), nichts Größeres auszusagen, als daß seine Pariser Berichte „die noch immer lebendige Großtat des modernen Journalismus geworden sind"; und diese Robinsone der literarischen Zurückgezogenheit berufen sich auf Heines Künstlerwort, daß seine Artikel „für die Bildung des Stils für populäre Themata sehr förderlich sein würden". Und wieder spürt man die Verbindung derer, die gleich weit vom Geiste wohnen: die in der Form und die im Stoffe leben; die in der Linie und die in der Fläche denken; der Ästheten und der Journalisten. Im Problem Heine stoßen sie zusammen. Von Heine leben sie fort und er in ihnen. So ist es längst nicht dringlich, von seinem Werke zu sprechen. Aber immer dringlicher wird die Rede von seiner Wirkung, und daß sein Werk nicht tragfähig ist unter einer Wirkung, die das deutsche Geistesleben nach und nach als unerträglich von sich abtun wird. So wird es sich abspielen: Jeder Nachkomme Heines nimmt aus dem Mosaik dieses Werks ein Steinchen, bis keines mehr übrig bleibt. Das Original verblaßt, weil uns die widerliche Grelle der Kopie die Augen öffnet. Hier ist ein Original, dem verloren geht, was es an andere hergab. Und ist denn ein Original eines, dessen Nachahmer besser sind? Freilich, um eine Erfindung zu würdigen, die sich zu einer modernen Maschine vervollkommnet hat, muß man die historische Gerechtigkeit anwenden. Aber wenn man absolut wertet, sollte man da nicht zugeben, daß die Prosa Heinrich Heines von den beobachterisch gestimmten Technikern, den flotten Burschen und den Grazieschwindlern übertroffen wurde? Daß diese Prosa, welche Witz

---

write about the day, so I will have to wait until my works become old. Then they'll be relevant.' Kraus also told his readers that he wanted to locate 'the chords of eternity' in the 'noises of the day.'" —PR

But Heinrich Heine—even the aesthetes who are rescuing his immortality in an island publishing house[44] (these gloriously impractical minds whose cerebral wrinkles trail away into ornament) have nothing more impressive to say about him than that his reports from Paris "have become the still-vital masterwork of modern journalism"; and these Robinsons of literary seclusion take Heine's artistic word for it that his articles "would be very useful in developing a style for popular themes." Here again you can sense the kinship of those who reside equally far from the Mind: those who live in form and those who live in content; who think in the line and who think in the surface; the aesthetes and the journalists. In the problem of Heine they collide. They live on off him and he in them. So it's by no means urgent to talk about his work. What is increasingly urgent is to talk about his influence, and about the fact that his work isn't capable of bearing up under an influence that German intellectual life will little by little cast off as unbearable. This is the way it will play out: each follower of Heine takes one tile from the mosaic of his work until no more remain. The original fades because the repellent glare of the copy opens our eyes. Here's an original that loses what it lends to others. And can you even call something an original when its imitators are better? Naturally, to appreciate an invention that has since perfected itself into a modern machine, you have to apply historical justice. But in making an absolute judgment, don't you have to concede that Heinrich Heine's prose has now been surpassed by the observationally inclined technicians, the style boys, and the swindlers of charm? That this prose, which signifies wit without perspective and perspectives without wit, was quite certainly surpassed by

44. Insel—literally "Island"—is the name of a venerable literary publisher.

ohne Anschauung und Ansicht ohne Witz bedeutet, ganz gewiß von jenen Feuilletonisten übertroffen wurde, die nicht nur Heine gelesen, sondern sich extra noch die Mühe genommen haben, an die Quelle der Quelle, nach Paris zu gehen? Und daß seiner Lyrik, im Gefühl und in der korrespondierenden Hohnfalte, Nachahmer entstanden sind, die's mindestens gleich gut treffen und die zumal den kleinen Witz der kleinen Melancholie, dem der ausgeleierte Vers so flink auf die Füße hilft, mindestens ebenso geschickt praktizieren. Weil sich ja nichts so leicht mit allem Komfort der Neuzeit ausstatten läßt wie einen lyrische Einrichtung. Sicherlich, keiner dürfte sich im Ausmaß der Übung und im Umfang intellektueller Interessen mit Heine vergleichen. Wohl aber überbietet ihn heute jeder Itzig Witzig in der Fertigkeit, ästhetisch auf Teetisch zu sagen und eine kandierte Gedankenhülse durch Reim und Rhythmus zum Knallbonbon zu machen.

Heinrich Heine, der Dichter, lebt nur als eine konservierte Jugendliebe. Keine ist revisionsbedürftiger als diese. Die Jugend nimmt alles auf und nachher ist es grausam, ihr vieles wieder

those feuilletonists who not only read Heine but took extra pains to go to the source of sources—to Paris? And that there have since appeared imitators of his poetry who manage the feelings and the newsman's wrinkle of disdain no less glibly, and who in particular are no less deft in making the little joke of the little melancholy, which the hurdy-gurdy verse helps so nimbly to its feet. Because, after all, nothing is easier to outfit with every modern convenience than a lyrical arrangement. It's true that nobody would dare compare himself to Heine in the extent of his output and the scope of his intellectual interests. But today every Itzak Wisecrack[45] can probably outdo him when it comes to making an aesthetic anesthetic[46] and using rhyme and rhythm to turn candied husks of thought into cherry bombs.

Heinrich Heine the poet lives only as a canned youthful sweetheart. None is in greater need of reassessment than this one. Youth soaks up everything, and it's cruel to take many things

45. Again with the antisemitism.

Reitter informatively adds: "'Itzig,' the term of opprobrium Kraus uses here, gained prominence through a character in Gustav Freytag's novel *Debit and Credit*, the unscrupulous *Ostjude* (Eastern Jew) Feitel Itzig. But Itzig was also the name of an important figure in the German-Jewish Enlightenment, Daniel Itzig (1723–1799), whose son Elias had it changed to Hitzig, which sounded less Jewish. Heine, in his poem 'Jehuda ben Halevy,' while chiding Hitzig for altering the family nomenclature, has some fun with the phonetic proximity of 'Itzig' to 'Hitzig.' Thus, with 'Itzig Witzig' (Itzak Wisecrack), Kraus is smearing Jewish journalists with a term whose meaning had changed since Heine's time, as well as slighting Heine's style of wordplay."

46. In the original, it's "*ästhetisch auf Teetisch zu sagen.*" Reitter comments: "'Aesthetic' in German sounds like 'tea table.' The pun, with its trivializing and ultimately meaningless irony, originated with Heine."

I'm indebted to Reitter for suggesting "cherry bomb" later in the sentence and for his help with numerous other problematic lines.

abzunehmen. Wie leicht empfängt die Seele der Jugend, wie leicht verknüpft sie das Leichte und Lose: wie wertlos muß eine Sache sein, damit ihr Eindruck nicht wertvoll werde durch Zeit und Umstand, da er erworben ward! Man ist nicht kritisch, sondern pietätvoll, wenn man Heine liebt. Man ist nicht kritisch, sondern pietätlos, wenn man dem mit Heine Erwachsenen seinen Heine ausreden will. Ein Angriff auf Heine ist ein Eingriff in jedermanns Privatleben. Er verletzt die Pietät vor der Jugend, den Respekt vor dem Knabenalter, die Ehrfurcht vor der Kindheit. Die erstgebornen Eindrücke nach ihrer Würdigkeit messen wollen, ist mehr als vermessen. Und Heine hatte das Talent, von den jungen Seelen empfangen und darum mit den jungen Erlebnissen assoziiert zu werden. Wie die Melodie eines Leierkastens, die ich mir nicht verwehren ließe, über die Neunte Symphonie zu stellen, wenns ein subjektives Bedürfnis verlangt. Und darum brauchen es sich die erwachsenen Leute nicht bieten zu lassen, daß man ihnen bestreiten will, der Lyriker Heine sei größer als der Lyriker Goethe. Ja, von dem Glück der Assoziation lebt Heinrich Heine. Bin ich so unerbittlich objektiv, einem zu sagen: sieh nach, der Pfirsichbaum im Garten deiner Kindheit ist heute schon viel kleiner, als er damals war? Man hatte die Masern, man hatte Heine, und man wird heiß in der Erinnerung an jedes Fieber der Jugend. Hier schweige die Kritik. Kein Autor hat die Revision so notwendig wie Heine, keiner verträgt sie so schlecht, keiner wird so sehr von allen holden Einbildungen gegen sie geschützt, wie Heine. Aber ich habe nur den Mut, sie zu empfehlen, weil ich sie selbst kaum notwendig hatte, weil ich Heine nicht erlebt habe in der Zeit, da ich ihn hätte überschätzen müssen. So kommt der Tag, wo es mich nichts angeht, daß ein Herr, der längst Bankier geworden ist, einst unter den Klängen von „Du hast Diamanten und Perlen" zu seiner Liebe schlich.

away from it later. How easily the soul of youth is impregnated, how easily things that are easy and slack attach themselves to it: how worthless a thing has to be for its memory not to be made precious by the time and circumstances of its acquisition! You're not critical, you're pious when you love Heine. You're not critical, you're blasphemous when you try to talk somebody who grew up with Heine out of his Heine. An assault on Heine is an invasion of the everyman's private life. It injures reverence for youth, respect for boyhood, veneration of childhood. To presume to judge firstborn impressions according to their merit is worse than presumptuous. And Heine had a talent for being embraced by young souls and thus associated with young experiences.[47] Like rating the melody of a hurdy-gurdy, to which I was unstoppably drawn, above Beethoven's Ninth, owing to a subjective urge. This is why grown-ups don't have to put up with anyone who wants to dispute their belief that Heine is a greater poet than Goethe. Yes, it's on the luck of association that Heinrich Heine lives. Am I so relentlessly objective as to say to someone: go, look, the peach tree in the garden of your childhood is quite a bit smaller than it used to be. He had the measles, he had Heine, and he gets hot in recollecting every fever of youth. Criticism should stay quiet here. No author needs reassessment as badly as Heine, no one bears up under it so poorly, no one is so protected from it by every fond illusion. But I have the courage to recommend it only because I'm hardly in need of it myself, because I failed to experience Heine at a time when I would have had to overrate him. There comes a day where it's no concern of mine that a gentleman who has long since become a banker once crept to his beloved

47. J. D. Salinger might be an example of an American writer whose reputation has similarly benefited from being read in people's youth. But consider here, too, the periodic arguments from Bob Dylan fans that Dylan deserves the Nobel Prize in Literature.

Und wo man rücksichtslos wird, wenn der Reiz, mit dem diese tränenvolle Stofflichkeit es jungen Herzen angetan hat, auf alte Hirne fortwirkt und der Sirup sentimentaler Stimmungen an literarischen Urteilen klebt. Schließlich hätte man der verlangenden Jugend auch mit Herrn Hugo Salus dienen können. Ich weiß mich nicht frei von der Schuld, der Erscheinung das Verdienst der Situation zu geben, in der ich sie empfand, oder sie mit der begleitenden Stimmung zu verwechseln. So bleibt mir ein Abglanz auf Heines Berliner Briefen, weil mir die Melodie „Wir winden dir den Jungfernkranz", über die sich Heine dort lustig macht, sympathisch ist. Aber nur in den Nerven. Im Urteil bin ich mündig und willig, die Verdienste zu unterscheiden. Die Erinnerung eines Gartendufts, als die erste Geliebte vorüberging, darf einer nur dann für eine gemeinsame Angelegenheit der Kultur halten, wenn er ein Dichter ist. Den Anlaß überschätze man getrost, wenn man imstande ist, ein Gedicht daraus zu machen. Als ich einst in einer Praterbude ein trikotiertes Frauenzimmer in der Luft schweben sah, was, wie ich heute weiß, durch eine Spiegelung erzeugt wurde, und ein Leierkasten spielte dazu die „Letzte Rose", da ging mir das Auge der Schönheit auf und das Ohr der Musik, und ich hätte den zerfleischt, der mir gesagt hätte, das Frauenzimmer wälze sich auf einem Brett herum und

under the strains of "You have diamonds and pearls."[48] And where you become rude at the sight of old brains still being affected by the charm with which this tearful materiality once captivated young hearts, and the syrup of sentimental moods adheres to literary judgments. When you get right down to it, the hankerings of youth could have been satisfied even by Herr Hugo Salus.[49] I don't fancy myself guiltless of giving a bit of culture the benefit of the situation in which I experienced it, or of confusing it with the attendant mood. I retain a warm glow from Heine's Berlin letters, for example, because the melody "We wind for you a bridal wreath," which Heine makes fun of there, is congenial to me. But only in my nerves. In my judgment, I am mature and willing to distinguish merits. The memory of how the garden smelled when your first love walked through it is of general concern to the culture only if you're a poet. You're free to overvalue the occasion if you're capable of making a poem out of it. When, once, in a booth at the Prater,[50] I saw a lady in tights floating in the air (which I now know was done with mirrors), and a hurdy-gurdy was accompanying her with "Last Rose," my eyes were opened to beauty and my ears to music, and I would have ripped to shreds the man who told me that the lady was waltzing around

48. "Du hast Diamanten und Perlen," one of the more famous poems in Heine's *Book of Songs*.
49. "Hugo Salus (1866–1929) was a German-Jewish poet (and gynecologist) based in Prague. He had discerning admirers, e.g., Max Brod, Rainer Maria Rilke, and Arnold Schönberg. But Kraus wasn't a fan; indeed, Kraus viewed Salus as an aesthete whose poetry exhibited the vices of the feuilleton. Its figures didn't stand up to close scrutiny, and its 'contemplative' tone masked an underlying superficiality. Or so Kraus repeatedly tried to show." —PR
50. The Viennese amusement park with the giant Ferris wheel featured in *The Third Man*.

die Musik sei von Flotow. Aber in der Kritik muß man, wenn man nicht zu Kindern spricht, den Heine beim wahren Namen nennen dürfen.

Sein Reiz, sagen seine erwachsenen Verteidiger, sei ein musikalischer. Darauf sage ich: Wer Literatur empfindet, muß Musik nicht empfinden oder ihm kann in der Musik die Melodie, der Rhythmus als Stimmungsreiz genügen. Wenn ich literarisch arbeite, brauche ich keine Stimmung, sondern die Stimmung entsteht mir aus der Arbeit. Zum Anfeuchten dient mir ein Klang aus einem Miniaturspinett, das eigentlich ein Zigarrenbehälter ist und ein paar seit hundert Jahren eingeschlossene altwiener Töne von sich gibt, wenn man daraufdrückt. Ich bin nicht musikalisch; Wagner würde mich in dieser Lage stören. Und suchte ich denselben kitschigen Reiz der Melodie in der Literatur, ich könnte in solcher Nacht keine Literatur schaffen. Heines Musik mag dafür den Musikern genügen, die von ihrer eigenen Kunst bedeutendere Aufschlüsse verlangen, als sie das bißchen Wohlklang gewährt. Was ist denn Lyrik im Heineschen Stil, was ist jener deutsche Kunstgeschmack, in dessen Sinnigkeiten und Witzigkeiten die wilde Jagd Liliencronscher Sprache einbrach, wie einst des Neutöners Gottfried August Bürger? Heines Lyrik: das

on a plank and the tune was by Flotow.[51] In criticism, though, unless you're speaking to children, you have to be allowed to call Heine by his true name.

His charm, according to his grown-up defenders, is a musical one. To which I reply: to be responsive to literature, you cannot be responsive to music, otherwise the melody and rhythm of music will suffice to create a mood.[52] I don't need a mood when I'm doing literary work; I create a mood in myself by working. To get the juices flowing, I use a tone from a miniature spinet that is actually a cigar box and which, if pressed on, emits a few old Viennese notes that have been locked inside it for a hundred years. I'm not musical; Wagner would disturb me in this situation.[53] And if I sought the same kitschy stimulus of melody in literature, I could produce no literature on such a night. Heine's music may, by the same token, suffice for musicians who require more significant disclosures from their own art than his little bit of euphony affords. What, then, is poetry in the Heinean style, what is that German taste in art into whose prettinesses and wittinesses the wild hunt of Liliencron's language burst, as the avant-gardist Gottfried August Bürger's once had?[54] Heine's

51. "Friedrich von Flotow (1812–1883), that is, whose 'The Last Rose' ('Die letzte Rose') comes from his opera *Martha* (1847)." —PR
52. To this line my friend Daniel Kehlmann, who is an actual Viennese and a deep student of Kraus, offers the comment: "Who the hell knows what Kraus is really saying here."
53. For somebody who claims not to be musical, Kraus knows an awful lot about music. But his resistance to music while working is a point of identification with me. I'm always amazed when writers report listening to Beethoven or Arcade Fire while at work. How do they pay attention to two things at once?
54. "Detlev von Liliencron (1844–1909), a late-blooming German writer of Nietzsche's generation, appealed to Kraus for a number of

ist Stimmung oder Meinung mit dem Hört, hört! klingelnder Schellen. Diese Lyrik ist Melodie, so sehr, daß sie es notwendig hat, in Musik gesetzt zu werden. Und dieser Musik dankt sie mehr als der eignen ihr Glück beim Philister. Der „Simplicissimus" spottete einmal über die deutschen Sippen, die sich vor Heine bekreuzigen, um hinterdrein in seliger Gemütsbesoffenheit „doch" die Loreley zu singen. Zwei Bilder: aber der Kontrast ist nicht so auffallend, als man bei flüchtiger Betrachtung glaubt. Denn die Philistersippe, die schimpft, erhebt sich erst im zweiten Bilde zum wahren Philisterbekenntnis, da sie singt. Ist es Einsicht in den lyrischen Wert eines Gedichtes, was den Gassenhauer, den einer dazu komponiert hat, populär werden läßt?

reasons. Foremost among these was a feature of Liliencron's style that other critics belittled: its rawness and apparent lack of refinement. In addition to printing some of Liliencron's poems in *Die Fackel*, Kraus liked to do what he's doing here, namely, play Liliencron's earthiness off against the aestheticism of Heine's heirs.

"Gottfried August Bürger (1747–1794) was a *Stürmer und Dränger*, a poet of the 'Storm and Stress' movement. But unlike, say, the young Goethe, Bürger was known for producing non-recondite verses that 'the people' could appreciate, which is why Bürger's work lends itself to being paired with Liliencron's. 'The Wild Hunter' ('Der wilde Jäger') is the title of a poem by Bürger."—PR

poetry: it is mood or opinion with the Hark! hark! of jingling bells. This poetry is melody—so much so that it demands to be set to music. And it owes more to this music than its own for its success with the philistines. *Simplicissimus* once poked fun at the kind of German who crosses himself to ward off Heine, only to sing his "Lorelei" later on, blissfully drunk on emotion, "nevertheless."[55] Two images: but the contrast isn't as glaring as it may seem at first glance. For the philistines who curse Heine don't rise to the true philistine confession until the second image, when they sing him. When a popular song is made out of a poem, is it insight into the poem's literary value that makes the song popular?[56]

55. "*Simplicissimus* was a German humor magazine that ran from 1896 to 1944 and was famous for its pictorial caricatures. (Not long after the Heine essay appeared, it printed a nasty sketch of Kraus, displeasing him in the extreme.) By juxtaposing images of a 'philistine' responding to Heine in very different ways, *Simplicissimus* had wittily evoked an oddity in Heine's reception, one that resulted from the infectiousness of his work. Both in life and in death, Heine was at once loved and reviled: we can add to our list of tentative superlatives that Heine was the most popular *and* the most hated German author of the nineteenth century. But it wasn't simply that Heine had many fans as well as many foes. Even some of his bigoted detractors couldn't resist his poems and especially, as Kraus will emphasize, the musical settings that had made them so popular. Even some of the people who abominated Heine in theory enjoyed him in practice, and didn't manage to hide or explain it."—PR

56. "Heine's tactic of framing his poems as 'songs,' from his early *Book of Songs* to his autumnal *Hebrew Melodies*, proved to be a brilliant success, for there was hardly a composer in Germany who failed to take Heine up on the invitation to set his words to music. In 1829, the year after the *Book of Songs* appeared, Franz Schubert set six of the poems. By the 1950s, the number of settings ran to about three thousand, which is surely some kind of record."—PR

Wie viele deutsche Philister wüßten denn, was Heine bedeuten soll, wenn nicht Herr Silcher „Ich wie nicht, was soll es bedeuten" in Musik gesetzt hätte? Aber wäre es ein Beweis für den Lyriker, daß diese Kundschaft seine unschwere Poesie auch dann begehrt hätte, wenn sie ihr nicht auf Flügeln des Gesanges wäre zugestellt worden? Ach, dieser engstirnige Heinehaß, der den Juden meint, läßt den Dichter gelten und blökt bei einer sentimentalen Melodei wohl auch ohne die Nachhilfe des Musikanten. Kunst bringt das Leben in Unordnung. Die Dichter der Menschheit stellen immer wieder das Chaos her; die Dichter der Gesellschaft singen und klagen, segnen und fluchen innerhalb der Weltordnung. Alle, denen ein Gedicht ihre im Reim beschlossene Übereinstimmung mit dem Dichter bedeutet, flüchten zu Heine. Wer den Lyriker auf der Suche nach weltläufigen Allegorien und beim Anknüpfen von Beziehungen zur Außenwelt zu betreten wünscht, wird Heine für den größeren Lyriker halten als Goethe. Wer aber das Gedicht als Offenbarung des im Anschauen der Natur versunkenen Dichters und nicht der im Anschauen des Dichters versunkenen Natur begreift, wird sich bescheiden, ihn als lust- und leidgeübten Techniker, als prompten Bekleider vorhandener Stimmungen zu schätzen. Wie über allen Gipfeln

How many German philistines would know what Heine means if Herr Silcher hadn't set "I know not what it means"[57] to music? But is it an argument for the poet that this clientele would have clamored for his undifficult poetry even if it hadn't been delivered to them on wings of song?[58] Oh, this narrow-minded hatred of Heine, which targets the Jew, tolerates the poet, and bleats along with a sentimental melody with or without a musician's later help. Art brings life into disorder. The poets of humanity restore chaos again and again; the poets of society do their singing and lamenting, their blessing and cursing, within a well-ordered world. All those for whom a poem amounts to an agreement between themselves and the poet, sealed with rhyme, flee to Heine. All those who wish to join the poet in his pursuit of urbane allegories and his establishment of relations with the outside world will consider Heine a greater poet than Goethe. But those who consider a poem to be the revelation of a poet lost in his observation of Nature, not of a Nature lost in the observations of the poet, will be satisfied to reckon Heine a technician skilled at pleasure and sorrow, a speedy outfitter of stock moods. When Goethe shares in—and shares with us—the "silence on

57. "Ich weiß nicht, was soll es bedeuten." According to Daniel Kehlmann, this is the one Heine poem that every German knows. "The poem is so famous, such a part of the German collective consciousness, that even the Nazis couldn't take it out of schoolbooks, anthologies, and calendars. Instead, they simply removed the name Heine from the books and wrote 'Author unknown' above the poem. This is infuriating, of course, but also funny in a certain way."

According to Paul Reitter, "Friedrich Silcher (1789–1860) was a German composer known mostly for his songs and, above all, for his popular setting of Heine's 'Lorelei.'"

58. "Kraus is playing off another Heine poem made famous by its musical setting: 'On Wings of Song' ('Auf Flügeln des Gesanges'). The key setting was Felix Mendelssohn's." —PR

Ruh' ist, teilt sich Goethe, teilt er uns in so groß empfundener Nähe mit, daß die Stille sich als eine Ahnung hören läßt. Wenn aber ein Fichtenbaum im Norden auf kahler Höh' steht und von einer Palme im Morgenland träumt, so ist das eine besondere Artigkeit der Natur, die der Sehnsucht Heines allegorisch entgegenkommt. Wer je eine so kunstvolle Attrappe im Schaufenster

every peak," he does it with such intensely felt kinship that the silence can be heard as an intimation.[59] But if a pine tree in the North stands on a barren peak and dreams of a palm tree in the Orient, it is an exceptional courtesy of Nature to oblige Heine's yearning allegorically. Seeing an artful fake like this in

59. Here is the opening of Goethe's famous poem:

Über allen Gipfeln
Ist Ruh,
In allen Wipfeln
Spürest du
Kaum einen Hauch

And again, in my amateur translation:

On every peak
Is silence.
In the top of every tree
You sense
Barely a breath.

Kraus was later prompted to call the poem a "national jewel," after an atrocious patriotic pastiche of it appeared in a newspaper during the First World War:

Under every sea—
Is the U-boat.
Of England's fleet
You note
Barely a smoke.

This kind of cleverness now mainly resides on the front page of the *New York Post.*

eines Konditors oder eines Feuilletonisten gesehen hat, mag in Stimmung geraten, wenn er selbst ein Künstler ist. Aber ist ihr Erzeuger darum einer? Selbst die bloße Plastik einer Naturan schauung, von der sich zur Seele kaum sichtbare Fäden spinnen, scheint mir, weil sie das Einfühlen voraussetzt, lyrischer zu sein, als das Einkleiden fertiger Stimmungen. In diesem Sinne ist Goethes „Meeresstille" Lyrik, sind es Liliencrons Zeilen: „Ein Wasser schwatzt sich selig durchs Gelände, ein reifer Roggenstrich schließt ab nach Süd, da stützt Natur die Stirne in die Hände und ruht sich aus, von ihrer Arbeit müd'". Der nachdenkenden Heidelandschaft im Sommermittag entsprießen tiefere Stimmungen als jene sind, denen nachdenkliche Palmen und Fichtenbäume entsprossen; denn dort hält Natur die Stirne in die Hände, aber hier Heinrich Heine die Hand an die Wange gedrückt . . . Man schämt sich, daß zwischen Herz und Schmerz je ein so glatter Verkehr bestand, den man Lyrik nannte; man schämt sich fast der Polemik. Aber man mache den Versuch, im aufgeschlagenen „Buch der Lieder" die rechte und die linke Seite durcheinander zu lesen und Verse auszutauschen. Man wird nicht enttäuscht sein, wenn man von Heine nicht enttäuscht ist. Und die es schon sind, werden es erst recht nicht sein. „Es zwitscherten

the show window of a confectioner or a feuilletonist might put you in a good mood if you're an artist yourself. But does that make its manufacturer one?[60] Even the plain outline of a perception of Nature, from which barely visible threads spin themselves out toward the soul, seems to me more lyrical than the dressing-up of ready-made moods, because it presupposes empathy. In this sense, Goethe's "Stillness and Sea" is lyric poetry, as are Liliencron's lines: "A river babbles its happy way across the land, a field of ripe rye gathers in the west, then Nature leans her head upon her hand and, weary from her work, takes rest." Deeper moods arise from a reflecting heathscape on a summer morning than from reflective palms and pine trees; for here Nature rests her head upon her hand, while there Heinrich Heine pressed his hand on Nature's cheek . . . You're ashamed that between fears and tears there ever existed such slick intercourse that went by the name of poetry; you're almost ashamed of polemics. But you should open the *Book of Songs* and try reading the right-hand and the left-hand pages higgledy-piggledy, interchanging the lines. You won't be disappointed, if you're not disappointed with Heine. And those who are already disappointed will, for the first time, not

60. My translation of the artful fake in question ("Ein Fichtenbaum steht einsam"):

A pine tree stands lonely
On a barren northern height.
It sleeps; it's covered by
White blankets of snow and ice.

It's dreaming of a palm tree
which, in a far-off Eastern place,
is grieving, silent and lonely,
Upon a burning rock face.

die Vögelein – viel' muntere Liebesmelodein." Das kann rechts und links stehen. „Auf meiner Herzliebsten Äugelein": das muß sich nicht allein auf „meiner Herzliebsten Mündlein klein" reimen, und die „blauen Veilchen der Äugelein" wieder nicht allein auf die „roten Rosen der Wängelein", überall könnte die Bitte stehen: „Lieb Liebchen, leg's Händchen aufs Herze mein", und nirgend würde in diesem Kämmerlein der Poesie die Verwechslung von mein und dein störend empfunden werden. Dagegen ließe sich etwa die ganze Loreley von Heine nicht mit dem Fischer von Goethe vertauschen, wiewohl der Unterschied scheinbar nur der ist, daß die Loreley von oben auf den Schiffer, das feuchte Weib aber von unten auf den Fischer einwirkt. Wahrlich, der Heinesche Vers ist Operettenlyrik, die auch gute Musik vertrüge. Im Buch der Lieder könnten die Verse von Meilhac und Halévy stehen:

Ich bin dein
Du bist mein
Welches Glück ist uns beschieden
Nein, es gibt
So verliebt
Wohl kein zweites Paar hienieden.

Es ist durchaus jene Seichtheit, die in Verbindung mit Offenbachscher Musik echte Stimmungswerte schafft oder tiefere satirische Bedeutung annimmt. Offenbach ist Musik, aber Heine

be. "The little birds, they chirped so fine / Glad lovesongs did my heart entwine." That can stand right or left. "In those darling little eyes of thine": this need not simply rhyme with "My dear darling's mouth as red as wine" and "blue little violets of thine eyes sublime" or, again, with "thine little red-rosy cheeks divine"; at every point the plea could stand: "Dear little darling, rest thy little hand upon this heart of mine," and nowhere in this dear little chamber of poesy would the transposition of mine and thine be felt as a disturbance. On the other hand, Heine's entire "Lorelei," say, could not be substituted for Goethe's "Fisher," even though the only seeming difference is that the Lorelei influences the boatman from above, whereas the watery woman influences the fisher from below. Truly, Heinean verse is operetta lyrics, which even good music isn't ruined by. Meilhac and Halévy's lines wouldn't be out of place in the *Book of Songs*:

I am thine
Thou art mine
What heavenly luck is ours
A pair of doves
So much in love
Cannot be found beneath the stars.

This is exactly the sort of shallowness that, in combination with Offenbach's music, generates genuine emotive value or takes on deeper satirical significance.[61] Offenbach is music, but Heine is

61. "In the beginning was Eros: Kraus formed an attachment to Offenbach (1819–1880) in 1900, when he saw the beautiful actress Annie Kalmar performing in Offenbach's *Tales of Hoffmann* (one of the few "serious" operas he wrote). The association of Offenbach's music with Kalmar, whom Kraus came to adore, gave it a special personal resonance for him. By 1909, he had also started to theorize about Offen-

ist bloß der Text dazu. Und ich glaube nicht, daß ein echter Lyriker die Verse geschrieben hat:

> Und als ich euch meine Schmerzen geklagt,
> Da habt ihr gegähnt und nichts gesagt;
> Doch als ich sie zierlich in Verse gebracht,
> Da habt ihr mir große Elogen gemacht.

Aber es ist ein Epigramm; und die Massenwirkung Heinescher Liebeslyrik, in der die kleinen Lieder nicht der naturnotwendige Ausdruck, sondern das Ornament der großen Schmerzen sind, ist damit treffend bezeichnet. Jene Massenwirkung, durch die der Lyriker Heine sich belohnt fühlt. Es ist ein Lyriker, der in einer Vorrede schreibt, sein Verleger habe durch die großen Auflagen, die er von seinen Werken zu machen pflege, dem Genius des Verfassers das ehrenvollste Vertrauen geschenkt, und der stolz auf die Geschäftsbücher verweist, in denen die Beliebtheit dieser Lyrik eingetragen stehe. Dieser Stolz ist so wenig verwunderlich wie diese Beliebtheit. Wie vermöchte sich eine lyrische Schöpfung, in der die Idee nicht kristallisiert, aber verzuckert wird, der allgemeinen Zufriedenheit zu entziehen? Nie, bis etwa zur Sterbenslyrik, hat sich eine schöpferische Notwendigkeit in Heine zu diesen Versen geformt, daß es Verse werden mußten; und diese Reime sind Papilloten, nicht Schmetterlinge: Papier-

---

bach's aesthetic virtues. This was the time when Kraus really began taking aim at both the Viennese feuilleton and the established cultural institutions that had facilitated its rise. Not coincidentally, it was also the time when Kraus started to celebrate noncanonical forms and figures—vaudeville, a theater troupe that spoke Jewish dialect, Else Lasker-Schüler, Offenbach—for having more to offer than their prestigious counterparts, which lacked fantasy and were, in his opinion, dangerously out of touch with reality. In a 1909 essay on Offenbach, for

merely the words for it. And I don't believe that a real poet wrote the lines:

And when I wailed to you about my pain,
You all just yawned in mute disdain;
Yet when I set it out in lyrical phrases,
You couldn't wait to sing my praises.

But it's an epigram; and it perfectly captures the mass appeal of Heine's love poetry, in which the little songs are merely the ornament of big sorrows, not their naturally inevitable expression. The same mass appeal by which the poet Heine feels so rewarded. This is a poet who writes, in one of his prefaces, that his publishers have shown the most gratifying faith in his genius by means of the large first printings they're wont to make of his work, and who points proudly to the account books in which the popularity of his poetry stands registered. How, indeed, could lyrical work in which ideas are candied, rather than crystallized, fail to be greeted with universal satisfaction? At no point before, say, his deathbed poetry did verse become for Heine such a creative necessity that it had to be verse; and these rhymes are papillotes, not butterflies: paper ruffles often folded for no other reason

---

example, Kraus points up the contrast between the emptiness of official theater culture and the 'thought-provoking nonsense' of Offenbach's operettas. The latter have the potential to be a true '*Gesamtkunstwerk*,' Kraus claims, for they capture the absurdity characteristic of modern life. In the 1920s Kraus adapted and translated Meilhac and Halévy's libretti, and he began to give 'speech-song' readings of Offenbach—a lot of them. During the last decade of his life he devoted more than a third of his stage performances to Offenbach (123 of 346)."—PR

krausen, oft nur eben gewickelt, um einem Wickel vorzustel-
len. „Das hätte ich alles sehr gut in guter Prosa sagen können",
staunt Heine, nachdem er eine Vorrede versifiziert hat, und fährt
fort: „Wenn man aber die alten Gedichte wieder durchliest, um
ihnen, behufs eines erneuerten Abdrucks, einige Nachfeile zu
erteilen, dann überrascht einen unversehens die klingelnde Ge-
wohnheit des Reims und Silbenfalls . . ." Es ist in der Tat nichts
anderes als ein skandierter Journalismus, der den Leser über
seine Stimmungen auf dem Laufenden hält. Heine informiert
immer und überdeutlich. Manchmal sagt ers durch die blaue
Blume, die nicht auf seinem Beet gewachsen ist, manchmal direkt. Wäre das sachliche Gedicht „Die heiligen drei Könige" von
einem Dichter, es wäre ein Gedicht. „Das Öchslein brüllte, das
Kindlein schrie, die heil'gen drei Könige sangen." Das wäre die
Stimmung der Sachlichkeit. So ist es doch wohl nur ein Bericht.
Ganz klar wird das an einer Stelle des Vitzliputzli:

> Hundertsechzig Spanier fanden
> Ihren Tod an jenem Tage;
> Über achtzig fielen lebend
> In die Hände der Indianer.
> Schwer verwundet wurden viele,
> Die erst später unterlagen.
> Schier ein Dutzend Pferde wurde
> Teils getötet, teils erbeutet.

Einer indianischen Lokalkorrespondenz zufolge. Und wie die
Sachlichkeit, so das Gefühl, so die Ironie: nichts unmittelbar,
alles handgreiflich, aus jener zweiten Hand, die unmittelbar nur
den Stoff begreift. Im Gestreichel der Stimmung, im Gekitzel
des Witzes.

than to demonstrate a fold. "I could have said all of that very well in good prose," an amazed Heine writes after setting a preface in verse, and he continues: "But when one reads through the old poems again to polish them up with a view to republication, one is unexpectedly surprised by the jingling routine of the rhyme and meter . . ." It is indeed nothing but a journalism that scans: that keeps the reader minutely informed about his moods. Heine is always and overplainly informative. Sometimes he says it with blue flowers from someone else's garden, sometimes directly. If the factual poem "The Holy Three Kings" had been written by a poet, it would be a poem. "The little ox bellowed, the little child screamed, and the three holy kings did sing." This would be the mood of factuality. In Heine's hands, though, it's merely a dispatch. This becomes quite clear in a passage of the "Vitzliputzli":[62]

> One hundred sixty Spaniards
> Met their death that day;
> More than eighty others
> Were taken by the Indians.
> Seriously wounded, too, were many
> Who only later died.
> Nearly a dozen horses were lost,
> Some killed, some captured.

According to our local correspondent. And, as with the factuality, so with the feeling, so with the irony: nothing immediate, everything utterly graspable with that second hand that can grasp nothing but the material. In the petting of mood, in the tickling of wit.

62. "'Vitzliputzli,' a long and biting poem by Heine, is about the conquistadores' guileful victory over the Aztecs and the revenge plans of the Aztec god who wants to torment Europe." —PR

Die Tore jedoch, die ließen
Mein Leibchen entwischen gar still;
Ein Tor ist immer willig,
Wenn eine Törin will.

Diesen Witz macht kein wahrer Zyniker, dem seine Geliebte echappiert ist. Und kein Dichter ruft einem Fräulein, das den Sonnenuntergang gerührt betrachtet, die Worte zu:

Mein Fräulein, sein Sie munter,
Das ist ein altes Stück;
Hier vorne geht sie unter,
Und kehrt von hinten zurück.

Nicht aus Respekt vor dem Fräulein, aber aus Respekt vor dem Sonnenuntergang. Der Zynismus Heines steht auf dem Niveau der Sentimentalität des Fräuleins. Und der eigenen Sentimentalität. Und wenn er gerührt von sich sagt: „dort wob ich meine zarten Reime aus Veilchenduft und Mondenschein", dann darf man wohl so zynisch sein wie er und ihn – Herr Heine, sein Sie munter – fragen, ob er nicht vielleicht schreiben wollte: dort wob

But the fools made my darling
Slip silent to a rendezvous;
A fool is always willing
When a foolish girl is too.

This joke isn't made by any real cynic whose love has given him
the slip. And no poet calls these words to a girl who is moved by
the sunset she is watching:

My girl, now don't you frown,
This happens all the time;
In front here it goes down
And comes back up from behind.

Not out of respect for the girl; out of respect for the sunset.[63]
Heine's cynicism is at the same level as the girl's sentimentality.
And as his own sentimentality. And when, greatly moved, he says
of himself, "there I wove my tender Rhymes out of Balm and
Moonlight," you may well want to be as cynical as he is and ask
him—Herr Heine, now, don't you frown—whether he didn't perhaps mean to write "there I wove my tender Rhymes *for* Balm &

63. Boy, does Kraus nail what's wrong with Heine's sunset poem. And
yet, when I was twenty, I found this poem hilarious. I welcomed its
puncturing of the earnestness of the other German literature I'd been
reading. I thought, wow, this guy is one of *us*. Heine has remained popular with Germans because they feel the same way I did: he's a relief
from the heaviness of so much of German culture. For Germans,
experiencing Heinean irony is like escaping to a Latin country where
life is freer and lighter; they read him the way they flock to the Mediter-
ranean for their vacations.
   The German term "Romantic irony" is synonymous with Heine (even
if Heine saw himself as a post-Romantic author and the Romantics

ich meine zarten Reime für Veilchenduft und Mondenschein, und ob dies nicht eben jene Verlagsfirma ist, auf deren Geschäftsbücher er sich soeben berufen hat. Lyrik und Satire – das Phänomen ihres Verbundenseins wird faßlich –: sie sind beide nicht da; sie treffen sich in der Fläche, nicht in der Tiefe. Die Träne hat kein Salz, und dieses Salz salzt nicht. Wenn Heine, wie sagt man nur, „die Stimmung durch einen Witz zerreißt", so habe ich den Eindruck, er wolle dem bunten Vogel Salz auf den Schwanz streuen; ein altes Experiment: der Vogel entflattert doch. Im Fall Heine glückt die Illusion, wenn schon nicht das Experiment. Man kann ihm das Gegenteil beweisen; ihm, aber nicht den gläubigen Zuschauern. Er wurde nicht nur als der frühe Begleiter von Allerwelts lyrischen Erlebnissen durchs Leben mitgenommen, sondern immer auch dank seiner Intellektualität von der Jugendeselei an die Aufklärung weitergegeben. Und über alles wollen sie aufgeklärt sein, nur nicht über Heine,

---

promoted their own brand of irony). I first encountered it in 1979, in Munich, where I was enrolled in a junior-year-abroad program run by Wayne State University. Imagining that American students might be homesick on a major holiday, the program's director, Frau Doktor Riegler, annually organized a formal Thanksgiving dinner to which professors and other dignitaries were invited, and for some reason Frau Doktor Riegler singled me out to give a speech at the dinner. I wrote the kind of faux-philosophical confection I'd perfected as a style reporter for my college newspaper, and Frau Doktor Riegler vetted it and approved it. When I delivered the speech, though, I inflected its serious passages with an irony borrowed from the Talking Heads—in the years before I discovered Kraus, David Byrne was my number one hero—and I got a lot of laughs and made some progress toward impressing the Bryn Mawr girl I was bent on impressing. Afterward, Frau Doktor Riegler chided me for having deceived her about the nature of my

Moonlight," and whether this might not be the very publishing house to whose account books he was just referring.[64] Poetry and satire—the phenomenon of their alliance becomes comprehensible: neither of them is there, they meet on the surface, not in the depths. This tear has no salt, and this salt doesn't salt. When Heine—what is the phrase?—"punctures the mood with a joke," I have the impression that he wants to sprinkle salt on the tail of the pretty bird: an old experiment; the bird still flutters away.[65] With Heine, the illusion succeeds, if not the experiment. You can prove the contrary to him; to him, but not to his credulous audience. He wasn't simply taken along through life as an early accompanist of everyday lyrical experiences, he was also always, by virtue of his intellectualism, passed along by people's youthful idiocy to their more enlightened selves. And they want to be

---

speech. "What you did," she said, "is called Romantic irony, Herr Franzen. Very clever of you." Kraus would say that I was imitating Heine *before I'd even read him*. I was doing what smart-ass adolescents do, undermining substance with irony because they don't have substance yet themselves, or because they're afraid of the substance that they do have, afraid of the intensity of their own emotion at the sight of a sunset, or afraid (as in my case, on Thanksgiving) of how powerfully they love their childhood home. Heine's poem about the girl and the sunset is smart-ass. It shouldn't wear well as you get older, and Kraus was incensed that grown-up Germans, who'd taken up Heine in their own smart-ass days, continued to place him alongside Goethe, a poet of real substance who respected sunsets.

64. Balm and Moonlight in the original are "*Veilchenduft*" and "*Mondschein*," which, as Reitter notes, would have been recognizable as German-Jewish surnames, or as parodies of them.

65. "According to an old superstition, sprinkling salt on the tail of a bird would cause it to become crazy—and thus catchable." —PR

und wenn sie schon aus seinen Träumen erwachen, bleibt ihnen noch sein Witz.

Dieser Witz aber, in Vers und Prosa, ist ein asthmatischer Köter. Heine ist nicht imstande, seinen Humor auf die Höhe eines Pathos zu treiben und von dort hinunter zu jagen. Er präsentiert ihn, aber er kann ihm keinen Sprung zumuten. Wartet nur! ist der Titel eines Gedichtes:

> Weil ich so ganz vorzüglich blitze,
> Glaubt ihr, daß ich nicht donnern könnt'!
> Ihr irrt euch sehr, denn ich besitze
> Gleichfalls fürs Donnern ein Talent.

> Es wird sich grausenhaft bewähren,
> Wenn einst erscheint der rechte Tag;
> Dann sollt ihr meine Stimme hören,
> Das Donnerwort, den Wetterschlag.

> Gar manche Eiche wird zersplittern
> An jenem Tag der wilde Sturm,
> Gar mancher Palast wird erzittern
> Und stürzen mancher Kirchenturm!

Das sind leere Versprechungen. Und wie sagt doch Heine von Platen?

> Eine große Tat in Worten,
> Die du einst zu tun gedenkst! –
> O, ich kenne solche Sorten
> Geist'ger Schuldenmacher längst.

> Hier ist Rhodus, komm und zeige
> Deine Kunst, hier wird getanzt!

enlightened about everything, just not about Heine, and even if they awaken from his dreams they still have his wit.

This wit, however, in verse and prose, is an asthmatic cur. Heine isn't capable of driving his humor to the height of pathos and chasing it down from there. He trots it out, but he can't make it jump. "Just Wait!" is the title of a poem.

> Because I flash with such success
> You think at thundering I can't excel!
> But you're all wrong, for I possess
> A talent for thundering as well.
>
> Dreadful it will stand the test,
> When come the proper day and hour;
> You shall hear my voice at last,
> The thunderous word, the weather's power.
>
> The wild storm on that day will cleave
> Full many an oak tree tall,
> Full many a palace wall will heave
> And many a steeple fall!

These are empty promises. After all, what does Heine say about Platen?

> In words, a splendid deed
> That you intend to do someday!—
> How well I know this breed
> Who borrow time but do not pay.
>
> Here is Rhodes, now come and show
> Your art, this is your chance!

Oder trolle dich und schweige,
Wenn du heut nicht tanzen kannst.

„Gleichfalls fürs Donnern ein Talent" haben – das sieht ja dem Journalismus ähnlich. Aber von Donner kein Ton und vom Blitz nur ein Blitzen. Nur Einfälle, nur das Wetterleuchten von Gedanken, die irgendwo niedergegangen sind oder irgendwann niedergehen werden.

Denn wie eigene Gedanken nicht immer neu sein müssen, so kann, wer einen neuen Gedanken hat, ihn leicht von einem andern haben. Das bleibt für alle paradox, nur für jenen nicht, der von der Präformiertheit der Gedanken überzeugt ist, und davon, daß der schöpferische Mensch nur ein erwähltes Gefäß ist, und davon, daß die Gedanken und die Gedichte da waren vor den Dichtern und Denkern. Er glaubt an den metaphyischen Weg des Gedankens, der ein Miasma ist, während die Meinung kontagiös ist, also unmittelbarer Ansteckung braucht, um übernommen, um verbreitet zu werden. Darum mag ein schöpferischer Kopf auch das aus eigenem sagen, was ein anderer vor ihm gesagt hat, und der andere ahmt Gedanken nach, die einem schöpferischen Kopf erst später einfallen werden. Und nur in der Wonne sprachlicher Zeugung wird aus dem Chaos eine Welt. Die leiseste Belichtung oder Beschattung, Tönung und Färbung eines Gedankens, nur solche Arbeit ist wahrhaft unverloren, so pedantisch, lächerlich und sinnlos sie für die unmittelbare Wirkung auch sein mag, kommt irgendwann der Allgemeinheit zugute und bringt ihr zuletzt jene Meinungen als verdiente Ernte ein, die sie heut mit frevler Gier auf dem Halm verkauft. Alles Geschaffene bleibt, wie es da war, eh es geschaffen wurde. Der Künstler holt es als ein Fertiges vom Himmel herunter. Die Ewigkeit ist ohne Anfang. Lyrik oder ein Witz: die Schöpfung liegt zwischen dem Selbstverständlichen und dem Endgültigen.

Or hold your tongue and go,
If today you cannot dance.

"A talent for thundering as well"—that sounds like journalism, doesn't it? But from thunder not a sound and from the lightning only a twinkle. Only glimmerings, only the heat lightning of thoughts that went down somewhere or will sometime.

For just as an original thought need not always be new, so the person who has a new thought can easily have got it from someone else. This will remain a paradox for everyone except those who believe that thoughts are preformed, and that the creative individual is merely a chosen vessel, and that thoughts and poems existed before thinkers and poets—those who believe in the metaphysical way of thought, which is a miasma, whereas opinion is contagious, that is, it requires direct contact in order to be caught, in order to spread. Thus a creative head may say originally what somebody else has already said, and someone else may already be imitating a thought that won't occur to the creative head until later. And it's only in the rapture of linguistic conception that a world grows out of chaos. The subtlest illumination or shading of a thought, the tinting, the toning: only work like this goes truly unlost; no matter how pedantic, laughable, and meaningless it may seem at the time, it will eventually come to benefit the general public and yield, in the end, as a well-deserved harvest, those opinions that today are sold unripe with wanton greed. Everything that's created remains as it was before it was created. The artist fetches it down from the heavens as a finished thing. Eternity has no beginning. Poetry or a joke: the act of creation lies between what's self-evident and what is permanent.[66]

66. Daniel Kehlmann notes that this line simply isn't fully understandable. But it's clearly of a piece with the paradoxical conception of originality which Kraus is advancing in this paragraph: that every con-

Es werde immer wieder Licht. Es war schon da und sammle sich wieder aus der Farbenreihe. Wissenschaft ist Spektralanalyse: Kunst ist Lichtsynthese. Der Gedanke ist in der Welt, aber man hat ihn nicht. Er ist durch das Prisma stofflichen Erlebens in Sprachelemente zerstreut, der Künstler schließt sie zum Gedanken. Der Gedanke ist ein Gefundenes, ein Wiedergefundenes. Und wer ihn sucht, ist ein ehrlicher Finder, ihm gehört er, auch wenn ihn vor ihm schon ein anderer gefunden hätte.

So und nur so hat Heine von Nietzsche den Nazarenertypus antizipiert. Wie weitab ihm die Welt Eros und Christentum lag, welche doch in dem Gedicht „Psyche" mit so hübscher Zufälligkeit sich meldet, zeigt er in jedem Wort seiner Platen-Polemik. Heine hat in den Verwandlungen des Eros nur das Ziel, nicht den Weg des Erlebnisses gesehen, er hat sie ethisch und ästhetisch unter eine Norm gestellt, und hier, wo wir an der Grenze des erweislich Wahren und des erweislich Törichten angelangt sind,

---

ceivable thought has always existed (hence the "permanent" here), and that writers find their way, through language, from the particulars of their time and place ("what's self-evident") to the same permanently existing thoughts. As evidence for this conception, Kraus observes elsewhere (in "Nestroy and Posterity") that aperçus from different languages and different centuries all have strikingly similar cadences. This notion of the latency of thought in language seems to me both somewhat correct and somewhat self-serving, in that it applies best to Kraus's own aphoristic style of writing (less well, say, to novels) and that originality is a vexed subject for a satirist whose work is fueled by the writing of others. I get the sense here of Kraus chafing against the confines of his particular gifts—for mimicry, in particular—and defending himself against charges that his work is derivative or parasitic. He protests perhaps too much.

Let there be light, again and again. It was already there and can reassemble itself from the spectrum. Science is spectral analysis: art is the synthesis of light. Thought is in the world, but it isn't had. It's refracted by the prism of material experience into elements of language; the artist binds them into a thought. A thought is a discovered thing, a recovered thing. And whoever goes looking for it is an honorable finder; it belongs to him even if somebody before him has already found it.

In this and only in this way did Heine anticipate Nietzsche with the idea of a Nazarene type.[67] He demonstrates, with every word of his polemic against Platen, how far removed he was from the world of Eros and Christianity, which nevertheless shows up in his poem "Psyche" with such neat serendipity. In the transformations of Eros, Heine was able to see only the goal of experience, not the way of it; he applied ethical and aesthetic norms to it, and here, where we arrive at the border between the demonstrably true and the demonstrably silly, he anticipated not

67. "Building off of his ideas about spiritualism and sensualism, Heine, in his book *Ludwig Börne* (1840), sets up a dichotomy between the 'Nazarene' and 'Hellene' types. The former are ascetic, contemptuous of beauty, and fixated on abstract ideals (like Christian nihilists, in Nietzsche's terminology); Hellenes are just the opposite. Heine then uses this duality to explain why his relationship with Ludwig Börne (1786–1837), a progressive critic who looked like a natural ally, had been destined to sour. Given that Heine is a Hellene and Börne a Nazarene, they never really had a chance. But *Ludwig Börne* is a book that abounds with inconsistencies, and spiritualists and Nazarenes don't always come off so badly. Indeed, Heine lauds both the Old and the New Testament, and his stress on the value of spiritualism amounts to a further affinity with Nietzsche—never mind Kraus's claim that Heine anticipates Nietzsche in only one way. For in a formulation akin to the Dionysian-Apollonian interplay in Nietzsche's *The Birth of Tragedy*,

hat er vielmehr den seligen Herrn Maximilian Harden antizipiert. In dieser berühmten Platen-Polemik, die allein dem stofflichen Interesse an den beteiligten Personen und dem noch
stofflicheren Vergnügen an der angegriffenen Partie ihren Ruhm
verdankt und die Heines Ruhm hätte auslöschen müssen, wenn
es in Deutschland ein Gefühl für wahre polemische Kraft gäbe

Heine writes, in *Ludwig Börne*, that the most sublime art results from
precisely a confluence of opposites: 'Shakespeare is at once Jew and
Greek, or with him perhaps both elements, spiritualism and art, have
permeated each other in a conciliatory way, and developed into a higher
whole.'"—PR

Nietzsche but the late Herr Maximilian Harden.[68] In the famous
Platen polemic—which owes its fame solely to our pulp interest
in the persons involved and to the even pulpier pleasure we get
from the body parts of the persons under attack, and which
would have to have destroyed Heine's reputation if there existed
in Germany a feeling for true polemical power instead of the

68. "Once Kraus's mentor, Maximilian Harden (1861–1927) had become Kraus's enemy by the time he wrote 'Heine and the Consequences.' That they split shouldn't have surprised anyone. What else
tends to happen when you have two big egos—who share a love of in-
vective—relating to each other within a mentor-mentee dynamic? But
if the break was a matter of time, it was also a function of principle. In
1907 Harden used the platform of his newspaper *The Future* to expose
Count Philip Eulenberg, a close adviser to Wilhelm II, as a homo-
sexual. This act—as well as the moralizing that accompanied it—ran
counter to a cause that Kraus had been pushing for years. Since 1902,
Kraus had been insisting that modern journalism's pursuit of sex scan-
dals has the same dangerous effect as the regulation of sexual conduct
through modern 'ethics laws.'

"Kraus liked to play up his proclivity for erotic exploration—
'because it is illegal to keep wild animals, and house pets give me no
pleasure, I'd rather stay unmarried'—and for him the threat of public
shaming promotes a conformity that makes life less colorful and less
fun. Even worse is that this threat shuts down ethical deliberation
where consenting adults should be honing their ethical faculties, in the
most intimate sphere: the bedroom. Thus Kraus believed that, like the
'ethics court,' Harden's treatment of Eulenberg did nothing but produce 'unethical individuals,' and Kraus said as much in print. His doing
so, or having done so, gives his reference to Harden in 'Heine and the
Consequences' its meaning. It's what allows the line about Heine anticipating Harden to serve as a segue into Kraus's critique of Heine's
'Platen polemic,' a section of *The Baths of Lucca* (1830) that takes aim at
the homosexuality of another aristocrat, Count von Platen. While he

und nicht bloß für das Gehechel der Bosheit, in dieser Schrift
formt Heine sein erotisches Bekenntnis zu den Worten:

> Der eine ißt gern Zwiebeln, der andere hat mehr Gefühl für
> warme Freundschaft, und ich als ehrlicher Mann muß aufrich-

was feuding with Harden, Kraus boasted that he had, in effect, 'rubbed
out' his opponent. This is why Kraus gave a subsequent polemic the title
'Maximilian Harden: An Obituary' (1908), and also why he speaks here
of 'the late Maximilian Harden.'" —PR

mere carping of meanness—in this document, Heine chooses to make his erotic confession with the words:[69]

The one likes to eat onions, the other has more of a feeling for warm friendship, and I as an honest man must frankly confess

69. "It was Heine who started the fight with Platen, or, more properly, with Count August von Platen-Hallermünde, a poet whose homosexuality was a kind of open secret. Heine acknowledged Platen's gifts as a writer, to be sure: his talent as a sonneteer was undeniable. But Heine, who regarded homosexuality as a perversion, also felt that there was something off about Platen's poetry. Even before the 'Platen polemic,' Heine had connected Platen's lyrical inclinations—i.e., his attachment to ancient Greek and Persian verse forms and his choice of motifs—with his sexual leanings. Indeed, Heine had complained that he could hear a 'sighing after pederasty' in Platen's work. This, though, was in private. Publicly, Heine contented himself at first with pouring scorn on the Persia-inspired formalism with which Platen was associated. The idea here was to disparage another formalistic poet as well, one whose sexual orientation wasn't an issue, so jokes about homosexuality would have been difficult to pull off. But even without such humor, the initial affront was too much for Platen. His response stemmed in part from his high opinion of himself—he saw himself as Goethe's successor—and in part from his low opinion of Heine, which, in turn, stemmed partly from a snobbish antisemitism. Without really knowing much about Heine, Platen swiftly set about trying to put him in his (Jewish) place. The counterattack took the form of a play, *The Romantic Oedipus*, which appeared in 1829, and contains quite a few antisemitic barbs. Having recently been subjected to an even sharper anti-Jewish obloquy, Heine was in no mood to accept Platen's insults as a fair settling of the score. Instead he opted for escalation, and thus the 'Platen polemic' came to be. It begins with a mischievous bit of editing: Heine lops off part of a line of Platen's poetry, so that what's left reads, 'I am like woman to man.' From there Heine keeps going and going: not even Platen's use of antisemitic discourse escapes the charge of effeteness.

tig gestehen, ich esse gern Zwiebeln, und eine schiefe Köchin ist mir lieber, als der schönste Schönheitsfreund.

Das ist nicht fein, aber auch nicht tief. Er hatte wohl keine Ahnung von den Varietäten der Geschlechtsliebe, die sich am Widerspiel noch bestätigt, und spannte diese weite Welt in das grobe Schema Mann und Weib, normal und anormal. Noch im Sterben ist ihm ja die Vorstellung von der Kuhmagd, die „mit dicken Lippen küßt und beträchtlich riecht nach Mist", geläufig, wiewohl sie dort nur eine bessere Wärme als der Ruhm geben soll und nicht als die warme Freundschaft. Wer so die Seele kennt, ist ein Feuilletonist! Feuilletonistisch ist Heines Polemik durch die Unverbundenheit, mit der Meinung und Witz nebeneinander laufen. Die Gesinnung kann nicht weiter greifen als der Humor. Wer über das Geschlechtsleben seines Gegners spottet, kann nicht zu polemischer Kraft sich erheben. Und wer die Armut seines Gegners verhöhnt, kann keinen bessern Witz machen, als den: der Ödipus von Platen wäre „nicht so bissig geworden, wenn der Verfasser mehr zu beißen gehabt hätte".

As Heine brings his case against Platen to a close, he demonstrates how much more forcefully he can hurl antisemitic abuse. Heine's readers weren't impressed, however. Most thought that he had crossed the line; Goethe, for instance, remarked that assaults like Heine's have no place in the world of letters."—PR

that I like to eat onions, and a crooked female cook is dearer to me than the most beautiful friend of beauty.[70]

This isn't gentlemanly, but it isn't profound, either. He apparently had no concept of the diversity of sexual love, which confirms itself even in the things it rejects, and he crammed this wide world into the crude schema of man and woman, normal and abnormal. Indeed, even on his deathbed, the image that comes to hand is of the milkmaid who "kisses with thick lips and strongly smells of cow chips," although here she's only supposed to be more warming than fame, not warm friendship.[71] The person who understands the soul this way is a feuilletonist! Heine's polemic is feuilletonistic in the disconnectedness with which opinion and wit run alongside each other. The outlook can reach no further than the humor can. A person who makes fun of his adversary's sex life is incapable of rising to polemical power. And a person who ridicules his adversary's poverty can make no better joke than this: Platen's *Oedipus* would "not have been so biting if its author had had more to bite on." Bad opinions can only make

70. Daniel Kehlmann unpacks this: "'Warm' in German is a code word for gay. So the sentence means: 'The one [I, Heine] may enjoy eating onions [may be Jewish], but the other [Platen] has more feeling for men [is gay], and to me even a crooked cook [an ugly, coarse woman] is preferable to a gay aesthete.' Heine destroyed Platen by outing him, and Kraus, in turn, can't forgive him for that. Rightly so, I think."

71. Kehlmann again: "Kraus is quoting a late poem of Heine's in which Heine avows that this manure-smelling milkmaid is dearer to him than his entire posthumous reputation as a poet. Kraus isn't finding fault with the thought itself, but he considers it dishonest and finds the image of the cook and the milkmaid, which recurs constantly in Heine, stale to the point of cliché. To Kraus, when it comes to sexuality, Heine is narrow-mindedly judgmental in a journalistic way."

Exactly. What Platen did with boys is vile.

Schlechte Gesinnung kann nur schlechte Witze machen. Der Wortwitz, der die Kontrastwelten auf die kleinste Fläche drängt und darum der wertvollste sein kann, muß bei Heine ähnlich wie bei dem traurigen Saphir zum losen Kalauer werden, weil kein sittlicher Fonds die Deckung übernimmt. Ich glaube, er bringt das üble Wort, einer leide an der „Melancholik", zweimal. Solche Prägungen – wie etwa auch die Zitierung von Platens „Saunetten" und die Versicherung, daß er mit Rothschild „famillionär" verkehrt habe – läßt er dann freilich den Hirsch Hyacinth verantworten. Und dieser Polemiker spricht von seiner guten protestantischen Hausaxt! Eine Axt, die einen Satz nicht beschneiden kann! Seiner Schrift gegen Börne geben die wörtlichen Zitate aus Börne das Rückgrat, aber wenn er darin Börne sprechend vorführt, spürt man ganz genau, wo Heine über Börne hinaus zu schwätzen beginnt. Er tuts in der breitspurigen Porzellangeschichte. Auf Schritt und Tritt möchte man redigieren,

bad jokes. The play of wit and word, which compresses whole worlds of contrast onto the tiniest of surfaces and can therefore be the most valuable kind of play, must, in Heine's hands, as in the hands of the dismal Saphir, become a slack pun, because there are no moral funds to underwrite it.[72] I believe he twice makes awful reference to somebody having a bad case of "melancolic." Such coinages—as also, for example, his quotations from the "sownets" of Platen or his avowal that he and Rothschild have been on "famillionaire" terms—he naturally then blames on Hirsch-Hyacinth.[73] This from a polemicist who talks about his trusty Protestant kitchen hatchet! A hatchet that can't even trim a sentence! The structural backbone of his attack on Börne consists of direct quotations from Börne, and every time he brings Börne out to speak you can detect quite precisely the point at which Börne stops and Heine's own yakking takes over.[74] He does it in the heavy-handed porcelain story.[75] At every step, you

72. "Moritz Saphir (1795–1858) was a German-Jewish satirist and journalist who has often been seen as forming some kind of cultural continuum with his fellow German Jews Börne and Heine, even though, as Kraus implies, Saphir's humor tended to be considerably lower brow." —PR

73. Hirsch-Hyacinth is a character in Heine's *The Baths of Lucca.*

74. "In *Ludwig Börne,* Heine quotes both the conversations he had with Börne and Börne's *Letters from Paris* (1830–34), where Börne blasts Heine for lacking political seriousness. It's in the *Letters* that Börne describes Heine as someone with 'talent' but no 'character.' Strangely, Heine often cites Börne's damaging accusations and formulations without doing anything to debunk them." —PR

75. "*Ludwig Börne* includes an extended anecdote about porcelain. As Heine has it, Börne once explained to him that it was by publicly smashing a tea service that Napoleon tamed Europe's aristocrats. Fearing for their beloved porcelain, they became more compliant. Next, according to Heine, Börne proceeded to confess that upon acquiring a

verkürzen, vertiefen. Einen Satz wie diesen: „Nächst dem Durch-
zug der Polen, habe ich die Vorgänge in Rheinbayern als den
nächsten Hebel bezeichnet, welcher nach der Juliusrevolution die
Aufregung in Deutschland bewirkte, und auch auf unsere Lands-
leute in Paris den größten Einfluß ausübte", hätte ich nicht
durchgehen lassen. Die Teile ohne Fassung, das Ganze ohne Kom-
position, jener kurze Atem, der in einem Absatz absetzen muß,
als müßte er immer wieder sagen: so, und jetzt sprechen wir von
etwas anderm. Wäre Heine zum Aphorismus fähig gewesen, zu
dem ja der längste Atem gehört, er hätte auch hundert Seiten
Polemik durchhalten können. Von Börne, der in dieser Schrift
als sittlich und geistig negierte Person den Angreifer überragt,
sagt er: „Alle seine Anfeindungen waren am Ende nichts anderes, als der kleine Neid, den der kleine Tambour-Maitre gegen
den großen Tambour-Major empfindet – er beneidete mich ob
des großen Federbusches, der so keck in die Lüfte hineinjauchzt,
ob meiner reichgestickten Uniform, woran mehr Silber, als er,
der kleine Tambour-Maitre, mit seinem ganzen Vermögen be-
zahlen konnte, ob der Geschicklichkeit, womit ich den großen
Stock balanciere usw." Die Geschicklichkeit ist unleugbar, und
der Tambour-Major stimmt auch. In Börnes Haushalt sieht
Heine „eine Immoralität, die ihn anwidert", „das ganze Reinlich-
keitsgefühl seiner Seele" sträubt sich in ihm „bei dem Gedanken,
mit Börnes nächster Umgebung in die mindeste Berührung
zu geraten". Er weiß die längste Zeit auch nicht, ob Madame

'sumptuous' tea service of his own, he began to appreciate how those
aristocrats felt. He even started to worry about how his activities as a
critic might affect his porcelain. How would his porcelain fare if he had
to flee across the border and there was no time to pack carefully? In the
end, however, Börne gets his priorities in order. Heine closes out the
anecdote by (imaginatively) citing Börne as saying, '"But I am still
strong enough to break my porcelain bonds, and if the authorities make

want to revise, condense, deepen. "In addition to the passage of the Polish soldiers, I have characterized the occurrences in Rhenisch Bavaria as the next lever which, following the July Revolution, gave rise to the agitation in Germany and had the most profound influence even on our countrymen in Paris" is not a sentence I would have let stand. The parts without a frame; the whole without composition; that short-windedness that has to keep catching itself in a new paragraph, as if to say "So, and now let's talk about something else."[76] Had Heine been capable of aphorism (for which, indeed, the longest wind is needed), he could have made it through even a hundred pages of polemic. Of Börne, the ethically and intellectually rejected person who towers over the writer attacking him, he says, "In the end, all of his hostilities were nothing more than the petty jealousies that the little drummer boy feels for the great drum major—he envies me for the big plume that struts so boldly in the wind, and for my richly embroidered uniform, on which there's more silver than he, the little drummer boy, could buy with his entire life savings, and for the skill with which I twirl my baton, etc." The skill is undeniable; and the drum major is also dead-on. Heine sees in Börne's household "an immorality that disgusts" him; his "soul's entire feeling for purity" bristles "at the thought of coming in the slightest contact with Börne's immediate surroundings." He has also wondered for the longest time whether Madame Wohl is Börne's lover "or merely his wife."[77] This perfectly fine joke is

---

it hot for me, truly, the beautiful gilded teapot, and the scenes of marital bliss and St. Catherine's tower and the Guard Headquarters and the homeland, will all fly out the window, and I will be a free man again." ' "—PR

76. Cf. Hemingway vs. Faulkner.

77. "Having once been amorously involved with Jeanette Wohl, Börne later cohabited with her and her husband. Heine presents the arrange-

Wohl nicht die Geliebte Börnes ist „oder bloß seine Gattin". Dieser ganz gute Witz ist bezeichnend für die Wurzellosigkeit des Heineschen Witzes, denn er deckt sich mit dem Gegenteil der Heineschen Auffassung von der Geschlechtsmoral. Heine hätte sich schlicht bürgerlich dafür interessieren müssen, ob Madame Wohl die Gattin Börnes oder bloß seine Geliebte sei. Er legt ja noch im Sterbebett Wert auf die Feststellung, er habe nie ein Weib berührt, wußt' er, daß sie vermählet sei. Aber in dieser Schrift sind auch andere peinliche Widersprüche. So wird Jean Paul der „konfuse Polyhistor von Bayreuth" genannt, und von Heine heißt es, er habe sich „in der Literatur Europas Monumente aufgepflanzt, zum ewigen Ruhme des deutschen

---

ment in *Ludwig Börne* as being both unseemly and the result of sexual deficiencies on Börne's part. On the other hand, Heine also plays with the idea that it should have been difficult for Börne to sustain his erotic desire for Wohl. According to Heine, her face grew to resemble 'an old piece of matzoh.' It was insults of this kind that landed Heine in a near-fatal duel. *Ludwig Börne* scandalized a lot of people—Friedrich Engels called the book 'the most execrable thing ever written in German'—but it put Wohl's husband, Salomon Strauß, in a positively murderous frame of mind. After a few rounds of verbal sparring, Strauß issued a challenge, and on September 7, 1841, a shot from his pistol nicked Heine in the hip. There was, however, another side to the reception of *Ludwig Börne*. When friends tried to warn Heine that the book's content might cause trouble, he riposted, 'But isn't it beautifully written?' Over the years, quite a few readers would reinforce that opinion. Thomas Mann, for example, effused that *Ludwig Börne* features 'the most brilliant German prose before Nietzsche.' So by questioning the literary quality of the book, Kraus was expanding the objections to what was already Heine's most unpopular work. By implication, moreover, Kraus was upholding a principle dear to him: that ethical and stylistic problems tend to go together." —PR

characteristic of the rootlessness[78] of Heine's wit, for it pays off with the opposite of Heine's notion of sexual morality. Heine would have to have been curious, in a straightforward bourgeois way, as to whether Madame Wohl was Börne's wife or merely his lover. Indeed, on his deathbed he still sets great store by his avowal that he never touched a woman he knew was married. But there are yet more embarrassing contradictions in this piece. Jean Paul, for example, is called "the muddled polymath of Bayreuth," while Heine says, of himself, that he has "planted in the literature of Europe monuments redounding to the eternal

78. I suspect that the word "rootlessness" is loaded, since assimilated German-Jewish writers were commonly reproached, by both anti-semites and Zionists, for their rootlessness. According to the stereotype, they could be only mimics or parasites of more authentic literary tradi-tions—hence their overrepresentation in feuilletons. The best German-Jewish writers of the early twentieth century, Kafka and Benjamin as well as Kraus, were all searching for deeper identities in which to root themselves. Kraus, a world-class mimic, would have felt the reproach of rootlessness the most keenly. His defense, as Reitter argues in his excellent Kraus study, *The Anti-Journalist*, was to problematize the pairing of "imitation with superficiality and of originality with authen-ticity. It is as if the way to establish a truly radical position as a Jewish journalist was to take an avant-garde stand, *in both theory and practice*, on precisely these issues." The result, Reitter contends, was "a radical performance of German-Jewish identity."

Kafka seems to have recognized this aspect of Kraus's project while questioning its success as a tactic for escaping the terrible in-between position in which German-Jewish writers found themselves. Kafka is said to have remarked, "Karl Kraus locks Jewish writers in his hell, watches over them, disciplines them strictly. However, he forgets that he, too, belongs in this hell." Kafka was no doubt partly right about this: no matter how strenuously Kraus avowed that he was writing for posterity, posterity will always struggle with his having radically per-

Geistes" ... Der deutsche Geist aber möchte vor allem das nackte Leben retten; und er wird erst wieder hochkommen, wenn sich in Deutschland die intellektuelle Schmutzflut verlaufen haben wird. Wenn man wieder das Kopfwerk sprachschöpferischer Männlichkeit erfassen und von dem erlernbaren Handwerk der Sprachzärtlichkeiten unterscheiden wird. Und ob dann von Heine mehr bleibt als sein Tod?

Die Lyrik seines Sterbens, Teile des Romanzero, die Lamentationen, der Lazarus: hier war wohl der beste Helfer am Werke, um die Form Heines zur Gestalt zu steigern. Heine hat das Erlebnis des Sterbens gebraucht, um ein Dichter zu sein. Es war ein Diktat: sing, Vogel, oder stirb. Der Tod ist ein noch besserer Helfer als Paris; der Tod in Paris, Schmerzen und Heimatsucht, die bringen schon ein Echtes fertig.

Ich hör' den Hufschlag, hör' den Trab,
Der dunkle Reiter holt mich ab –

---

formed his German-Jewish identity on texts and controversies that grow ever more antiquated and inaccessible. But I think that Kraus was also genuinely liberated by his ferocious attachment to the German language and to a culturally transcendent spirit of literature running from Greek myth and Shakespeare through Goethe and Nestroy.

credit of the German Mind."[79] The German Mind, however, would mainly like to escape with its life; and it will rise again only when the intellectual flood of filth in Germany has run its course: when people again begin to appreciate the mental labor of linguistically creative manliness[80] and to distinguish it from the learnable manual labor of linguistic ticklings. And will there then be anything left of Heine but his death?

The deathbed poetry, parts of *Romancero, Lamentations, Lazarus*: here he no doubt had the best of all helpers in raising his form to the level of genuine figuration. It took the experience of dying to make Heine a poet. It was a dictate: sing, bird, or die. Death is an even better helper than Paris; death in Paris, pain and homesickness, they do finally accomplish something authentic.

I hear the trot, the hooves beat near,
The dark rider comes to fetch me here—

79. "Johann Paul Friedrich Richter (1763–1825) wrote under the name Jean Paul. The author of bildungsromane, edgy satires of the old regime, and novels that brood over the oppositions between poetry and reality, Jean Paul connected with some of the big intellectual movements of his age: the Enlightenment, Classicism, Romanticism. But he was always something of an outsider in the German literary culture. Having tried hard to diminish Goethe's standing, he was in turn largely dismissed by the Romantics. In 1804 he moved from Berlin to Bayreuth, and from then on he stayed away from the literary scene, while continuing to write. Thus Jean Paul took on an aura of independence, which formed part of his appeal for Kraus, his fellow loner."—PR

80. I.e., like Kraus's own. He could almost be a rapper here, boasting of his potency and belittling his adversary's. And I, as a late adolescent, was susceptible to it, as I was to the humor of a phrase like "would

Er reißt mich fort, Mathilden soll ich lassen,
O, den Gedanken kann mein Herz nicht fassen!

Das ist andere Lyrik, als jene, deren Erfolg in den Geschäfts-
büchern ausgewiesen steht. Denn Heines Wirkung ist das Buch
der Lieder und nicht der Romanzero, und will man seine Früchte
an ihm erkennen, so muß man jenes aufschlagen und nicht diesen. Der Tod konzentriert, räumt mit dem tändelnden Halbweltschmerz auf und gibt dem Zynismus etwas Pathos. Heines
Pointen, so oft nur der Mißklang unlyrischer Anschauung, stellen hier selbst eine höhere Harmonie her. Sein Witz, im Er-
löschen verdichtet, findet kräftigere Zusammenfassungen; und
Geschmacklosigkeiten wie: „Geh ins Kloster, liebes Kind, oder
lasse dich rasieren", werden seltener. Das überlieferte Mot „dieu
me pardonnera, c'est son métier" ist in seiner vielbewunderten
Plattheit vielleicht eine Erfindung jener, die den Heine-Stil
komplett haben wollten. Aber es paßt zum Ganzen nicht schlecht.
Im Glauben und Unglauben wird Heine die Handelsvorstellung

mainly like to escape with its life." I was blissfully unaware of the dangerous territory Kraus was entering with his talk of a "flood of filth"
unleashed by the Jew Heine. (The raw sincerity of the phrase, in this
context, contrasts with his more playful and sophisticated use of antisemitic tropes elsewhere in the essay.) But Kraus's call for a return to
purity, and his offer of a complete system for making sense of the world
in terms of its contamination: this I could respond to, the way a twenty-
two-year-old today might respond to local organic farming or to radical Islam.

He tears me away, from Mathilde I must part,
Oh, the thought will burst my heart!

This is a different poetry from the one whose success is proven in the account books. For Heine's influence derives from the *Book of Songs*, not the *Romancero*, and if you want to judge the accomplishments by the man, you have to open the former, not the latter. Death concentrates, death clears away the trifling underworld-weariness[81] and lends pathos to the cynicism. Heine's witticisms, so often just the dissonance of an unlyrical perspective, produce a higher harmony here. Compressed by its extinction, his wit finds more powerful fusions; and tasteless items such as "Get thee to a nunnery, dear child, or get thee a shave" become rarer.[82] The mot traditionally ascribed to him, "*Dieu me pardonnera, c'est son métier*,"[83] is perhaps, in its much-admired triteness, an invention of those who wanted Heine to remain true to his style to the end. But it suits the whole not badly. Both in belief and unbelief, Heine can't rid himself of the imagery of commerce. Love itself

---

81. *Halbweltschmerz*: literally "half-world-weariness," which in German combines 'demimonde' with 'weltschmerz.' Characteristic Krausian wordplay.
82. The Heine poem Kraus is referencing, "Old Rose" ("Alte Rose"), is notably nasty. Heine compares a beautiful girl whom he knew in his youth to a budding rose. He pursued her when she burst into bloom, but she fought him off with her thorns. Now, when she's old and faded, she's pursuing *him*, looking for love, but there's a bristle on a wart on her chin—a new kind of thorn. It sticks him as she tries to kiss him, and he tells her to shave. This kind of thing may be rarer in Heine's late poetry, but I'm with Kraus: it speaks to Heine's moral character.
83. "God will pardon me, that's his job."
   Reitter: "According to one witness, this was Heine's deathbed response to the question: How do things stand with you and God?"

nicht los. Selbst die Liebe spricht zum Gott der Lieder, „sie verlange Sicherheiten", und der Gott fragt, wieviel Küsse sie ihm auf seine goldene Leier borgen wolle. Indes, der Zynismus Heines, diese altbackene Pastete aus Witz und Weh, mundet dem deutschen Geschmack recht wohl, wenn ers auch nicht wahr haben will. Zu Offenbach, in dessen Orchester der tausendjährige Schmerz von der Lust einer Ewigkeit umtanzt wird, verhält sich dieser Schmerzspötter wie ein routinierter Asra zu einem geborenen Blaubart, einem vom Stamme jener, welche töten, wenn sie lieben.

. . . Was will die einsame Träne? Was will ein Humor, der unter Tränen lächelt, weil weder Kraft zum Weinen da ist noch zum Lachen? Aber der „Glanz der Sprache" ist da und der hat sich vererbt. Und unheimlich ist, wie wenige es merken, daß er von der Gansleber kommt, und wie viele sich davon ihr Hausbrot vollgeschmiert haben. Die Nasen sind verstopft, die Augen sind blind, aber die Ohren hören jeden Gassenhauer. So hat sich

says to the god of songs that "it demands guarantees," and the god asks how many kisses Love will advance him against his golden lyre. And meanwhile Heine's cynicism, this stale potpie of wit and woe, has become rather pleasing to the German palate, though the palate may not want to admit it. Compared with Offenbach, in whose orchestra the thousand-year misery is ringed by a dance of eternal delight, this ridiculer of misery looks like a trained Asra next to a born Bluebeard—to the kind that kills when it loves.[84]

. . . What does the lonely tear want?[85] What does a humor want which smiles through tears because both the strength to cry and the strength to laugh are lacking? But the "brilliance of language" isn't lacking, and it runs in the family. And it's uncanny how few people notice that it comes from chopped liver, and how many have spread it all over their household bread. Their noses are stuffed, their eyes are blind, but their ears are wide open to every hit song.[86] And so, thanks to Heine, the feuilleton has

84. "A reference to Offenbach's operetta *Bluebeard* (1866), which Kraus adored." —PR

Kraus is having fun with with Heine's poem "The Asra," which, in good Romantic fashion, is set in an exotic sultanate. Every evening, the sultan's beautiful daughter takes a walk in her garden and sees a young slave boy who's getting paler day by day. Finally she asks him who he is, and he tells her that he's from a Yemeni tribe, the Asra, "who die when they love." With the comparison with Offenbach, Kraus is mocking both the secondhand "misery" of the poem and the passive, unmasculine suffering of its author's persona.

85. "'What Does the Lonely Tear Want?' ('Was will die einsame Träne?') is the title of one of Heine's most famous 'songs.' Robert Schumann set the poem to music in 1840." —PR

86. Why was Kraus so angry? Consider the facts. He was a late child in a prosperous, well-assimilated Jewish family whose business generated

a large enough and steady enough income to make him financially independent for life. This in turn enabled him to publish *Die Fackel* exactly as he wished, without making concessions to advertisers or subscribers. He had a close circle of good friends and a much larger circle of admirers, many of them fanatical, some of them famous. He was an electrifying public speaker, capable of filling the largest theaters, which went a long way toward satisfying his youthful ambition to be an actor. Although he never married, he had some brilliant affairs and a deep long-term relationship with Sidonie. He seems to have suffered nothing like the conflicts with his father that Kafka had with his, nor to have regretted not having children. His only significant health problem was a curvature of the spine, and even this had the benefit of exempting him from military service. So how did a person so extremely fortunate become the Great Hater?

Kafka once diagnosed in German-Jewish writers a "terrible inner state," related to a bad relationship with Judaism. A bad inner state can certainly be discerned in Kraus's agon with Heine, as in a handful of other Kraus texts (including "He's Still a Jew" and his short play *Literatur*) and in his strikingly personal vendetta against certain Jews, including the publisher of the *Neue Freie Presse*. But Kraus's Jewish problem seems to me at most a supporting element in his larger project—his exposure of Austrian hypocrisies and corruption, his championing of language and literature he considered authentic and underappreciated. And although there was certainly plenty to be angry about in Austrian society, there's plenty to be angry about in every society; most people find ways to keep their anger from consuming their lives. You could understand a Viennese laborer with a sixty-hour workweek in bad conditions being enraged. But the privileged and sociable Kraus?

I wonder if he was so angry *because* he was so privileged. In "Nestroy and Posterity," the Great Hater defends his hatred like this: "acid wants the gleam, and the rust says it's only being corrosive." Kraus hated bad language because he loved good language—because he had the gifts, both intellectual and financial, to cultivate that love. And the person who's been lucky in life can't help expecting the world to keep

going his way; when the world insists on going wrong ways, corrupt and tasteless ways, he feels betrayed by it. He could have enjoyed a good life if only the bad world hadn't spoiled it. And so he gets angry, and the anger itself then further isolates him and heightens his sense of specialness. Being angry at newspapers beloved by the bourgeoisie was a way for Kraus to say "I don't belong to you" to a bourgeoisie whose upward striving was uncomfortably close to his own. His anger at the privileged writers who pulled strings to escape combat in the First World War was a kind of homeopathic attack on the even greater privilege that he himself enjoyed, the privilege of a morally pure medical excuse not to serve. He was a journalist who savaged other journalists, most of whom, unlike him, had to work for a living. Anger relieved some of the discomfort of his own privilege, by reassuring him that he was also a victim.

Kraus, like any artist, wanted above all to be an individual, and his anger can further be seen as a violent shrugging-off of categories that threatened his individual integrity. His privilege was just one of these categories. As the scholar Edward Timms writes in his magisterial study of Kraus, "He was a Jew by birth, an Austrian by nationality, a Viennese by residence, a German by language, a journalist by profession, bourgeois by social status and a rentier by economic position. Amid the ideological turmoil of Austria-Hungary, all of these ascribed identities seemed like falsifications." For much of his life Kraus was defiantly antipolitical; he seemed to form professional alliances almost with the intention of later torpedoing them spectacularly; and he was given to paradoxical utterances like "It is known that my hatred of the Jewish press is exceeded only by my hatred of the antisemitic press, while my hatred of the antisemitic press is exceeded only by my hatred of the Jewish press." Since it is also known that Kraus's favorite play was *King Lear*, I wonder if he might have seen his own fate in Cordelia, the cherished late child who loves the king and who, precisely because she's been the privileged daughter, secure in the king's love, has the personal integrity to refuse to debase her language and lie to him in his dotage. Privilege set Kraus, too, on the road to being an independent individual, but the world seemed bent on thwarting him. It disappointed him

the way Lear disappoints Cordelia, and in Kraus this became a recipe for anger. In his yearning for a better world, in which true individuality was possible, he kept applying the acid of his anger to everything that was false.

Let me turn to my own example, since I've been reading it into Kraus's story anyway.

I was a late child in a loving family that, although it wasn't nearly prosperous enough to make me a rentier, did have enough money to place me in a good public school district and send me to an excellent college, where I learned to love literature and language. I was a white male heterosexual American with good friends and perfect health, and beyond all this I had the immeasurably good fortune not only to discover very early what I wanted to do with my life but to have the freedom and the talent to pursue it. I had such an embarrassment of riches that I can barely stand to enumerate them here. And yet, for all my privileges, I became an extremely angry person. Anger descended on me so near in time to when I fell in love with Kraus's writing that the two occurrences are practically indistinguishable.

I wasn't born angry. If anything, I was born the opposite. It may sound like an exaggeration, but I think it's accurate to say that I knew nothing of anger until I was twenty-two. As an adolescent, I'd had my moments of sullenness and rebellion against authority, but, like Kraus, I'd had minimal conflict with my father, and the worst that could be said of me and my mother was that we bickered like an old married couple. Real anger, anger as a way of life, was foreign to me until one particular afternoon in April 1982. I was on a deserted train platform in Hannover. I'd come from Munich and was waiting for a train to Berlin, it was a dark gray German day, and I took a handful of German coins out of my pocket and started throwing them on the platform. There was an element of anti-German hostility in this, because I'd recently had a horrible experience with a penny-pinching old German woman, and it did me good to imagine other penny-pinching old German women bending down to pick the coins up, as I knew they would, and thereby aggravating their knee and hip pains. The way I hurled the coins, though, was more generally angry. I was angry at the world in a

way I'd never been before. The proximate cause of my anger was my failure to have sex with an unbelievably pretty girl in Munich, except that it hadn't actually been a failure, it had been a decision on my part. A few hours later, on the platform in Hannover, I marked my entry into the life that came after that decision by throwing away my coins. Then I boarded a train and went back to Berlin and enrolled in a class on Karl Kraus.

Paul Reitter kindly refines my theory and elaborates:

"Kraus hated his fellow German-Jewish writers for many reasons, not the least of which was that they wasted what he himself was so determined to use: privilege. Certainly many German-Jewish writers had money troubles, and Kraus, to his credit, was quite sensitive to the problem of penury—he helped keep the (German-Jewish) poets Peter Altenberg and Else Lasker-Schüler afloat. Yet a lot of fin de siècle German-Jewish authors were, as Kraus saw it, like him: well positioned to take some risks. Like him (and, say, Stefan Zweig), they were the children of the newly emancipated and prosperous *Gründerzeit* generation. If their fathers often tried to steer them into business, as Kraus himself suggests in his drama *Literatur*, there were resources to fall back on, something that ultimately made turning to letters much easier. Nor was there any lack of talent; Kraus always claimed that the German-Jewish literati had an abundance of that. But despite having so many advantages, these writers mostly chose to play it safe, reinforcing a bad paradigm of feuilletonism or parroting the latest style of expressionism, while treating such cultural authorities as the *Neue Freie Presse* with servile respect. The psychological needs and assimilationist tendencies that drove German-Jewish authors to do this were of interest to Kraus: hence the play *Literatur*, which Kafka esteemed and which, in fact, inspired his famous meditations on the 'terrible inner state' of German-Jewish writers. However, those needs and tendencies didn't excuse anything. As motives for bad linguistic behavior, they struck Kraus as tawdry.

"Could there be similar dynamics—minus the Jewish element—operating in some of our own contemporary literary scenes? The anecdotal evidence keeps piling up. Let's say that someone has given you a

dank Heine die Erfindung des Feuilletons zur höchsten Vollkommenheit entwickelt. Mit Originalen läßt sich nichts anfangen, aber Modelle können ausgebaut werden. Wenn die Heine-Nachahmer fürchten mußten, daß man sie entlarven könnte, so brauchten sie nur Heine-Fälscher zu werden und durften getrost unter seinem Namen en gros produzieren. Sie nehmen in der Heine-Literatur einen breiten Raum ein. Aber die Forscher,

---

recent novel. You can't recall seeing reviews of the book, but it looks like a high-end production. The press that published it is a very good one, and on its cover are blurbs from respected figures in the world of letters. Would you be surprised to learn that the author of the novel lives in Park Slope with a husband and two young children? Would you be surprised to read, on the author's website, that she grew up in Lake Forest, was educated at Brown, and teaches writing as an adjunct at the New School? When I encounter such author information, I sometimes wonder how the economics work. Advances are small, book sales are declining, teaching jobs don't pay well, and Park Slope is very expensive, as are kids. Maybe the family is just getting by. But in an age of soaring college tuition and health insurance costs, not many people from an affluent background are willing to take upon themselves the hazards of real, open-ended downward mobility. Maybe, then, the husband is a lawyer or in finance. Yet mixed couples aren't the norm, I'm told. If the husband is a fellow author, it may well be that the couple has gotten help from its baby-boomer parents. And if that's so, writing doesn't, and probably won't ever, pay the biggest bills.

"But there's still the desire as well as the pressure to succeed. For literati, as for professors of literature, the increasingly steep straight path to recognizable signs of accomplishment is to produce conventional work of high quality. I enjoy a lot of the writing created on this route, and I'm not about to echo Kraus's apocalyptic condemnation of the talented authors who take it. What feels sad, nevertheless, is that at a time when a relatively small percentage of the New York literary scene appears to be supporting itself through its writing, a high per-

evolved to the highest level of perfection. There's nothing to be done with an original, but copies can always be improved. When the imitators of Heine began to fear that somebody would expose them, all they had to do was become forgers of Heine, and they could go into mass production under his name. They take up a lot of space in the literature of Heine. But the experts who

---

centage of the scene is so very cautious. Indeed, the scene routinely demands of itself and others both cautiousness and the display of the most uncontroversial virtues (balance, moderation, warmth, etc.). God forbid that a novelist should be a little mean to her characters. Much more than in previous eras, we find such authorial harshness framed as reason enough for a (cautiously) negative review. Of course, sometimes the calls for niceness are themselves nasty. But in the more august places, that's certainly not the norm. One can be generally for civility in reviewing and still be alarmed by the fact a measured, polite, unfavorable appraisal of *Joseph Anton*, which appeared in *The New York Review of Books* (and exhibits a particular dislike for the 'egregiously uncharitable' treatment of exes in Rushdie's memoir), could win notoriety as a full-on 'takedown' job. Or consider that a few years ago, the critic and novelist Dale Peck got a lot of attention merely by being rude to some well-known writers. Consider also that even as brilliant a reviewer as the late John Leonard has been posthumously taken to task for the immoderation that was a function of his exuberance. So what if his riffing and ranting wasn't always comprehensible? It was unfailingly fun, and the style was his alone. But it made Leonard's *Times* reviewer 'yearn for a more straightforward or prioritized analysis.' Because, of course, critics should all sound more or less alike."

I might add that the tyranny of niceness, in contemporary fiction, is enforced by terror of the Internet and its ninth-grade social dynamics. Writers afraid of running afoul of the bloggers and the tweeters, of becoming universally "known" as *not a nice person*, can defend themselves with laudable sentiments: literacy and self-expression are good,

denen ihre Festellung gelingt, sind nicht sachverständig genug, um zu wissen, daß mit dem Dieb auch der Eigentümer entlarvt ist. Er selbst war durch einen Dietrich ins Haus gekommen und ließ die Tür offen. Er war seinen Nachfolgern mit schlechtem Beispiel vorangegangen. Er lehrte sie den Trick. Und je weiter das Geheimnis verbreitet wurde, umso köstlicher war es. Darum verlangt die Pietät des Journalismus, daß heute in jeder Redaktion mindestens eine Wanze aus Heines Matratzengruft gehalten wird. Das kriecht am Sonntag platt durch die Spalten und stinkt uns die Kunst von der Nase weg! Aber es amüsiert uns, so um das wahre Leben betrogen zu werden. In Zeiten, die Zeit hatten, hatte man an der Kunst eins aufzulösen. In einer Zeit, die Zeitungen hat, sind Stoff und Form zu rascherem Verständnis getrennt. Weil wir keine Zeit haben, müssen uns die Autoren umständlich sagen, was sich knapp gestalten ließe. So ist Heine wirklich der Vorläufer moderner Nervensyteme, als der er von Künstlern gepriesen wird, die nicht sehen, daß ihn die Philister besser vertragen haben, als er die Philister. Denn der Heinehaß der Philister gibt nach, wenn für sie der Lyriker in Betracht kommt, und für den Künstler kommt Heines Philisterhaß in Betracht, um die Persönlichkeit zu retten. So durch ein Mißverständnis immer aktuell, rechtfertigt er die schöne Bildung des

---

bigotry is bad, working people are the salt of the earth, love is more important than money, technology is fun, gentrification is a serious problem, animals have feelings, children are less corrupt than adults, and so on. To attempt a harsh critique of the electronic system that reduces writers to these bromides is to risk having it become common "knowledge" that you're a hater, a loner, not one of *us*.

succeeded in exposing the fraud aren't expert enough to realize that to expose the thief is to have exposed the owner.[87] He himself broke into the house with a skeleton key, leaving the door open behind him. He set a bad example for his successors. He taught them the trick. And the farther the trick spread, the more delicious it became. Thus the pieties of journalism demand that every editorial masthead today include at least a bedbug from Heine's "mattress grave." Every Sunday it creeps flatly through the columns and stinks the art out of our noses! But to be tricked out of a real life in this way is entertaining to us. In times that had time, art gave us one to resolve. In times that have the *Times*, form and content are split apart for faster understanding. Because we have no time, writers are obliged to say in many words what could have been succinctly put. So Heine really is the forerunner of modern nervous systems, praised by artists who fail to notice that the philistines have tolerated him a lot better than he tolerated philistines. For the philistines relent in their hatred of Heine when they take his poetry into account, while the artists take Heine's hatred of philistines into account in order to rescue his personality. And so, by means of a misunderstanding that never gets old, he vindicates the pretty coinage "cosmopolite," in

87. "Kraus bragged of possessing a savage proficiency in mimicking other writers, and some of his readers agreed. Walter Benjamin, for example, once commented that Kraus's literary impersonations were so intense and accurate that they felt 'cannibalistic.' One could almost see the 'blood dripping from his lips,' according to Benjamin. But Kraus may have been even prouder of how hard it was to copy his own style, of how it resisted mass consumption and reproduction in a way that Heine's, with its 'consequences,' hadn't. As Benjamin's friend Gershom Scholem put it, Kraus 'fought a war for incomprehensibility.' This is the spirit in which Kraus contends, in his Heine essay, that 'to expose the thief is to have exposed the owner.' Attempts to pass off imitations as

Wortes „Kosmopolit", in der sich der Kosmos mit der Politik versöhnt hat. Detlev von Liliencron hatte nur eine Landanschauung. Aber mir scheint, er war in Schleswig-Holstein kosmischer als Heine im Weltall. Schließlich werden doch die, welche nie aus ihrem Bezirk herauskamen, weiter kommen als die, die nie in ihren Bezirk hineinkamen.

Was Nietzsche zu Heine gezogen hat – er hatte den Kleinheitswahn, als er im Ecce homo schrieb, sein Name werde mit dem Heines durch die Jahrtausende gehen –, kann nur jener Haß gegen Deutschland sein, der jeden Bundesgenossen annimmt. Wenn man aber den Lazzaroni für ein Kulturideal neben dem deutschen Schutzmann hält, so gibt es gewiß nichts deutscheres als solchen Idealismus, der die weglagernde Romantik schon fürs

---

Heine's own work, as well as a parroting of Heine that reached the point of forgery—all that is unsavory stuff, of course. However, the scholars who have set about trying to identify the fraud, and present themselves as intervening on Heine's behalf, don't realize that they're just further 'exposing' the ur-offense, which is that Heine's style facilitates such criminal activity. Kraus made the same argument a little more directly just after 'Heine and the Consequences' had appeared in *Die Fackel*. Under the heading 'My Professional Opinion,' he quotes in full a poem whose authorship was being debated and then asserts that whether or not Heine actually wrote the poem doesn't matter. In either case, it's 'from Heine'—that is, ultimately Heine's doing." —PR

Titles like "My Professional Opinion," which mocks the earnest literary experts, make me love Kraus.

which the cosmos reconciled itself to politics. Detlev von Liliencron had a merely provincial outlook. But it seems to me that he
was more cosmic in Schleswig-Holstein than Heine was in the
cosmos. In the end, the people who never came out of their prov-
ince will go farther than the people who never came into one.[88]

What attracted Nietzsche to Heine—he had delusions of
smallness when, in *Ecce Homo,* he wrote that his and Heine's
names would go down together through the centuries—must
have been that hatred of Germany which embraces every ally it
can find. But when you hold up the *lazzarone* as a cultural ideal
alongside the German constable, there certainly seems to be nothing more German than such idealism, which takes a plagiarizing

88. I think there's a lot of truth in this, but Kraus also seems to be making an implicit claim about his own decision to remain rooted in Vienna, in contradistinction to Heine. Here's the story I tell myself about
his agon with Heine. Basically, Kraus arrives too late. He's an assimilated Jew who has an enormous facility with language but strikingly
less talent with "original" forms such as poetry, drama, and fiction. And
unfortunately there's already been a German-speaking Jew like him—
Heine—who, worse yet, became one of the most famous and influential writers of the previous century. Kraus needs room to live and to
work and to believe in the necessity of his work, and what does he have
to hold on to in his struggle against his famous precursor? His feeling
that there was something wrong with Heine—with the work, the man,
his language. And so the story that *he* tells himself is that Heine was a
proto-Kraus who betrayed his gifts by his moral failings and thereby
betrayed assimilated German Jews, too. Heine helped *create* the stereotype of the rootless, linguistically facile Jew. Without Heine, no feuilleton, yes. But also: without Heine, Kraus could simply have been a great
satirist who happened to be Jewish. Hence, I propose, the ferocity of
the attack in this essay, and the peculiarly moral tone of it. If Kraus also
sounds an antisemitic note, it's because he's trying to annihilate the bad
Jew, the stereotypical Jew, so as *not* to hate himself. That so many Gen-

tile German philistines are willing to forgive Heine's Jewishness only adds to his rage.

I, too, often make moral arguments about art, but on my better days I'm suspicious of them, because I'm aware of the envy, the powerlessness and self-pity, that lurks behind them. Back in the 1990s, I spent a lot of time assembling a moral case against John Updike. I was offended (rightly, I still think) by Updike's famous comparison of a writer's work to excretion: you take in life, digest it, and shit it out in paragraphs. Updike was very proud of his three-pages-per-day regularity, and I didn't need to know much about his personal history to imagine his mother crowing over the neatness and beauty of his daily bowel movements. My moral complaint was that Updike had tremendous, Nabokov-level talent and was wasting it, because he was too charmed by his daily dumps and too afraid of irregularity to take the kind of big literary risks that might have blocked him for a year or two. His lifelong penchant for alliteration was of a piece with this. It made reading even his otherwise fine stories about the Maples painful; I couldn't get through more than a few lines without running aground on the anal-retentive preciousness of his prose. Updike was exquisitely preoccupied with his own literary digestive processes, and his virtuosity in clocking and rendering the minutiae of daily life was undeniably unparalleled, but his lack of interest in the bigger postwar, postmodern, socio-technological picture marked him, in my mind, as a classic self-absorbed sixties-style narcissist. David Foster Wallace was the one who actually called Updike an asshole in print (in the *New York Observer*), but I felt the same way. If you'd suggested that I envied Updike for his unobstructed productivity or for all the women he got to go to bed with him (and then wrote about in graphic detail), I would only have restated my moral case more trenchantly.

Later on, after Updike ceased to seem like such a threat, I went through a period of feeling deeply censorious of Philip Roth, because he didn't seem to care about his many glaring technical deficiencies as a fiction writer, and because his admirers didn't seem to, either. Roth's writing seemed to me, as Kraus says of Heine's, "always and overplainly informative," which was why, I believed, the philistines had come to

tolerate him a lot better than he tolerated the philistines. As with Updike, my judgments had a flavor of Krausian moralism: Roth was lazy, Roth was an asshole, etc. Naturally, I believed that I was merely sticking up for vital aesthetic virtues—a fiction writer ought to be able to write good dialogue, create convincing and well-rounded female characters, and let a story tell itself without discursive intrusions—but these "vital" virtues happened to coincide with some of my own abilities as a fiction writer. To make my moral case against Roth, I had to ignore or downplay other plausible virtues, most notably Roth's heroic fearlessness of his readers' moral judgments, because I subterraneanly envied his fearlessness and wanted people to pay attention to *me* and not him. This was the kind of thing Nietzsche had in mind when he mocked the "slave" mentality of moral judgments.

"Heine and the Consequences" is the document of Kraus's struggle to overcome his great precursor. On his own terms, he may have succeeded; his best-known and most shattering work, *The Last Days of Mankind* (a documentary "drama" of the First World War), was written in the decade that followed. German readers, however, are not so convinced that he vanquished Heine. Daniel Kehlmann, for example, loves the essay and grants that Kraus scores a lot of points off Heine in it. "But," he says, "Heine is still wonderful, too."

Reitter offers a more fact-based counternarrative to mine:

"I agree that stereotypes about Jews and journalism weighed on Kraus: that's the whole point of *The Anti-Journalist*, my Kraus book. But for all of Kraus's sensitivity to how his writing was perceived, he was utterly convinced of its value and excellence. This was in notable contrast to many other gifted German-Jewish writers, including Schnitzler, Wittgenstein, and Kafka. The total absence of (Jewish) self-questioning in Kraus's personal communications is, indeed, remarkable. Kraus also thoroughly debunked the linguistic standards at the center of such self-questioning. He believed what he wrote about the bogusness of the genius-imitation hierarchy that antisemites never tired of invoking. His critique of it proceeded from the core of his understanding of language, as one of the more earnest lines of this essay makes clear: 'a creative head may say originally what somebody else

Ziel nimmt. Das intellektuelle Problem Heine, der Regenerator deutscher Luft, ist neben dem künstlerischen Problem Heine gewiß nicht zu übersehen: es läuft ja daneben. Doch hier ward einmal Sauerstoff in die deutschen Stuben gelassen und hat nach einer augenblicklichen Erholung die Luft verpestet. Daß, wer nichts zu sagen hat, es besser verständlich sage, diese Erkenntnis war die Erleichterung, die Deutschland seinem Heine dankt nach jenen schweren Zeiten, wo etwas zu sagen hatte, wer unverständlich war. Und diesen unleugbaren sozialen Fortschritt hat man der Kunst zugeschrieben, da man in Deutschland immerzu der Meinung ist, daß die Sprache das gemeinsame Ausdrucksmittel sei für Schreiber und Sprecher. Heines aufklärende Leistung in Ehren – ein so großer Satiriker, daß man ihm die Denkmalswürdigkeit absprechen müßte, war er nicht. Ja, er war ein so kleiner Satiriker, daß die Dummheit seiner Zeit auf die Nach-

---

has already said, and somebody else may already be imitating a thought that won't occur to a creative head until later.' Gershom Scholem, an enthusiastic early reader of the essay and a particularly alert observer of antisemitic discourse, was partaking of the essay's spirit when he wrote of Kraus: 'He never had an original thought in his life,' and 'that is meant here infinitely more as a compliment than as a criticism.'

"Charged with merely imitating genius, Heine responded by saying that since people can't seem to tell the difference between his imitation and the original, he'll go on imitating. Kraus wouldn't have been as self-effacing (never mind Heine's irony), and he wouldn't have accepted the implication that real genius and imitation are necessarily two different things. Unlike Heine, moreover, Kraus didn't have much trouble brushing off antisemitic slights (in part because, unlike Heine, he kept underestimating the danger of antisemitism). No doubt the low standing of his particular talents ate at Kraus, who was forever instructing readers to rate them higher; and he probably did blame Heine for fostering the development of a disadvantageous network of stereotypes

romanticism for something to be aspired to.[89] The intellectual problem of Heine, this refresher of German air, certainly should not be overlooked alongside the artistic problem of Heine: indeed, it runs alongside. And yet here, once, some oxygen was let into the room of Germany, and after a momentary improvement it tainted the air. That someone with nothing to say is better off saying it understandably: this perception was the relief for which Germany thanks its Heine after those difficult times when the people with something to say were all incomprehensible. And this undeniable piece of social progress has been attributed to art, since Germans are unshakable in their opinion that language is the means of expression common to both writers and speakers. With all due respect to Heine's enlightening achievement, he wasn't so great a satirist as to be deemed unworthy of a monument.[90] In fact, he was such a small satirist that the stupidity of

about Jewish writing. In the end, though, it's hard to see how these stereotypes led Kraus to the brink of hating himself. If the fierceness of his campaign against Heine seems telling, keep in mind that Kraus was similarly fierce in going after many other writers, both Jewish and non-Jewish."

89. This sentence is no easier to digest in the original. And yet it more or less makes sense, especially if you know that a *lazzarone* is a lowest-class Neapolitan beggar or idler.

90. "Should there be a Heine monument in Germany or Austria? When Kraus wrote 'Heine and the Consequences,' the question had been looming large in Germany and Austria for more than two decades. In 1906 Kraus himself entered the fray with a short piece entitled 'Around Heine,' in which he attacks both sides in the long-running monument debate. He dismisses the (thoroughly antisemitic) stand against a Heine monument as blustering 'idiocy,' but, typically, he seems more interested in flaying Heine's 'liberal' supporters, in part for their efforts to bring Heine into line with their own, less subversive lit-

welt gekommen ist. Gewiß, sie setzt sich jenes Denkmal, das sie ihm verweigert. Aber sie setzt sich wahrlich auch jenes, das sie für ihn begehrt. Und wenn sie ihr Denkmal nicht durchsetzt, so deponiert sie wenigstens ihre Visitkarte am Heine-Grab und bestätigt sich ihre Pietät in der Zeitung. Solange die Ballotage der Unsterblichkeit dauert, dauert die Unsterblichkeit, und wenn ein Volk von Vereinsbrüdern ein Problem hat, wird es so bald nicht fertig. Im Ausschuß der Kultur aber sitzen die Karpeles und Bartels, und wie immer die Entscheidung falle, sie beweist nichts für den Geist. Die niedrige Zeitläufigkeit dieser Debatte, die immerwährende Aktualität antiquierter Standpunkte ist so recht das Maß einer literarischen Erscheinung, an der nichts

---

erary values. Kraus concludes that Heine both does and doesn't deserve a monument, and that the real reason he shouldn't get one is that the one he would get would surely misrepresent him. Between the publication of 'Around Heine' and 'Heine and the Consequences,' Kraus revised his take on Heine, while the monument debate intensified in Austria. In 1907 Wilhelm II bought the palace on Corfu that Empress Elisabeth had owned, and he promptly shipped to France the Heine monument that 'Sissy,' a great Heine admirer, had unveiled in 1891. (This was actually the second Heine monument to be exiled; the first, commissioned by the city of Düsseldorf to mark the centenary of Heine's birth, was unveiled in 1899—in the Bronx.) Among the many Austrians who weighed in on whether Heine merited a monument was the young Adolf Hitler, who was adrift in Vienna in 1907. Oddly enough, it appears that Hitler belonged to the pro-monument camp. According to Reinhold Hanisch, a friend of his during his Vienna years, Hitler maintained that Heine was a great German poet and that Germany should memorialize him in stone. Germany's first Heine monument was unveiled in Frankfurt in 1913; the Nazis vandalized it not long after Hitler completed his rise to the chancellorship."—PR

his times has descended on posterity. Granted, this posterity builds itself the monument that it refuses to give him. But truly it also builds itself the one it wants for him. And if it doesn't follow through with its monument, it at least leaves its calling card on Heine's grave and reassures itself of its piety in the newspaper. As long as the secret balloting about his immortality continues, his immortality will continue, and when a nation of fraternity brothers has a problem, it won't be making an end of it so soon. But the cultural subcommittee is manned by the Karpeleses and the Bartelses, and whichever way the decision finally falls, it won't prove anything for the Mind.[91] The squalid all-in-due-courseness of this debate, the perennial timeliness of antiquated perspectives, is the perfect emblem for a literary phenomenon in

91. "Gustav Karpeles (1848–1909) was a proudly Jewish literary critic who, in 1868, had made the case that Heine was essentially a Jewish writer. Adolf Bartels (1862–1945) was the antisemitic literary critic who had been leading the fight to deny Heine a statue in Germany, his argument being that Heine was essentially a Jewish writer, and not a German one. By grouping together Karpeles and Bartels on the same 'cultural subcommittee,' Kraus is doing something he had done elsewhere, most notably in his critique of Zionism: he's pointing to structural parallels between the language of Jewish self-consciousness and that of antisemitic discourse. In Kraus's view, both sides were obsessed with identifying the Jewishness of works by secular Jewish writers; and as they tried to identify that Jewishness, critics of both Karpeles's and Bartels's ilk relied on crude ideas about how an author's Jewish heritage could manifest itself in his or her literary output." —PR

And, thus, Kraus's observation that it doesn't matter which side wins the debate.

ewig ist als der Typus, der von nirgendwo durch die Zeit läuft. Dieser Typus, der die Mitwelt staunen macht, weil er auf ihrem Niveau mehr Talent hat als sie, hat in der Kunst der Sprache, die jeder, der spricht, zu verstehen glaubt, schmerzlichen Schaden gestiftet. Wir erkennen die Persönlichkeiten nicht mehr, und die Persönlichkeiten beneiden die Techniker. Wenn Nietzsche Heines Technik bewundert, so straft ihn jeder Satz, den er selbst schrieb,

which nothing is eternal but the personality type, which runs through time from nowhere. This type, who amazes his contemporaries by having more talent on their level than they do, has inflicted grievous damage on the art of language, which everyone who speaks believes he can understand.[92] We no longer recognize the personalities, and the personalities envy the technicians.[93] If Nietzsche admires Heine's technique, then he is

92. "Kraus is working with a line by Goethe, a line that underscores the resemblance, in German, between the words 'speak' [*sprechen*] and 'language' [*Sprache*]—'*Ein jeder, weil er spricht, glaubt auch über die Sprache sprechen zu können*' ['every person believes, because he speaks, that he can speak about language']. Following Goethe, Kraus, too, is suggesting that as a result of the *sprechen-Sprache* resemblance, the German language is particularly vulnerable to the problem: all speakers see themselves as capable of comprehending it."—PR
93. Although the word "personality," as applied to people like Paris Hilton and Charles Barkley, has taken on adspeak flavor in English, Kraus is using it approvingly here.

Kraus will get into the problem of technology and the Mind more extensively in "Nestroy and Posterity." But a lot of good writers have lately been fretting, mostly in private, about what it means that they can't interest themselves in Facebook and Twitter. I think it means that they have personalities. This feels like strangely meager consolation, though, when you see the rest of the world giving itself heedlessly (I almost wrote "headlessly") to the new technologies.

Immersing myself in Kraus in my twenties helped innoculate me against technology envy. I internalized his distrust and made it my own, even though, in the early 1980s, technology to me meant little more than TV, airliners, nuclear weaponry, and the minibus-size computer at the seismology lab where I worked part-time. Because I'd used computers in high school and college and was an early adopter of computerized word processing, I've persisted in the quaint conviction that technology is a tool, not a way of life. The metastatic and culturally

Lügen. Nur einer nicht: „Die Meisterschaft ist dann erreicht, wenn man sich in der Ausführung weder vergreift noch zögert". Das Gegenteil dieser untiefen Einsicht ist die Sache des Künstlers. Seine Leistung sind Skrupel; er greift zu, aber er zaudert, nachdem er zugegriffen hat. Heine war nur ein Draufgänger der Sprache; nie hat er die Augen vor ihr niedergeschlagen. Er schreibt das Bekenntnis hin: „Der Grundsatz, daß man den Charakter eines Schriftstellers aus seiner Schreibweise erkenne, ist nicht unbedingt richtig; er ist bloß anwendbar bei jener Masse von Autoren, denen beim Schreiben nur die augenblickliche Inspiration die Feder führt, und die mehr dem Worte gehorchen, als befehlen. Bei Artisten ist jener Grundsatz unzulässig, denn diese sind Meister des Wortes, handhaben es zu jedem beliebigen Zwecke, prägen es nach Willkür, schreiben objektiv, und ihr Charakter verrät sich nicht in ihrem Stil". So war er: ein Talent, weil kein Charakter; bloß daß er die Artisten mit den Journalisten verwechselt hat. Und die Masse von Autoren, die dem Wort gehorchen, gibt es leider nur spärlich. Das sind die Künstler. Talent haben die andern: denn es ist ein Charakterdefekt. Hier spricht Heine seine unbedingte Wahrheit aus; er braucht sie gegen Börne. Aber da er objektiv schreibt und als Meister des Worts dieses zu jedem beliebigen Zwecke handhabt, so paßt ihm das Gegenteil gegen Platen. In ihm sein, „ungleich dem wahren Dichter, die Sprache nie Meister geworden"; er sei „dagegen Meister geworden in der Sprache, oder vielmehr auf der Sprache, wie ein Virtuose auf einem Instrumente". Heine ist objektiv. Gegen Börne: „Die Taten der Schriftsteller bestehen in Worten".

transformative technological advances of the last two decades have struck me as vindications of Kraus's warnings. In 1910 he was already not impressed; and his work showed me the way to not being impressed myself. But even I am not immune to feelings of dread and, yes, envy when I see books being routed by electronics in the sexiness contest.

given the lie by every sentence he himself ever wrote. Except one: "You have attained mastery when you neither err nor hesitate in the execution."[94] The converse of this shallow insight is the artist's business. His achievement is scruples. He seizes, but, after seizing, he hesitates. Heine was a go-getter of the language; never did he cast his eyes down before her. Here is how his credo reads: "The axiom that we may know the character of an author from his style is not unconditionally correct; it is applicable merely to that mass of authors who depend upon momentary inspirations to guide their pens, and who obey the word more than they command it. With artistes, this axiom is inadmissible, for these are masters of the word, they manipulate it to whatever end they please, coin it according to their whim, write objectively, and their character does not betray itself in their style." And that's what he was: a talent, because no character; except he confused the artistes with the journalists.[95] As for the mass of authors who obey the word, they are unfortunately very few. These are the artists. Talent is what the others have: for it is a character defect. Here Heine utters his unconditional truth; he needs it against Börne. But since he writes objectively and, as a master of the word, manipulates it to whatever end he pleases, the opposite suits hims against Platen. In Platen, "unlike the true poet, the language has never become master"; he has, "rather, become a master in the language, or, rather, on the language, like a virtuoso on an instrument." Heine is objective. Against Börne: "The deeds of an author consist in words." Against Platen: he calls his

---

94. From an aphorism in Nietzsche's *Dawn* (1881).
95. "Kraus is reworking, and repurposing against Heine, yet another of Heine's own lines, which is itself a reworking of a line by Börne. Heine writes in the long poem *Atta Troll* (1847), 'No talent, and yet a character!'"—PR

Gegen Platen: er nenne seine Leistung „eine große Tat in Worten" – „so gänzlich unbekannt mit dem Wesen der Poesie, wisse er nicht einmal, daß das Wort nur bei dem Rhetor eine Tat, bei dem wahren Dichter aber ein Ereignis ist."

Was war es bei Heine? Nicht Tat und nicht Ereignis, sondern Absicht oder Zufall. Heine war ein Moses, der mit dem Stab auf den Felsen der deutschen Sprache schlug. Aber Geschwindigkeit ist keine Hexerei, das Wasser floß nicht aus dem Felsen, sondern er hatte es mit der andern Hand herangebracht; und es war Eau de Cologne. Heine hat aus dem Wunder der sprachlichen Schöpfung einen Zauber gemacht. Er hat das höchste geschaffen, was mit der Sprache zu schaffen ist; höher steht, was aus der Sprache geschaffen wird. Er konnte hundert Seiten schreiben, aber nicht die Sprache der hundert ungeschriebenen Seiten gestalten. Wenn nach Iphigeniens Bitte um ein holdes Wort des Abschieds der König „Lebt wohl!" sagt, so ist es, als ob zum erstenmal in der Welt Abschied genommen würde, und solches „Lebt wohl!" wiegt das Buch der Lieder auf und hundert Seiten von Heines Prosa. Das Geheimnis der Geburt des alten Wortes war ihm fremd. Die Sprache war ihm zu Willen. Doch nie brachte sie ihn zu schweigender Ekstase. Nie zwang ihn ihre

achievement "in words, a splendid deed"—"so entirely unfamiliar with the essence of poesy that he doesn't even know that the word is a deed only for a rhetorician, whereas for a true poet the word is an event."

Which was it for Heine? Neither deed nor event but intention or accident. Heine was a Moses who tapped his staff on the rocks of the German language. But speed isn't sorcery, the water didn't flow from the rock, he simply brought it up with his other hand; and it was eau de cologne.[96] Heine turned the miracle of linguistic creation into a magic act. He achieved as much as can be achieved with language; greater still is what can be created *out* of language. He could write a hundred pages, but he couldn't shape the language of the hundred pages that weren't written. When Iphigenie[97] begs for a kind parting word and the king says to her, "Farewell!" it's as though leave were being taken for the first time in the world, and a "Farewell!" like this outweighs the *Book of Songs* and a hundred pages of Heine's prose. The mystery of the birth of the old word was foreign to him.[98] The language was at his command. Yet never did she reduce him to silent

96. Here is Reitter's helpful parsing in *The Anti-Journalist*: "Kraus's Heine is a Jewish parvenu. He deals in the sweet, non-nourishing superficialities of Western culture. But again, as a Moses, Heine remains a transformative moment for the Jews. Thus Kraus suggests that Heine's feuilletonistic writing, a verbal eau de cologne, has a kind of foundational significance in German-Jewish culture, or, for the turn-of-the-century Jewish literati, 'the consequences.' If Heine is a foppish Moses in assimilated Jewish culture, his textual legacy, feuilletonism, would amount to its saccharine sacred text."
97. The heroine of the Goethe tragedy *Iphigenie auf Tauris*.
98. This is Kraus's most concise formulation of the paradox of linguistic originality. "Farewell," a very old word, is born anew by Goethe's use of it in *Iphigenie*.

Gnade auf die Knie. Nie ging er ihr auf Pfaden nach, die des profanen Lesers Auge nicht errät, und dorthin, wo die Liebe erst beginnt. O markverzehrende Wonne der Spracherlebnisse! Die Gefahr des Wortes ist die Lust des Gedankens. Was bog dort um die Ecke? Noch nicht ersehen und schon geliebt! Ich stürze mich in dieses Abenteuer.

ecstasy. Never did her favor force him to his knees. Never did he follow paths invisible to the profane reader's eye, approaching the place where love first begins. Oh, the marrow-burning rapture of experiences in language! The danger of the word is the delight of thought. What turned the corner there? Not even seen and already loved! I plunge into this adventure.

Nestroy und die Nachwelt

ZUM 50. TODESTAGE

NESTROY¹ AND POSTERITY

ON THE FIFTIETH ANNIVERSARY
OF HIS DEATH

1. Johann Nestroy (1801–1862) was a leading figure in the golden age of Viennese theater, in the first half of the nineteenth century. Although virtually unknown outside Austria (owing in part to the Austrian inflection of his lower-class characters' language), he was widely loved at home for his comic genius. Like Shakespeare, Nestroy was an

Wir können sein Andenken nicht feiern, indem wir uns, wie's einer Nachwelt ziemt, zu einer Schuld bekennen, die wir abzutragen haben. So wollen wir sein Andenken feiern, indem wir uns zu einer Schuld bekennen, die wir zu tragen haben, wir Insassen einer Zeit, welche die Fähigkeit verloren hat, Nachwelt zu sein... Wie sollte der ewige Bauherr nicht von den Erfahrungen dieses Jahrhunderts lernen? Seitdem es Genies gibt, wurden sie als Trockenwohner in die Zeit gesetzt; sie zogen aus und die Menschheit hatte es wärmer. Seitdem es aber Ingenieure gibt, wird das Haus unwohnlicher. Gott erbarme sich der Entwicklung! Er lasse die Künstler lieber nicht geboren werden, als mit

---

inveterate borrower of well-worn plots, which he executed with unapologetic panache, and he had a Shakespearean gift for rendering his buffoons at once ridiculous and sympathetic. His language was brilliant and his plot structures were crisp, but because so much of his work was mistakable for what Kraus will here call "routine," and because comedy is everywhere (and especially in Germany) held in lower esteem than tragedy, his reputation at the time of Kraus's celebration of him was closer to Gilbert and Sullivan's than to Shakespeare's.

In "Nestroy and Posterity" (1912), Kraus was doing the inverse of what he'd done two years earlier in "Heine and the Consequences"—

We cannot celebrate his memory the way a posterity ought to, by acknowledging a debt we're called upon to honor, and so we want to celebrate his memory by confessing to a bankruptcy that dishonors us, we inhabitants of a time that has lost the capacity to *be* a posterity . . . How could the eternal Builder fail to learn from the experiences of this century? For as long as there have been geniuses, they've been placed into a time like temporary tenants, while the plaster was still drying; then they moved out and left things cozier for humanity. For as long as there have been engineers, however, the house has been getting less habitable. God have mercy on the development! Better that He not

championing an underrated writer rather than taking down an overrated one. The reader should be warned that the Nestroy essay is, in places, even denser than the Heine. But here again Kraus is leveraging a seemingly intramural literary fight into a very broad cultural critique, which is the essence of his method: he jumps directly from a small ill (the fact that Nestroy is underrated, misread, and substantially forgotten) to the largest of ills (the dehumanizations of technology, the false promises of Progress and Enlightenment). The stakes here are even higher and more directly relevant to our own times.

dem Trost, wenn sie auf die Nachwelt kommen, würde diese es besser haben. Diese! Versuche sie es nur, sich als Nachwelt zu fühlen, und sie wird über die Zumutung, ihren Fortschritt dem Umweg des Geistes zu verdanken, eine Lache anschlagen, die zu besagen scheint: Kalodont ist das Beste. Eine Lache, nach einer Idee des Roosevelt, instrumentiert von Bernhard Shaw. Es ist die Lache, die mit allem fertig und zu allem fähig ist. Denn die Techniker haben die Brücke abgebrochen, und Zukunft ist, was

allow artists to be born than with the consolation that this future of ours will be better for their having lived before us. This world! Let it just try to feel like a posterity, and, at the insinuation that it owes its progress to a detour of the Mind, it will give out a laugh that seems to say: More Dentists Prefer Pepsodent. A laugh based on an idea of Roosevelt's and orchestrated by Bernhard[2] Shaw. It's the laugh that's done with everything and can do whatever. For the technicians have burned the bridges, and the

2. *Sic.* Although it's no excuse for misspelling his name, Kraus hated Shaw for some of the same reasons he hated Heine. "For Kraus," says Daniel Kehlmann, "Shaw is the prototype of the modern, shallow, media-compatible journalist-litterateur whose fame rests largely on having interesting opinions and giving original interviews: who talks to every newspaper and doesn't have the least interest in language itself." Even in *Pygmalion*, which appears to be preoccupied with language, Henry Higgins is presented as a *scientist* of spoken English. Shaw gives Higgins a big and predictable emotional blind spot—our egghead has a lesson to learn about the human heart, etc.—while remaining palpably infatuated with Higgins's smarty-pants scientific hauteur.

Regarding Roosevelt, Paul Reitter comments: "No fan of America, Kraus disliked Theodore Roosevelt, who seemed so very American; he even commented snidely on Roosevelt's game attempt, in 1910, to speak a little German to a German choral group. In this sentence, though, Kraus has in mind Roosevelt's push for technological progress, his modernizing streak. Kraus wasn't a technophobe in his everyday life. In 1914, when Vienna had few automobiles and many automobile accidents (see the first scene in Musil's *The Man Without Qualities*), Kraus bought a car and had himself driven around by a chauffeur. Nor was Kraus averse, later on, to air travel. But around 1908 he came to believe that our technological capabilities and our imaginative faculties were going in opposite directions—the former were going up and, as a result, the latter down—and this thought really scared him. It's what

sich automatisch anschließt. Diese Geschwindigkeit weiß nicht, daß ihre Leistung nur wichtig ist, ihr selbst zu entrinnen. Leibesgegenwärtig, geisteswiderwärtig, vollkommen wie sie ist, diese Zeit, hofft sie, werde die nächste sie übernehmen, und die Kinder, die der Sport mit der Maschine gezeugt hat und die Zeitung genährt, würden dann noch besser lachen können. Bange machen gilt nicht; meldet sich ein Geist, so heißt es: wir sind komplett. Die Wissenschaft ist aufgestellt, ihnen die hermetische Abschließung von allem Jenseitigen zu garantieren. Die Kunst verjage ihnen die Sorge, welchem Planeten soeben die Gedanken ihrer Vorwelt zugutekommen. Was sich da Welt nennt, weil

---

made him into the 'apocalyptic satirist.' In the essay 'Apocalypse' (1908), he writes, 'Culture can't catch its breath, and in the end a dead humanity lies next to its works, whose invention cost us so much of our intellect that we had none left to put them to use. We were complicated enough to build machines and too primitive to make them serve us. We operate a worldwide system of traffic along a narrow route in the brain.'"

Culture can't catch its breath: to me the most impressive thing about Kraus as a thinker may be how early and clearly he recognized the divergence of technological progress from moral and spiritual progress. A succeeding century of the former, involving scientific advances that would have seemed miraculous not long ago, has resulted in high-resolution smartphone videos of dudes dropping Mentos into liter bottles of Diet Pepsi and shouting "Whoa!" while they geyser. Technovisionaries of the 1990s promised that the Internet would usher in a new world of peace, love, and understanding, and Twitter executives are still banging the utopianist drum, claiming foundational credit for the Arab Spring. To listen to them, you'd think it was inconceivable that Eastern Europe could liberate itself from the Soviets without the benefit of cell phones, or that a bunch of Americans revolted against the British and produced the U.S. Constitution without 4G capability.

future is: whatever follows automatically.[3] This velocity doesn't realize that its achievement is important only in escaping itself. Present in body, repellent in spirit, perfect just the way they are, these times of ours are hoping to be overtaken by the times ahead, and hoping that the children, spawned by the union of sport and machine and nourished by newspaper, will be able to laugh even better then. There's no scaring them; if a spirit comes along, the word is: we've already got everything we need. Science is set up to guarantee their hermetic isolation from anything from the beyond. Let art chase away their worries about which planet happens to be benefiting from the thoughts of the world

3. Nowadays, the refrain is that "there's no stopping our powerful new technologies." Grassroots resistance to these technologies is almost entirely confined to health and safety issues, and meanwhile various logics—of war theory, of technology, of the marketplace—keep unfolding automatically. We find ourselves living in a world with hydrogen bombs because uranium bombs just weren't going to get the job done; we find ourselves spending most of our waking hours texting and e-mailing and tweeting and posting on color-screen gadgets because Moore's law said we could. We're told that, to remain competitive economically, we need to forget about the humanities and teach our children "passion" (to use Thomas Friedman's word in a 2013 *Times* column) for digital technology and prepare them to spend their entire lives incessantly re-educating themselves to keep up with it. The logic says that if we want things like Zappos.com or home DVR capability—and who wouldn't want them?—we need to say goodbye to job stability and hello to a lifetime of anxiety. We need to become as restless as capitalism itself.

Not only am I not a Luddite, I'm not even sure the original Luddites were Luddites. (They had no systematic beef with technology; it simply seemed practical to them to smash the steam-powered looms that were putting them out of work.) In developing this book, I'm relying on software and silicon to facilitate discussions with Kehlmann and Reitter in two other time zones, and I'm enchanted with everything about

es in fünfzig Tagen sich selbst bereisen kann, ist fertig, wenn es sich berechnen kann. Um der Frage: Was dann? getrost ins Auge zu sehen, bleibt ihr noch die Zuversicht, mit dem Unberechenbaren fertig zu werden. Sie dankt den Autoren, die ihr das Problem, sei es durch Zeitvertreib abnehmen, sei's durch Bestreitung. Aber sie muß jenem fluchen, dem sie – tot oder lebendig – als Mahner oder Spielverderber zwischen Geschäft und Erfolg begegnet. Und wenns zum Fluch nicht mehr langt – denn zum Fluchen gehört Andacht –, so langt's zum Vergessen. Und kaum besinnt sich einmal das Gehirn, daß der Tag der großen Dürre angebrochen ist. Dann verstummt die letzte Orgel, aber noch saust die letzte Maschine, bis auch sie stille steht, weil der Lenker das Wort vergessen hat. Denn der Verstand verstand nicht, daß er mit der Entfernung vom Geist zwar innerhalb der Generation wachsen konnte, aber die Fähigkeit verlor, sich fortzupflanzen.

my new Lenovo ultrabook computer except its name. (Working on something called an IdeaPad tempts me to refuse to have ideas.) I don't mind technology as my servant; I mind it only as my master. But not long ago, when I was intemperate enough to call Twitter "dumb" in public, the response of Twitter addicts was to call me a Luddite. Nyah, nyah, nyah! It was as if I'd said it was "dumb" to smoke cigarettes, except that in this case I had no medical evidence to back me up. People did worry, for a while, that cell phones might cause brain cancer, but the purported link has been revealed to be feeble to nonexistent, and now nobody has to worry anymore.

anterior to them.[4] This thing that calls itself a world because it can tour itself in fifty days is finished as soon as it can do the math.[5] To look the question "What then?" resolutely in the eye, it still has the confidence to reckon with whatever doesn't add up. It's grateful to the authors who relieve it of the problem, whether by diversion or by dispute. But it has to curse the one—living or dead—whom it encounters as admonisher or spoilsport between business and success. And when cursing no longer suffices—because cursing implies reverence—it's enough to forget. And the brain has barely an inkling that the day of the great drought has dawned. Then the last organ falls silent, but the last machine goes on humming until even it stands still, because its operator has forgotten the Word.[6] For the intellect didn't understand that, in the absence of spirit, it could grow well enough within its own generation but would lose the ability to reproduce

4. No matter how many times I read it, I can't make full sense of this sentence, although it does help, a little bit, to plug in the example of the anterior thoughts of the Framers of our Constitution and their benefit to our current planet. Kehlmann also helpfully notes: "The sentence elaborates on a line of thought that Kraus began in his poem 'To Eternal Peace': that there's nothing more noble than the pleasure (a pleasure experienced by Kant, whom the poem is about) of knowing that future generations will have things better than one's own. Our present does exactly the opposite, not only not working for later generations but actually making things worse for them."

5. Kehlmann considers it a near certainty that somewhere in an earlier edition of *Die Fackel* is a reference to someone's having circled the world in fifty days—a reference that Kraus's readers would have recognized here. Reitter suspects the reference is to Jules Verne's *Around the World in Eighty Days*, amended to fifty because it's fifty years since Nestroy's death.

6. "The phrase about the operator forgetting the Word comes from Goethe's poem 'The Sorcerer's Apprentice.'"—PR

Wenn zweimal zwei wirklich vier ist, wie sie behaupten, so verdankt es dieses Resultat der Tatsache, daß Goethe das Gedicht „Meeresstille" geschrieben hat. Nun aber weiß man so genau, wieviel zweimal zwei ist, daß man es in hundert Jahren nicht mehr wird ausrechnen können. Es muß etwas in die Welt gekommen sein, was es nie früher gegeben hat. Ein Teufelswerk der Humanität. Eine Erfindung, den Kohinoor zu zerschlagen, um

itself.[7] If two times two really is four, the way they say it is, it's owing to the fact that Goethe wrote the poem "Stillness and Sea." But now people know the product of two times two so exactly that in a hundred years they won't be able to figure it out. Something that never before existed must have entered the world. An infernal machine of humanity.[8] An invention for shattering the Koh-i-noor to make its light accessible to everyone

7. Here's a little glimpse of what's getting lost in translation: in the original, "the intellect didn't understand" is the beautifully repetitive *der Verstand verstand nicht*. Although the translator is mostly just grinning and bearing these losses, he thought he'd mention this one.

8. In the original, for "humanity," Kraus unexpectedly uses the Latinate *Humanität* rather than the Germanic *Menschlichkeit*. Kehlmann says: "My guess is that it's an echo of Nietzsche, 'O Voltaire, o humanity [*Humanität*], o idiocy!' All of Kraus's contemporary readers would have heard a faint echo of Nietzsche and his loathing of Enlightenment in that word. But that's just a guess." Following a tip from a fellow scholar, Reitter notes that Kraus is also probably echoing an often-cited rhyme by the Austrian writer Franz Grillparzer (1791–1872):

Der Weg der neuern Bildung geht:
Von Humanität,
Durch Nationalität,
Zur Bestialität.

(The road of modern education leads:
From humanity,
Through nationality,
To barbarity.)

I'd like to unpack this sentence fragment further, since, of all of Kraus's lines, it's probably the one that has meant the most to me. An "infernal machine" is an explosive or destructive device constructed to

sein Licht allen, die es nicht haben, zugänglich zu machen. Fünfzig Jahre läuft schon die Maschine, in die vorn der Geist hinein-
getan wird, um hinten als Druck herauszukommen, verdünnend,
verbreitend, vernichtend. Der Geber verliert, die Beschenkten
verarmen, und die Vermittler haben zu leben. Ein Zwischending
hat sich eingebürgert, um die Lebenswerte gegeneinander zu
Falle zu bringen. Unter dem Pesthauch der Intelligenz schließen
Kunst und Menschheit ihren Frieden . . . Ein Geist, der heute
fünfzig Jahre tot ist und noch immer nicht lebt, ist das erste
Opfer dieses Freudenfestes, über das seit damals spaltenlange
Berichte erscheinen. Wie es kam, daß solch ein Geist begraben

---

deliberately cause harm; the German term, *Teufelswerk* (literally
"devil's work"), sharpens the Krausian paradox of the phrase "of humanity." Kraus in this passage is evoking the Sorcerer's Apprentice—
the unintended unleashing of supernaturally destructive consequences.
Although he's talking about the modern newspaper, his critique applies, if anything, even better to contemporary techno-consumerism.
For Kraus, the infernal thing about newspapers was their fraudulent
coupling of Enlightenment ideals with a relentless and ingenious pursuit of profit and power. With techno-consumerism, a humanist rhetoric of "empowerment" and "creativity" and "freedom" and "connection"
and "democracy" abets the frank monopolism of the techno-titans; the
new infernal machine seems increasingly to obey nothing but its own
developmental logic, and it's far more enslavingly addictive, and far
more pandering to people's worst impulses, than newspapers ever were.
Indeed, what Kraus will later say of Nestroy could now be said of Kraus
himself: "He attacks his small environs with an asperity worthy of a
later cause." The profits and reach of Moriz Benedikt, the publisher of
the *Neue Freie Presse*, were pitifully small by the standards of today's
tech and media giants. The sea of trivial or false or empty data is thousands of times larger now. Kraus was merely prognosticating when he
envisioned a day when people had forgotten how to add and subtract;

who doesn't have it.[9] For fifty years now it's been running, the machine into which the Mind is put in the front to emerge at the rear as print, diluting, distributing, destroying. The giver loses, the recipients are impoverished, and the middlemen make a living. A hybrid thing has settled in to subvert the values of life by turning them against each other. In the pestilential miasma of the intellect, art and mankind make their peace . . . A spirit who's been dead for fifty years today, and who still isn't alive, is the first victim of this festival of joy, about which reports by the column have appeared ever since. How it happened that a spirit like this was buried:[10] it could only be the enormous content of his

---

now it's hard to get through a meal with friends without somebody reaching for an iPhone to retrieve the kind of fact it used to be the brain's responsibility to remember. The techno-boosters, of course, see nothing wrong here. They point out that human beings have always outsourced memory—to bards, historians, spouses, books. But I'm enough of a child of the sixties to see a difference between letting your spouse remember your nieces' birthdays and handing over basic memory function to a global corporate system of control.

9. The Koh-i-noor, at 106 metric carats, was once the largest known diamond. It now resides in the crown of Britain's Queen Elizabeth II.

10. Reitter notes: "When Kraus published 'Nestroy and Posterity,' in May of 1912, Nestroy was generally considered, for all his popularity, to be no more than an author skilled at vernacular farces—a fun and sometimes vulgar form of entertainment that didn't ultimately have much depth. Only Kraus and a few others thought he was a great artist."

Kehlmann continues: "Kraus's persistent championing of Nestroy had consequences: Nestroy today is acknowledged to be perhaps the greatest comic genius in Austrian literature. His plays are produced and he's read in school; he's a classic whose literary status is no longer in dispute—at least in Austria. In Germany, people maybe know just the name. His plays are neither read nor produced. And this has nothing to

wurde: es müßte der große Inhalt seines satirischen Denkens sein, und ich glaube, er dichtet weiter. Er, Johann Nestroy, kann es sich nicht gefallen lassen, daß alles blieb, wie es ihm mißfallen hat. Die Nachwelt wiederholt seinen Text und kennt ihn nicht; sie lacht nicht mit ihm, sondern gegen ihn, sie widerlegt und bestätigt die Satire durch die Unvergänglichkeit dessen, was Stoff ist. Nicht wie Heine, dessen Witz mit der Welt läuft, der sie dort traf, wo sie gekitzelt sein wollte, und dem sie immer gewachsen war, nicht wie Heine wird sie Nestroy überwinden. Sondern wie der Feige den Starken überwindet, indem er ihm davonläuft und ihn durch einen Literarhistoriker anspucken läßt. Gegen Heine wird man undankbar sein, man wird die Rechte der Mode gegen ihn geltend machen, man wird ihn nicht mehr tragen. Aber immer wird man sagen, daß er den Horizont hatte, daß er ein Befreier war, daß er sich mit Ministern abgegeben hat und zwischendurch noch die Geistesgegenwart hatte, Liebes-

---

do with their being hard to follow: the right way to produce him, as Kraus himself will point out, is not in Austrian dialect but in clear High German with a slight Austrian intonation. The problem is that the Prussian canon has, in general, very little room for Austrian writers and, in particular, no interest in humor. This is a subject too complex to be treated properly even in footnotes as deviant as ours. But Goethe and Schiller were explicitly opposed to humor in literature, there was never a Voltaire in German letters, and even a comic genius like Nestroy or a master of witty polemic like Kraus finds very little traction with readers and theatergoers in Germany. Germans and humor: the old, great, sad problem . . . !"

"Kraus himself had quite a bit to say about this problem," Reitter adds. "He was predictably hard on what he once called 'the overwhelm-

satirical thinking, and I believe he continues to create. He, Johann Nestroy, cannot tolerate that everything he found intolerable remained in place. Posterity repeats his text and doesn't recognize him; it doesn't laugh with him, it laughs against him, it refutes and confirms his satire through the undying nature of the subject matter.[11] Unlike Heine, whose wit agrees with the world, who touched it where it wanted to be tickled, and whom it could always handle—the world won't vanquish Nestroy the way it did Heine. It will do it the way the coward overcomes the strong man, by running away from him and getting a literary historian to spit on him. People will be ungrateful to Heine, they'll enforce the laws of fashion against him, they won't wear him anymore. But they'll always say that he had wide horizons, that he was an emancipator, that he rubbed shoulders with statesmen and still had the presence of mind to write a love poem now

---

ing humorlessness of German literature.' And where it did attempt to be funny, according to him, it tended to be filthy in the most puerile way: 'No experience is more important to German humorists than the process of digestion.'"

11. By "subject matter," Kraus appears to mean "the object or content of satire" (we're up against the tricky word "*Stoff*" again), but I don't think he gives us enough information here to understand the final phrase. I'd understand it better if he'd written "perennial fascination" instead of "undying nature," but unfortunately he didn't. Kehlmann's comment may nevertheless be illuminating: "'*Stoff*' is a key word for Kraus. In his opinion, we shouldn't be laughing at the content of satire, because the only thing that matters is our aesthetic enjoyment of how the content is arranged—the form, in other words."

gedichte zu machen. Anders Nestroy. Keinen Kadosch wird
man sagen. Keinem Friedjung wird es gelingen, nachzuweisen,
daß Der eine politische Gesinnung hatte, geschweige denn jene,

and then. Not so Nestroy. No Kaddish will be said.[12] No Fried-jung[13] will succeed in demonstrating that *he* had a political out-look, let alone the kind of outlook that turns a political outlook

12. Pretty clearly a reference to Heine's transformative importance to later generations of German-Jewish writers, and to the maintenance of his reputation by newspapers controlled and substantially written by German Jews. "They take care of their own," is perhaps the unsavory implication here, "and Nestroy, being Gentile, doesn't have that advan-tage." Reitter adds: "At least some of Kraus's readers would have known that 'no Kaddish will be said' is a Heine quotation. The source is Heine's poem 'Memorial Service' ('Gedächtnisfeier')."

13. "Heinrich Friedjung (1851–1920) was an assimilated Jewish histo-rian and journalist who wrote for the *Neue Freie Presse* and shared its dual commitments to liberalism and a German patriotism that could go over into a saber-rattling nationalism. He had, in short, all the mak-ings of a Kraus target. But it was through a sensational act of gullibility that Friedjung got Kraus's full attention. In 1909, it looked as if the Serbian response to Austria's annexation of Bosnia might give the Austrian-Hungarian government the opportunity to invade Serbia. Thus the government found itself in need of a moral justification for the war it wanted. The Austrian foreign minister turned to none other than Friedjung, handing him forged documents that he proceeded to run with. Writing in the *Neue Freie Presse*, Friedjung tried to make the case that the Austro-Hungarian regional administration in Bosnia had entered into a conspiracy with the anti-Habsburg government in Bel-grade. Soon, however, the Serbs backed down. The threat of war abated, whereupon the regional administration that Friedjung had accused of treason brought a libel suit against him—and won. For Kraus, the really damning thing was a point that Friedjung had managed to prove *in his defense*: he hadn't known that the documents on which he'd based his claims were forgeries. Kraus's essay on the affair ('The Trial of Friedjung,' 1909) contains some memorable remarks about the forces driving Austrian history—'its events are a function of the conflict be-tween stupidity and randomness'—but his focus is on the related issue

die die politische Gesinnung erst zur Gesinnung macht. Was lag ihm am Herzen? So viel, und darum nichts vom Freisinn. Während draußen die Schuster für die idealsten Güter kämpften,

---

of the state of reading in Austria. 'Austria in *orbe ultima*: in a world that's been deceived, Austria has kept its credulity longer than anyone else. It is journalism's most willing victim, for it not only believes what it sees in print, it believes the opposite when it sees that in print, too.' The reason Friedjung merits only one mention in 'Nestroy and Posterity' is that Kraus had just written an essay dealing exclusively with Friedjung's (1908) attempt to interpret Nestroy as a 'mockingbird' with a liberal outlook. Unsurprisingly, Kraus wasn't about to let stand the ultimate bad reader's reading of Nestroy, but here, according to Kraus, Friedjung may actually have been aware of the tendentiousness of his interpretation. Finding some dark solace in that, Kraus writes, 'Only this time it isn't quite believable that Herr Friedjung is acting out of honest belief.'"—PR

into an outlook in the first place. What mattered to him? So much, and therefore nothing of liberalism.[14] While the cobblers outside were fighting for the most ideal of wares, he was having

14. "So, was Kraus, whose experimental style influenced Brecht and Schönberg, a reactionary modernist? Walter Benjamin once suggested as much. His essay 'Karl Kraus' (1931) describes its subject's work as a mix of 'reactionary theory and revolutionary practice.' But as Benjamin himself knew, this formulation was misleading.

"The original motto of *Die Fackel* was 'What we kill.' In 1899, on the first page of the first issue, Kraus proclaimed that 'nothing' would move him from a 'standpoint' that was openly polemical and radically independent—as opposed to Vienna's better newspapers, which feigned openness and impartiality but in fact adhered to liberal pieties and played to the material interests of their backers. Beholden to no one and to no party line, Kraus would be able to 'carry out polemics from all perspectives,' as he put it a little later. Yet even as he underscored his independence, he didn't shy from tying it to an agenda that invited him to be taken for a progressive reformer. In the first issue of *Die Fackel* he announced his intention to expose the obfuscations of the established press so that it would be easier to 'recognize the urgent social matters.' Another early mission statement emphasized that *Die Fackel* would 'give the oppressed a voice.'

"Kraus wasted no time in making good on his pledges. He hammered away at all sides in reporting on the dysfunction in Austria's parliament, and in 1900 he took up the cause of the Galician coal miners who had gone on strike against 'their exploiters.' This helped win him a following among workers' groups in Vienna. If there had been Viennese prostitutes' groups, he might have had a following among them, too. The plight of prostitutes resonated with Kraus, and he addressed it repeatedly in covering what he saw as emblematic instances of disenfranchisement and injustice. In his essay 'Medal of Honor' (1909), he relates the story of a prostitute whose client didn't tip her but instead gave her a decorative medal, which she proceeded to put on. Unfortunately for her, this was potentially against the law. It also 'aroused,' to

use Kraus's phrasing, the indignation of the brothel's patrons, who turned her in. At her second trial—the first judge pronounced her innocent, but the prosecutor appealed the decision—the judge reinterpreted the status of the decorative cross, and the prostitute was fined twenty crowns for 'unauthorized wearing of a military medal.' As Kraus saw it, the case illustrated not just the extreme fatuousness and hypocrisy of the legal system's attempts to preserve decency, but also the system's perverse tendency to come down hardest on the very people it failed to protect. He ends the piece by declaring that the real 'whore' in the story is justice in Austria.

"Of course, Kraus took other kinds of stands, too. He heaped scorn on the supporters of Alfred Dreyfus. He belittled the women's movement (and wrote unkind aphorisms about women: 'at night, all cows are black, even the blond ones'). And in the years before the First World War, which he famously decried, Kraus sided with the old Austrian social order. After the war, he went through something of a socialist phase, but then, to Bertolt Brecht's dismay, he gave his imprimatur to Engelbert Dollfuß, Austria's right-wing chancellor from 1932 until 1934; Kraus believed that Dollfuß might effectively resist the reach of Nazi Germany and was thus the 'lesser evil' in Austrian politics. But Kraus's political interventions, or really his peregrinations up and down the political spectrum, aren't the main reason he's so hard to place politically. He had two primary programs in trying to improve society, and while these programs were always interdependent, they had different political valences. Reactionary theory and revolutionary practice didn't just coexist in Kraus's work: they fed off each other.

"For Kraus—as for, say, Marx—liberal faith in progress was the worst sort of ideology. Technological progress was being driven by hubris and greed, and it was increasing civilization's destructive capabilities, not just its productive ones, and Kraus was frightened by the enormous potential for abuse. An aphorism from around 1908 reads: 'Progress celebrates the pyrrhic victory over nature.' Another: 'Progress will make wallets out of human skin.' A key factor for Kraus was that technology and modernization were diminishing the space that the imagination needed to thrive. Once the popular imagination has atro-

phied, the likelihood that technology will be misused hardens into a certainty. Lamenting Austria's relationship to Germany, in 1908, Kraus wrote, 'Until the hypertrophy of our technological development, which our brains can't handle, leads to a general catastrophe, it is the fate of people who eat meat and were born to mothers to be swallowed up by people who were born to machines and are nourished by them.' When the general catastrophe then arrived, in the form of the First World War, Kraus believed that it was caused in large part by a failure of the Austrian imagination, which wasn't strong to begin with, and which had been fatally enfeebled by the mass press, at a moment of unparalleled technological might. Not long after the war began, Kraus claimed that the very signature of our time is the threat our lack of imagination has come to pose: 'in this time in which what people could no longer imagine is precisely what happens, and in which what they can no longer imagine has to happen, and if they could have imagined it, it wouldn't have happened . . .'

"Part of Kraus's response to this diagnosis might be characterized as romantic conservatism. Often with nostalgia for better days he hadn't experienced himself, Kraus fought to keep open space for the imagination by campaigning against the modern things that got in its way: the feuilleton, with its addictive, and thus lucrative, offering of prepackaged emotional responses to the news; psychoanalysis, which, according to Kraus, 'analyzes the dreams into which the disgust it elicits tries to escape'; etc. But another part of Kraus's response was to promote Enlightenment in the Kantian sense—that is, to call for mental maturity: 'I want the fruit of my labors to be that reading is done with sharper eyes.' Kraus, to be sure, sometimes directed his readers to see his writing as the result of a kind of mystical submission to language: 'I have only mastered the language of others. Language itself does whatever it wants to with me.' Yet he stressed, as well, that an important purpose of his 'revolutionary,' extremely challenging style was to force readers to read more alertly, in the hope of revitalizing the Austrian mind. His audience 'shouldn't necessarily read different newspapers, they should read differently.'

"They should speak and write differently, too. Kraus exhorted his readers to think as hard as they could about their linguistic options.

hat er die Schneider Couplets singen lassen. Er hat die Welt nur in Kleingewerbetreibende und Hausherren eingeteilt, in Heraufgekommene und Heruntergekommene, in vazierende Hausknechte und Partikuliers. Daß es aber nicht der Leitartikel, sondern die Welt war, die er so eingeteilt hat, daß sein Witz immer den Weg nahm vom Stand in die Menschheit: solch unverständliches Kapitel überblättert der Hausverstand. Blitze am engen Horizont, so daß sich der Himmel über einem Gewürzgewölbe öffnet, leuchten nicht ein. Nestroy hat aus dem Stand in die Welt

---

Doing so was, he believed, the best practice for ethical decision making. Because our deliberating over language usually takes place with neither the threat of punishment nor the prospect of gain hanging over it, it can teach us, in a uniquely unconstrained way, to hesitate, to have 'scruples,' and to be sensitive to nuance and thus to particularity. There was a time when these ideas resonated; more even than Kraus's claims about journalism and the Great War, they're what prompted critics to credit him with seeing, as one of them put it, 'the connection between mistreated words and mistreated bodies.'

"It's also been said that Kraus's Enlightenment project was a bust. Elias Canetti, for example, argued that Kraus was too authoritarian a figure to encourage intellectual independence in other people, and that his style overwhelmed readers more than it stimulated their critical faculties. That Kraus had an Enlightenment project, which is one of Canetti's points of departure, is harder to contest. And that Kraus never gave up on the project, regardless of its success or unsuccess, is impressive, especially given his low opinion of the people whom he was able to reach. He was only half joking when he quipped that the worst thing his audience members could say about him was: 'I know Kraus personally.'"—PR

Kehlmann points out that *Die Fackel*'s original motto, "*Was wir umbringen*," is a play on the hackneyed newspaper motto "*Was wir bringen*"—"What we bring." So I might suggest a less literal translation: "We bring you the noose."

his tailors sing lampoons.[15] He limited his partitioning of the world to small businessmen and landlords, to the up-and-coming and the down-and-out, to pensioners and unemployed porters. But that it was the world, not the editorial page, that he partitioned like this; that his wit was forever taking the road from social standing to humanity: conventional wisdom leafs past a chapter as incomprehensible as that.[16] Flashes on a narrow horizon—the heavens opening over a grocery store—are not enlightening. Nestroy's thinking proceeded from social status into the

15. "A reference to Nestroy's farce about the revolution of 1848, *The Lady and the Tailor* (1849), which Friedjung had framed as an expression of Nestroy's liberal convictions. Kraus would later back away from his attempt to distance this particular work, as well as Nestroy in general, from liberal politics. During the early 1920s, when Kraus was alarmed by the Fascist movements in Germany and Austria, he set about showing that the play 'isn't undemocratic.'" —PR

16. To return, in a roundabout way, to the connection between Kraus's anger and his privilege, I should note that his political sympathies were substantially conservative when he wrote this essay. Hence his irritation at the spectacle of Heine, an outspoken if somewhat inconsistent liberal, being lionized by the latter-day liberal press, which Kraus believed overvalued Heine's artistic achievements because his politics were correct. Where conservative American critics such as Dinesh D'Souza directly apply the crude label "PC" to work like Alice Walker's, Kraus here more subtly, but in a similarly conservative spirit, mocks the word "enlightened." (He does this in "Heine and the Consequences," too: "And they want to be enlightened about everything, just not about Heine.") Since almost everything Kraus says about Nestroy applies to himself as well, his insistence that Nestroy was neither liberal nor antiliberal clearly connects with his own rather contortionist efforts to remain politically indefinable, at least in public.

In private, Kraus was a privileged rentier with a strong stake in the status quo. Indeed, part of what intoxicated him about Sidonie Nád-

herný, when he met her in 1913, was that she belonged to the landed aristocracy: he fell in love not only with her but with her family's country estate. His long-running satiric preoccupation with financial malfeasance—first with the petty corruptions of Vienna's prewar liberal press, later with the rampant profiteering, by Jewish businessmen especially, in the First World War—can be seen as a way of elevating himself above the money-minded liberal bourgeoisie. It was only at the end of the war that Kraus became fully disillusioned with the monarchy and came out for the Socialists, and even this conversion was shaky and short-lived.

The works of Kraus's two playwright heroes, Shakespeare and Nestroy, are rooted in worlds of fixed social standing. The wonderful contrast between the diction of Dogberry and the diction of Beatrice, and between Nestroy's servants and Nestroy's masters, depends on firm distinctions between social classes. Satire, too, thrives on contrasts, and so the prospect of liberal democracy, in which everyone is identically entitled and eventually comes to speak identically, threatened Kraus's very foundations as an artist. This specter of uniformity—modernity's effacement of *difference*—would later haunt thinkers as various as the anthropologist Claude Lévi-Strauss, with his notion of "cultural entropy," and the postmodern novelist William Gaddis, with his lament for a lost era of Status in which high art was high and low was low. The uncomfortable dissonances of their positions (Lévi-Strauss's "Please don't change until we've thoroughly studied you" and Gaddis's "Please hold still while I kick you") are versions of the more general discomfort with which creative people view the levelings of modernity. To write well about slum dwellers, or about Andaman islanders, you need to have sympathy with them—precisely the kind of liberal sympathy that also makes you want better schools for the slums or Western-style amenities for the Andaman Islands. Good narrative art thus tends toward liberalism. But good artists also crave contrast. Unless you want to tell the same story of global monoculture's triumph over differences, again and again, you want slum dialogue to keep sounding distinctively like the slums, and you don't want Andaman islanders to start using the same iPhones and wearing the same sensible sneakers as Americans;

you want them to keep doing intensely, interestingly Andaman is-
lander things. This makes you a conservative. Or, actually, *worse* than a
conservative, because you, as an artist, want to be able to move liberally
and sympathetically among various classes and cultures—just like
Shakespeare did—*while secretly hoping that everyone who's not an artist
will stay fixed in place.* This is the monstrous sort of privilege that can be
claimed only by a person like Cordelia, who feels entitled to speak un-
welcome truths and still be loved. It's part of the dubious moral character that artists are famed for. And it helps makes sense of how furiously
Kraus rejected political categories. He wasn't just resisting the linguistically debased slogancering of politics. He was insisting on the
artist's uniquely privileged place in society. He argued for maintaining
differences because he knew that his kind of art—maybe all good
art—depends on it.

Clive James, in a perceptive piece in the *Australian Literary Review*, contends that after the First World War Kraus began to lose his
way as a satirist. James notes that Kraus's humor and his anger with the
liberal bourgeoisie, especially the Jewish bourgeoisie, remained viable
only as long as the genteel old order survived: Kraus could safely in-
dulge in a little antisemitism because the antisemites were still arguing
within the rule of law, and because he could do antisemitism more
deftly and wickedly than the antisemites themselves. Even the titanic
horror of the First World War was susceptible to his methods, because
people of all ethnicities were collectively suffering; because what Kraus
calls *Verstand* (intellect, reason), in the form of war theory, was responsible for it; and because, as Reitter points out, his satirical targets didn't
change all that much. (Reitter notes that "what Kraus had decried before the war was also operating during the war: the benightedness and
incompetence of aristocratic leaders, the posturing and complicity of
the bourgeois literati, the gleeful cruelty of the troglodyte elements in
Austrian society, and, of course, the rapacity and warping effects of the
press.") But then along came the irrational Nazis and demolished the
old Viennese order that Kraus had raged against and thrived in.

That Kraus had "nothing to say" about Hitler is a fact so widely accepted that it once cleared *The New Yorker*'s fact-checkers and appeared

in its pages. It's true that he did once write "I can't think of anything to say about Hitler." But this was the first line of a *book-length document* about Hitler and the Nazis. Published posthumously as *The Third Walpurgis Night*, it bravely and clear-sightedly takes their measure, and Daniel Kehlmann considers it Kraus's finest work. To me, though, it has the feel of a despairing exercise. The problem, as James points out, is that the Nazis were not lying (ten years before the Final Solution, they were already saying plainly what they intended to do to the Jews) or were so obviously lying as not to require satirical exposure, and that they were generally too dangerous to be laughed at. And so Kraus's last book isn't funny the way so much of his earlier work was, and its takeaway—that the Nazis were evil and insane—doesn't retain the biting relevance of his ideas about literature or of his critique of modern media.

James doesn't claim that Kraus's artistic dilemma vis-à-vis the Nazis was unique. Indeed, he seems to suggest that no form of writing can be effective in the face of irrational and genocidal violence—that only the counter-application of rational violence will avail. (His piece was published during the Iraq War.) What this says to me about art is that it's the child of a well-ordered house. Kraus was the kind of privileged child who was angriest, and therefore funniest, *en famille*. When something alien or irrational comes along and smashes the house's windows, the game ceases to be fun.

To which Reitter illuminatingly adds:

"One of the disorienting things about reading Kraus today is that he often sounds simultaneously un-PC and PC. In a PC way, he bashes the liberal culture of the press for its leveling of difference, but he does this in a way that's calculated to sound wildly un-PC (which of course has the effect of introducing more difference into the discussion). His critique in 'Heine and the Consequences' is a great example: the problem with feuilletonists is at once their mindless worship of a canon (Heine) *and* their difference-leveling false subjectivity. The feuilletonists all 'taste alike.' The early *Fackel* is full of such lines: 'the newspaper speaks like the world, because the world speaks like the newspaper,' 'the tone is always the same.' Thus Kraus's PC-seeming predilection for

minor and marginalized forms (vaudeville, Jewish-dialect theater, Nestroy, etc.) is *very much in keeping with* his hatred of the liberal culture of the time, which he saw as an assimilation-driven, impossibly snobbish agent of conformity, with a narrow and culturally chauvinist notion/fetish of *Bildung*. It's also worth noting that Kraus's early (and perspicacious) critique of Zionism was that it was often assimilationism masquerading as a movement devoted to sustaining difference. Zionism was the Jews' 'imitation nationalism,' to cite a phrase that Kraus likely inspired. This can be a pretty PC argument these days, and KK made it in 1898!

"And here's a sad irony: Kraus's fight against the cliché has lent itself to being characterized in clichéd terms. Even Clive James does some of that, for all the perceptiveness of his piece. To read James on *Die Fackel*, you'd think that Kraus 'tirelessly' went after every platitude and sloppy formulation that bothered his ears. Thus, 'Nothing got past him.' Or at least, 'Anyone who let slip a loose phrase lived to rue it if Kraus caught him.' What these well-worn overstatements obscure is that Kraus was interested in the emblematic infelicities, the ones that he could reveal to be both a symptom and a cause of social ills. At its best, Kraus's cultural criticism presents us with a feedback loop wherein bad circumstances and motives lead to bad prose that makes the world vastly worse. The press may have begun to gain the upper hand, the virtual reality of the media may have begun to determine the external reality that it's supposed to cover—'shadows now throw bodies,' in Kraus's formulation—but Kraus didn't imagine that the language of the press developed independently of its material conditions. Often, in fact, the importance of language misuse is that it allows us to recognize a dangerous underlying corruption: 'that one is a murderer doesn't necessarily tell us something about his style; but his style can tell us that he's a murderer.' Because James misses this point, it's easy for him to accuse Kraus of being more one-sided about historical causality than he was. According to James, Kraus, the language-obsessed satirist, failed to appreciate sufficiently that 'the world is made up of more than language.' Similarly, James reproaches Kraus for coming 'close to suggesting that the war had been caused by bad journalism,' then adds, with an implied

gedacht, Heine von der Welt in den Staat. Und das ist mehr. Nestroy bleibt der Spaßmacher, denn sein Spaß, der von der Hobelbank zu den Sternen schlug, kam von der Hobelbank, und von den Sternen wissen wir nichts. Ein irdischer Politiker sagt uns mehr als ein kosmischer Hanswurst. Und da uns die Vermehrung unserer intellektuellen Hausmacht am Herzen liegt, haben wir nichts dagegen, daß die irdischen Hanswurste Nestroy gelegentlich zum Politiker machen und ihn zwingen, das Bekenntnis jener liberalen Bezirksanschauung nachzutragen, ohne

---

sigh of impatience, 'if only it had been that simple.' James also conjectures that Kraus 'might have found instruction in the despotic past, had he been more historically minded.'

"There's certainly something to the last claim. Kraus showed no inclination for tracking how historical events unfold over time, or for figuring out how complex webs of factors produce them. You could say that he analyzed key features of his age in a series of aphorisms, some funny and some not, which he supported with thousands of pages of commentary and painstaking, often breathtaking work with the evidence, but which he didn't try to put into meaningful narrative contexts (see 'Heine and the Consequences'). For me, what's striking about *The Third Walpurgis Night* isn't so much the lack of humor or effective satire as the absence of aphoristic insights. This absence, incidentally, may explain the book's odd shape. Without such insights to ground him (he often built upon the aphorisms that he inserted into his essays), Kraus appears to be at sea. He goes on and on: *The Third Walpurgis Night* is probably five times longer than Kraus's second-longest essay. Of course, much of what Kraus writes in it has merit. The book is, indeed, 'clear-eyed.' It contains detailed accounts of Nazi violence, and it forcefully calls out cultural authorities—men such as Gottfried Benn and Martin Heidegger—whose support helped legitimate the Nazi movement by conferring upon it the cachet of poetry and philosophy in the country that fancied itself the land of *Dichter und Denker*. But Kraus's performance nevertheless feels 'wrong-footed,' to use James's

world, Heine's from the world into the state. And that is more.[17] Nestroy remains a joker because his jokes, which shot from the workbench to the stars, came from the workbench and we know nothing of the stars. An earthly politician says more to us than a cosmic buffoon. And since what matters to *us* is increasing our stores of conventional wisdom, we don't mind if some earthly buffoons occasionally make Nestroy into a politician and force him to speak the kind of liberal precinct-opinion without which we can no longer conceive of a dead satirist. The

---

word. Liberally translated, Kraus's opening line reads 'No ideas about Hitler occur to me' ('*Mir fällt zu Hitler nichts ein*'), and it proves to be an apt warning. Kraus wasn't able to muster for Nazism the kinds of provocative aphoristic distillations that serve as the basis for so much of his work. The closest he gets in *The Third Walpurgis Night* is that famous first sentence."

Right. The wit of Kraus's aphorisms was grounded in a comprehensible world and was always therefore, at some level, optimistic. To say that "shadows now throw bodies" is not only to invoke a former world in which bodies threw shadows but to imply that this proper relation could be restored if people would stop swallowing the media's manipulation of reality. Nazi ideology was beyond any such redemption—there was no way to flip it over, via paradoxical aphorism, into something potentially meliorable.

I might add that James not only propagates a smallening cliché about Kraus but implicitly buys into an aggrandizing cliché about Saddam Hussein—namely, that his threat to the world bore comparison with Hitler's. Bad journalism may not have *caused* the Iraq invasion (which James seems to believe was a necessary response to Hitler-level evil), but Judith Miller's shoddy reporting on WMDs, in the *Times*, did do a lot to neutralize opponents of the war. Her WMD shadows threw bodies.

17. In other words, Heine is more "important" than Nestroy. Kraus means this ironically, as the following sentences make clear.

die wir uns einen toten Satiriker nicht mehr denken können. Die Phraseure und Riseure geben dann gern zu, daß er ein Spottvogel war oder daß ihm der Schalk im Nacken saß. Und dennoch saß er nur ihnen im Nacken und blies ihre Kalabreser um. Und dennoch sei jenen, die sich zur Kunst herablassen und ihr den Spielraum zwischen den Horizonten gönnen, so von der individuellen Nullität bis zur sozialen Quantität, mit ziemlicher Gewißheit gesagt: Wenn Kunst nicht das ist, was sie glauben und erlauben, sondern die Wegweite ist zwischen einem Geschauten und einem Gedachten, von einem Rinnsal zur Milchstraße die kürzeste Verbindung, so hat es nie unter deutschem Himmel einen Läufer gegeben wie Nestroy. Versteht sich, nie unter denen, die mit lachendem Gesicht zu melden hatten, daß es im Leben häßlich eingerichtet sei. Wir werden seiner Botschaft den Glauben nicht deshalb versagen, weil sie ein Couplet war. Nicht einmal deshalb, weil er in der Geschwindigkeit auch dem Hörer etwas zuliebe gesungen, weil er mit Verachtung der Bedürfnisse des Publikums sie befriedigt hat, um ungehindert empordenken zu können. Oder weil er sein Dynamit in Watte wickelte und seine Welt erst sprengte, nachdem er sie in der Überzeugung befestigt hatte, daß sie die beste der Welten sei, und weil er die Gemütlichkeit zuerst einseifte, wenn's ans Halsabschneiden ging, und sonst nicht weiter inkommodieren wollte. Auch werden wir, die nicht darauf aus sind, der Wahrheit die Ehre vor dem Geist zu geben, von ihm nicht deshalb geringer denken, weil er oft mit der Unbedenklichkeit des Originals, das Wichtigeres vorhat, sich das Stichwort von Theaterwerkern bringen ließ. Der Vorwurf, der Nestroy gemacht wurde, ist alberner als so manche Fabel, die er einem französischen Handlanger

phraseurs and *riseurs* are then happy to admit that he was a mock-ingbird and a cutup. And nevertheless, he was only cutting them down and blowing off their Calabrian hats.[18] And nevertheless, to those who condescend to art and grant it free play between the horizons—that is, from the individual nullity to the social quan-tity—let it be said with considerable certainty: If art is not what they conceive and condone but instead is the stretch from some-thing seen to something thought—the shortest link from the gutter to the Milky Way—then there has never been a runner under the German sky like Nestroy. Never, it goes without say-ing, among those who brought the news, with laughing faces, that life is arranged in an ugly way.[19] We won't deny credence to his message because it was a lampoon. Not even because, in his rush, he also sang something for the listener; because, in his con-tempt for the needs of the audience, he satisfied them, so that his thoughts could soar unhindered. Or because he swaddled his dy-namite in cotton and blew up his world only after reinforcing its conviction that it was the best of all possible worlds, and because he laid on the soft soap of congeniality before he started slitting throats, and otherwise didn't wish to inconvenience anyone. Nor, not being interested in honoring truth before spirit,[20] will we think less of him because he often, with the carelessness of an original who has more important things on his mind, borrowed punch lines from stagehands. The reproof that was leveled against Nestroy is sillier than any plotline he lifted from a French flunky,

18. "Calabrian hats (*Kalabreser*) were the felt hats favored by the revolutionaries of 1848."—PR
19. I.e., people like Heine.
20. Kehlmann, the Viennese and major Kraus fan: "I have no idea what he means with this phrase. It doesn't make sense to me." Nor to me. But the sense of the sentence as a whole is that the originality of Nestroy's spirit matters more than the non-originality of his plots.

abnahm, alberner als sich irgendeines der Quodlibets im Druck liest, die er dem Volk hinwarf, das zu allen Zeiten den Humor erst ungeschoren läßt, wenn es auch den Hamur bekommt, und damals sich erst entschädigt wußte, wenn es mit einem Vivat der versammelten Hochzeitsgäste nach Hause ging. Er nahm die Schablone, die als Schablone geboren war, um seinen Inhalt zu verstecken, der nicht Schablone werden konnte. Daß auch die niedrige Theaterwirkung hier irgendwie der tieferen Bedeutung zugute kam, indem sie das Publikum von ihr separierte, und daß es selbst wieder tiefere Bedeutung hat, wenn das Orchester die Philosophie mit Tusch verabschiedet, spüren die Literarhistoriker nicht, die wohl fähig sind, Nestroy zu einer politischen Überzeugung, aber nicht, ihm zu dem Text zu verhelfen, der sein unsterblich Teil deckt. Er selbst hatte es nicht vorgesehen. Er schrieb im Stegreif, aber er wußte nicht, daß der Ritt übers Repertoire hinausgehen werde. Er mußte nicht, wiewohl jede Nestroysche Zeile davon zeugt, daß er es gekonnt hätte, sich in künstlerische Selbstzucht vor jenen zurückziehen, die ihn nur für einen Lustigmacher hielten, und der mildere Stoß der Zeit versagte der Antwort noch das Bewußtsein ihrer Endgiltigkeit, jenen seligen Anreiz, die Rache am Stoff im Genuß der Form zu

sillier than the printed look of any of those potpourris that he used to toss to the people, who, then as now, won't give humor a free pass unless they're also given their hardy-har-har, and who, in those days, weren't convinced they'd got their money's worth unless they went home with a cheer for the assembled wedding guests.[21] He chose the routine, which had been born as a routine, in order to conceal his substance, which could never be a routine. That even the low theatrical effects here somehow contributed to the deeper meaning, by separating the audience from it—and that, again, there's deeper meaning even in the fanfare with which the orchestra sends off philosophy—escapes the literary historians, who may well be capable of helping Nestroy to a political conviction, but not to the text that encompasses the immortal part of him.[22] He himself hadn't bargained for this. He wrote on the fly, but he didn't know the flight would extend beyond the repertoire. Although every Nestroyan line attests that he was capable of it, he didn't have to withdraw into artistic self-discipline in the face of those who considered him nothing more than a humorist, and the milder jarring of his times denied his response the consciousness of its finality—that blessed incentive

21. Untranslatable wordplay in here. In the original, "humor" is *Humor* and "hardy-har-har" is *Hamur*, which was Viennese slang for "humor." The implication is that Viennese audiences would forgive genuine wit in a playwright only if he or she also gave them comforting, earthy, low-class laughs.
22. "For all Kraus's dismissiveness toward literary historians, his relations with them weren't all bad. Otto Rommel, who was the leading Nestroy scholar in Kraus's day, publicly stated how much he admired Kraus; and when, in private, Rommel told Kraus that he had made it possible for him to understand Nestroy, Kraus proudly reported this acknowledgment in the *Fackel*." —PR

besiegeln. Er hätte, wäre er später geboren, wäre er in die Zeit des journalistischen Sprachbetrugs hineingeboren worden, der Sprache gewissenhaft erstattet, was er ihr zu verdanken hatte. Die Zeit, die das geistige Tempo der Masse verlangsamt, hetzt ihren satirischen Widerpart. Die Zeit hätte ihm keine Zeit mehr zu einer so beiläufigen Austragung blutiger Fehde gelassen, wie sie die Bühne erlaubt und verlangt, und kein Orchester wäre melodisch genug gewesen, den Mißton zwischen seiner Natur und der nachgewchsenen Welt zu versöhnen. Sein Eigentlichstes war der Witz, der der Bühnenwirkung widerstrebt, dieser planen Einmaligkeit, der es genügen muß, das Stoffliche des Witzes an den Mann zu bringen, und die im rhythmischen Wurf das Ziel vor dem Gedanken trifft. Auf der Bühne, wo die Höflichkeit gegen das Publikum im Negligé der Sprache einhergeht, war Nestroys Witz nur zu einer Sprechwirkung auszumünzen, die, weitab von den Mitteln einer schauspielerischen Gestaltung, wieder nur ihm selbst gelingen konnte. Sein Eigentlichstes hätte eine zersplitterte Zeit zur stärkeren Konzentrierung im Apho-

to seal revenge on the material in his enjoyment of form.[23] If he'd been born later, if he'd been born into these times of journalistic language fraud, he would have conscientiously repaid everything he owed to language. Times that retard the intellectual tempo of the masses incite their satirical counterpart. These times would have left him no time for as casual a prosecution of a bloody feud as the stage permits and insists on, and no orchestra would have been harmonious enough to resolve the dissonance between his nature and the world that grew up after it. His essence was the joke that runs counter to the stage effect, the flat onceness that has to be satisfied with finding a mate for the joke's material and which, in its rhythmic salvo, hits the target before the thought.[24] On the stage, where politeness toward the audience parades around in the negligee of language, Nestroy's wit could only be coined in the currency of rhetoric, which, far removed from the actor's tools of characterization, was something again only he could pull off.[25] Fragmented times would have driven his essence

23. I invite the reader to skip over the second half of this sentence. As Kehlmann says, "The sentence is overinstrumented. Basically Kraus is saying that Nestroy lived in better times, which is to say less apocalyptic times, and so he was spared the feeling of finality and didn't have to use form (the satirical brilliance of the sentences) to revenge himself on his content (the things he was writing about). Not a great sentence of Kraus's, I don't think. But the next sentence belongs with it and helps make sense of it."
24. Kehlmann again: "My guess about what Kraus means by 'onceness' is that an audience hears a stage line only once and can't go back and reread it, which means that you have to be simple and immediately understandable when you write for the theater."
25. There's a whole little outbreak of subpar sentences in here. Kehlmann's best guess about this one: "It's possible that Kraus means that Nestroy achieves rhetorical effects so strong that they function independently of the quality of the actor." Reitter adds: "On second (or

rismus und in der Glosse getrieben, und das vielfältigere Gekreische der Welt hätte seiner ins Innerste des Apparats dringenden Dialektik neue Tonfälle zugeführt. Seiner Satire genügte vorwiegend ein bestimmter Rhythmus, um daran die Fäden einer wahrhaft geistigen Betrachtung aufzuspulen. Manchmal aber sieht sich die Nestroysche Klimax an, als hätten sich die Termini des jeweils perorierenden Standesbewußtseins zu einer Himmelsleiter gestuft. Immer stehen diese vifen Vertreter ihrer Berufsanschauung mit einem Fuß in der Profession, mit dem andern in der Philosophie, und wenn sie auch stets ein anderes

---

fifth) thought, I'm not so sure. I think that KK is still referring to Nestroy the actor here. His point is that, as an actor, Nestroy had a particular talent for the rhetorical part of the performance. This creates another link between Nestroy and Kraus, since Kraus's public readings were essentially rhetorical performances whose success wasn't a function simply of his writing but of his voice and delivery as well."

I must say that it's a relief to see Kehlmann and Reitter struggling with Kraus's language. I first started translating Kraus in 1983, entirely on my own, and because so many of his sentences yielded beauty and meaning if I engaged in sufficient solitary struggle with them, I naturally assumed it was my fault when some of them didn't; I wasn't a native German speaker, after all. But this is the dangerous thing about literary difficulty: the farther the writer moves away from transparent, readily graspable language (and you can't move much farther away than Kraus did and still hope to convey coherent thoughts), the greater the temptation to cut corners. I don't think Kraus himself cuts very many, but once you start writing sentences that are deliberately opaque on first reading, the door is open to writing sentences that remain opaque on the hundredth reading. There's a kind of moral hazard here—literary difficulty inclines readers to excuse the writer, since negative statements ("There is no conceivable way to make sense of this") are notoriously resistant to proof—and it's one that less scrupulous avant-gardists still exploit in a big way.

to concentrate itself in aphorism and glosses, and the world's more varied screechings would have introduced new cadences to his dialectic in its penetration to the core of the apparatus.[26] In his satire, one particular rhythm above all suffices as a winding post for the threads of an observation that is truly of the spirit. But sometimes a Nestroyan climax will look as if the terminologies of class feeling, perorating in succession, had arranged themselves as the steps of a Jacob's ladder. These lively exponents of their professional point of view are always standing with one foot in their trade and the other in philosophy, and if their face is

26. "Accused by Franz Werfel of letting a Yiddishism slip into his prose, Kraus responded that the word in question wasn't actually a Yiddishism, and even if it were one, so what? 'My style screeches with all the noises of the world,' Kraus boasted elsewhere. Something like that statement goes for Nestroy's style as well, in Kraus's reading of it." —PR

Kraus, whose own specialties were aphorisms and glosses, is making a rather outrageously self-justifying claim in this sentence: "If Nestroy were writing now, he'd be doing what I'm doing." Or, conversely, "If I'm not writing plays like Nestroy did, it's because I live in more urgently bad times." Kraus did, to be sure, write one monumental play, *The Last Days of Mankind*, a satire of Austrian corruption and lies and self-deceptions in the First World War, but it's remarkably lacking in conventional drama. Its backbone consists of vertabim quotation and exaggerated mimicry of a remarkable variety of sources, along with glosses and aphorisms provided by the character of the Grumbler. It's quite a presumption to imagine that this is the kind of thing Nestroy would have written if he'd been born seventy-five years later.

And yet, says Kehlmann, "I completely agree with Kraus about Nestroy's particular gifts as a writer. It's true that his plays are fully conventional from the standpoint of story, but his linguistic creativity, his wit, and his aphoristic power are tremendous; at their best, they really are comparable only to Shakespeare's. Nestroy isn't a born dramatist, à

la Schiller—that he wrote for the stage was really more a matter of circumstance, and it's hard not to think that under different circumstances he might well have produced aphoristic prose. Of course Kraus is being self-serving here, but what he's saying about Nestroy isn't so unreasonable or far-fetched."

To thrive as a man, you need to find ways both to admire your father and to surpass him. If the kinship is literary, which is to say metaphorical, you may also need to deny false paternity, as Kraus does in "Heine and the Consequences." Because Heine is the famous and widely beloved Kraus precursor, Kraus tries to annihilate him, highlighting the differences between Heine's work and his own and pointing toward Heine's fundamentally bad character: if Heine had been born seventy-five years later, he would still have been a feuilletonist. Because Nestroy, on the other hand, is the neglected and undervalued Kraus precursor, Kraus praises him, stresses his kinship with him, and posits that different times would have made him a different kind of writer. Kraus may conceivably have had submerged assimilationist motives in choosing a Gentile as a literary father, but the really important argument he's making is that Nestroy was a great writer uncomfortably stuck in the wrong genre—thus leaving the son (Kraus) free to find the right genre and fulfill his potential. To champion Nestroy is at once to make him a more satisfactory father and to demonstrate the champion's own superior strength. Nestroy in 1912 needed Kraus's help, and Kraus needed to provide it.

When I went to Berlin, in the fall of 1981, I was actively seeking literary fathers. In a college playwriting workshop, I'd spontaneously generated a story about a conspiracy in my hometown, and my theater professor, Lee Devin, had said I'd better take a look at Pynchon (also, curiously, at the thriller writer Richard Condon). Because I intended to turn my story idea into a novel in Berlin, I took along *Gravity's Rainbow*—a brick of a paperback that might have been a brick of firecrackers, so deliciously full of explosive potential did it seem.

(Somewhat random aside: I loved fireworks, and so did my father. Every Fourth of July morning he took me out past the county line into a jurisdiction where they were legal. He bought himself a brick of fire-

crackers, half of which he would save for setting off in our front yard on New Year's Eve, and we went down to a gravel bar on the Meramec River, where he worked through the other half of his brick while I ignited bottle rockets and smoke bombs. For the first few years we were accompanied by a neighbor of ours, a colleague of my father's at the railroad, and by his pyromaniacal son, Fred. I remember Fred's father lighting firecrackers with the cigarettes he chain-smoked. He died of lung cancer when I was only eight or nine. His name was Karl Kraus.)

In my last semester of college I'd read some essays of Harold Bloom in which there was a lot of talk about "strong" and "weak" poets. Since I was going to be writing novels anyway, I figured it would be much more fun and satisfactory to be a strong one. Of course, the whole thing was preposterous, since Bloom's theory was steeped in Freud and turned on the literary ephebe's willful but *unconscious* misreading of his (always *his*, never *her*) strong precursor's work: my Unconscious would have to have been awfully feeble if reading some literary criticism had been all it took for me to stage direct it. But I was impressed by how smart Bloom and the other theorists were. For a while, I believed that studying them would help me produce the kind of texts that they considered good, as if they were Julia Child and I wanted to master the art of French cooking. I hoped they'd show me shortcuts to becoming a strong novelist, so that I could avoid the suffering of various agons (which sounded highly unpleasant) and the embarrassment of being unconscious of motives that any halfway competent Bloomian critic would be totally conscious of. I was like Hardy's Jude the Obscure, who is under the impression that all you need to be able to read Latin is the trick of decoding it into English, and who is stricken to learn that each Latin word and conjugation has to be laboriously memorized.

When I started reading the Pynchon, in the suburban basement of the family that hosted me for my first five weeks in Berlin, I was simultaneously reading Bloom's *Anxiety of Influence*, as if Pynchon were a deadly virus and literary theory the hazmat suit that would let me safely handle it. But the suit did not avail. Pynchon still made me ill, both literally and figuratively. To compound my literary self-consciousness, I was spending between two and six hours every day

typing letters to my secret fiancée, V. Before I left for Berlin, V and I had agreed that our letters to each other would double as journals; our innermost thoughts would be communal property. And so I made a carbon copy of every page I wrote to her, partly to create a journal but partly also on the crazy presumption that our correspondence would eventually be seen as one for the ages; what bound me and V together, more than anything else, was our literary ambition.

it's like the bitter irony of my picking up <u>Gravity's Rainbow</u> when I can't write these days, oh what a mess, I find Bloom's style revolting in hindsight, his Manifesto a travesty like late Nietzsche, but I recognize Pynchon as my major precursor, the better he is the more I want to hate him but the less I can, a strange state of affairs, such as my reading list of novels in the last five years respectably large yet somehow managing to avoid all Joyce, Faulkner, Proust, Dostoyevsky, Flaubert, Austen, Stendhal, Mailer, my God, you'd think I've hardly read a thing, what fear what fear, my suitcase stuffed with more irony, you name— Derrida, Bloom, Burke, Jameson twice, Lacan, Marcuse, Lukacs, Barthes—it, but how many novels? just one, of course, cover reading "The most important work of fiction yet produced by any living writer," influence, why fight it? does Irving? well, it hardly matters with Irving, but there's almost nothing he does in <u>Garp</u> that Pynchon doesn't do better, or Heller, and it seems that Pynchon's Irving is just one among a dozen tricks the book is pulling off, how can you <u>write</u> in America anymore? how keep going without big genius? well, I hear you saying, who knows that one or both of us isn't a genius, who says you have to be the best?

[. . .]

You scowl from my picture of you in your black tank top, arms as fluid and smooth as air, a coffee cup in one hand, a cigarette in the other. I hope you're thinking, oh come on Jon, take it easy now, it's all the same letter (call it V., title of Pynchon's oh god great first novel, how could he? how could he?—"THOMAS PYNCHON is known almost exclusively through his writing. In all other respects, he craves and guards his privacy. The public facts about his life are few and far

between"—from the blurb About the Author at the back of Bantam Book #0-553-14761-7, His Most Highly Praised Novel.) You still scowl. I know, I know.

[. . .]

I'd almost swear that this is a Pynchon toxin numbing my spirit. Why else do I want to go back to p. 321, where I left off reading after lunch?

A year earlier, my departmental adviser had suggested that I apply for a Fulbright grant for study in Germany. My chances of getting one were good: the German government, understandably intent on promoting international cooperation after the Second World War, contributed heavily to the Fulbright program, which, as a result, gave nearly as many fellowships for Germany as for the rest of the world combined. To make sure I went to Germany's most interesting city, Berlin, I crafted a proposal, consisting almost entirely of bullshit, to use certain archives in Berlin to study expressionist theatrical productions. My letter of acceptance arrived on the same day and in the same mail-room where V, with whom I was falling in love and would soon be sleeping, got her letter of rejection from the Fulbright people. She'd applied to go to Italy—unlike Germany, Italy was cool!—but so had a thousand other people.

I don't remember what prompted me to propose to V, six months later. Probably I'd said something wrong (I was always saying the wrong thing that summer) and wanted to make her feel better. We were living with throngs of cockroaches in a sublet at the corner of 110th Street and Amsterdam Avenue, in New York; I've still never seen thicker Lucite security partitions than the ones in the liquor store downstairs from us. To throw my mother off the scent of my relationship with V, I'd told her that a whole bunch of my college friends were living in the apartment, not just V and me. My mother had met V only once, at our college graduation, and had conceived an intense disapproval of her. ("She's very intellectual" was the nicest thing she ever managed to say about her.) To my lie about our living arrangements I soon added conceal-ment of our engagement and of my intention to spend my Berlin year

working on a novel; my mother considered the idea of my becoming a novelist a dangerous and irresponsible fantasy. I pretended to her that my Fulbright would set me up to be a journalist, a lawyer, an international banker, or, at the very least, a German professor. She, for her part, hoped that, while in Germany, I would develop a taste for blond, sharp-cheekboned, un-V-like women along the lines of the daughters of her good Austrian friend, Ilse.

Where was my father in this? He was retiring, that summer, at the age of sixty-six and a half, from his forty-year career as a civil engineer. Admiring him was not a problem for me, but surpassing him was: I'd heard it said that he was the best railroad bridge and track engineer in the United States. I also had a troubling sense of false paternity. My father was a formidable intellectual arguer and a good, clear writer, but he knew and cared nothing about literature. He was a tower of honesty and integrity, whereas I was an inveterate concealer of pertinent information, sometimes even an outright liar, and was intending to make a career of writing stories that weren't factually true. My best near-term option for surpassing him was to be more deferential to a woman, more solicitous and sympathetic, than he was to my mother. Longer term, I would have to become the nation's best at what *I* did—hence the insane magnitude of my literary ambitions at twenty-two. To get anywhere with the long-term project, I needed the example of a different kind of father.

A few days after I left for Berlin, my mother was hospitalized with a near-fatal pulmonary embolism. I now think that it's a mistake to metaphorize illness, and certainly my mother's long troubles with blood clots weren't aggravated by her emotions the way other of her ailments were, but back then the timing of her hospitalization seemed to me inescapably significant. Her youngest child had just flown the nest for good, and for the first time in her life she had my father at home with her, being depressed and generally forcing all the marital issues that his busy work life had allowed them to suppress. I was constituted to feel responsible for this, and I began to make the argument, first privately and then to V, that I couldn't break the news of our engagement until my mother's health was better, for fear of worsening it with the shock of the news.

Of course, being twenty-two, I typically thought about my parents only when I felt obliged to write them a letter; they were mostly a distraction from the important subject of me. But my daily anxiety levels were very high. I self-medicated with cigarettes, a habit I not only concealed from my parents but was attempting to hide from my host family by sneaking around outside their house. In the great tradition of Fulbright anxiety (a phenomenon treated most comically in Ben Lerner's novel *Leaving the Atocha Station*), I felt anxious about the weird impression I was making on my host family, anxious about concealing my engagement, anxious about chaining myself to my portable typewriter and writing self-referential letters instead of improving my German and gathering exotic material, anxious about committing myself to marriage before I'd sampled the charms of blond, sharp-cheekboned women, anxious about the new buildup of tactical nuclear weapons on both sides of the German border, anxious about being a smoker, anxious about my laziness as a scholar, anxious about finding a place to live in the extremely tight low-end Berlin housing market, anxious about the many ways in which I half knew that V and I weren't right for each other, and anxious about the badness of the story I was writing as an exercise, a fluffy confection that concerned a young man named Wallace Wallace Wallace and was so steeped in my recent reading of John Irving that there was even a bear in it.

Harold Bloom, however, was telling me I was supposed to be anxious about Pynchon:

I'm a great sublimator. Not finding an apartment, the simple raw fear, becomes not finding an apartment when you and I are poor, in two years. This fear gives way to the worry that you're not the Practical Type. Worry about Practical Types practically stops the typing: how can I sit in here when my thoughts should be flooding outward? But what is this worry, if not pynchon-anxiety? since pynchon appears to have done almost everything in the world, he's just bursting with details that can be had only through experience. But why pynchon-anxiety? Why decide he's the Major Precursor? Because of the style-crisis I'm locked in with the Wallace story and with these letters. As you've been seeing, I'm

to the point where I'll destroy style rather than imitate someone else's. But style-destruction is, if only momentarily, a very anti-literary thing to do to oneself; it sounds like it might be connected to the doubts I've been having about our neat lives as authors.

Gravity's Rainbow seemed to me a novel of dizzying capability. Its melding of the gonzo and the literary was so effortless and brilliant it felt inevitable, and it dealt squarely with the two contemporary issues that weighed on me the most: the nuclear peril and the impenetrably complex modern System that rendered individuals powerless. Pynchon's narrative voice was scarily authoritative the way my father's was, and the street wisdom of his entropic proto-hippie antihero, Tyrone Slothrop, was like that of my much older brother Tom, whom I revered. I was doubly a little pisher, and the book pushed all my buttons in this regard.

To defend myself against it, all I really had was my engagement to V. The engagement was conventional, for one thing, and I already had some awareness that I was destined to live and work within convention, both because it had served me well (I'd known how to play the game of getting a Fulbright) and because I'd seen how my brother's unconventionality had estranged him from my parents. The engagement was also predicated on achieving a relationship of equals with V, one that fully respected her subjectivity. *Gravity's Rainbow* was an absolute boy-novel, a rockets-and-erections book, its female characters fundamentally sex objects. When, in subsequent letters to V, I experimented with riffs that mimicked the novel's raunchy tone and attitudes, she wrote back sharply to register her moral distaste, and the lesson I drew was that you couldn't write like Pynchon and sustain an I-Thou relationship with a woman. I had to reject Pynchon's sexism the way I rejected my father's. It also quickly became apparent that Pynchon's turn on novelistic convention—reading every coincidence as evidence of conspiracy—was a trick without a future. Pynchon wholly owned it, and there was no point in competing with him on his turf:

What astounds me is how easy it is to make up a plot like that, and that no one before pynchon ever did it. But now no one else can do it. He is,

as Lee Devin told me two and a half years ago, the Master of Paranoid Conspiracy.

[. . .]

The pynchon-anxiety has diminished, by the way, since Sunday morning (yesterday); the anxiety that remains is strangely antipynchonesque: ominous coincidences, but no chance of a conspiracy behind them. For instance, the end of a sentence near the bottom of page 404: " . . . a repulsive black gob of the foul-smelling substance wrapped in a scrap torn from an old Enbeski Qazaq for 17 August of last year." Not the best spot of writing in the book, but at least all the details seem reasonable, except for the date [August 17 is my birthday], which appears nowhere else in the first 535 pages, which seems to have been planted as a sign for watchful me, a message from pynchon to the effect, "I KNOW YOU'RE READING THIS AND I KNOW WHO YOU ARE." I have come to expect coincidences like this, though.

[. . .]

I haven't given up on this idea of how susceptible we, or at least I, are to the toxins in the things we read. I only read GR for about two hours yesterday, three at most. But the whole night was filled with it. It really is as Weasel Bloom describes it: influenza. And far more dangerous when it happens with a novel than with a critical theory. It could cripple you for life. So to read, or not to read? "He gets back to the Casino just as big globular raindrops, thick as honey, begin to splat into giant asterisks on the pavement, inviting him to look down at the bottom of the text of the day, where footnotes will explain all." This is why I'm having such a hard time with the man. Heller or Vonnegut I can live with, because they're about as stylistically interesting (or annoying) as a translation of Chekhov. But not pynchon—who also provides us with a tour de force through every sexual act ever dreamed of (shit-eating, piss-drinking and incest included (hardly appealing, you say, but—)), who wants us to know he knows exactly what a brick of hash looks like, exactly what WWII Europe was like, down to the minutest detail (V[ ], he was two when the war started, eight when it ended), exactly what it feels like to have destroyed yourself with cocaine, exactly how much chemistry, math, physics, and Pavlovian psy-

Gesicht haben, so ist es doch nur Maske, denn sie haben die eine und einzige Zunge Nestroys, die diesen weisen Wortschwall entfesselt hat. Was sie sonst immer sein mögen, sie sind vor allem Denker und Sprecher und immer in Gefahr, coram publico den Gedanken über dem Atem zu kurz kommen zu lassen. Dieser völlig sprachverbuhlte Humor, bei dem Sinn und Wort sich

---

chology he has mastered—it goes on and on, stealing names, phrases, techniques and making them so totally his own that the universe of possibilities seems <u>distinctly</u> smaller for his having written one book, one lousy book. It's so BIG. That's the problem.

Rereading these letters, with the aim of quoting from them at embarrassing length here, I'm struck by how much more authentic and persuasive my cries of pain were than the resolution I arrived at. I don't know if this is an effect of hindsight, but I have the same feeling about the passages in my letters where I reaffirm my love of V and promise her that everything is going to be okay with us. The anxieties sound real, the optimism somewhat pat:

I'll get over Pynchon somehow. Maybe through criticism, some discontinuity, some dialectic, that will enable me to forget him. It's still only faith, but it hasn't been destroyed: Novels aren't called novel for nothing: they're about the times and about time. That's the pun that Thomas Mann thought he invented, calling <u>Der Zauberberg</u> a Zeitroman. [...] You watch Mann do his numerological/philosophical/historicosymbolic tricks and it's as exciting as <u>Star Wars</u>, just vastly clever, and done in full seriousness too. And then you see the same themes, sometimes even the same phrases and sentences, popping up in Kafka, Rilke, Mann and Döblin, popping up unintentionally, where not even Bloom could make a case for Influence, positive or negative—and suddenly it's all right again: these guys aren't talking about the Problem of Falling (which Bloom maintains is always the same problem for poets, whose task of finding new solutions grows harder by the generation), they're

always changing, it's really just a mask, because they have Nestroy's one and only tongue, which has unleashed this sage torrent of words. Whatever else they may be, they are, above all, thinkers and speakers and are always in danger, on the public stage, of shortchanging their thought to save their breath. This utterly language-infatuated humor, in which word and sense

---

talking about how lousy it is to see the moral individual dying off in the face of advancing modern society, or something like that. It's all about time.

And that seemed to be the end of it. I stopped talking about Pynchon in my letters, and soon after that, having been shamed by V's criticisms, I expunged all traces of his gonzo style. My engagement to V was a freely chosen clampdown, a truncator of anxious-makingly open-ended trains of thought, a bulwark against the boy-novel phallicism I'd found so dangerously attractive in *Gravity's Rainbow*. At a Thanksgiving dinner hosted by the Berlin coordinator of the Experiment in International Living, Frau Heilgendorff, I was deep in a flirtatious conversation with the prettiest woman at the table, a blond and high-cheekboned German, when Frau Heilgendorff swooped down and said pointedly, "Jonathan, how is your *fiancée*? When is your *fiancée* coming over to see you?" End of conversation. Besides being annoyed, I felt obscurely that the word "fiancée" misrepresented me. And yet in the weeks and months that followed, as my fear of giving my parents the news of my engagement mounted to excruciating heights, I persisted in thinking that I was afraid of exposing a truth that I'd been lying about, rather than of exposing something false that I was trying to will into truth. To distract myself from my fear, I took my best rational, conscious shot at one-upping Pynchon and began to write a novel of my times in which the conspirators themselves were sympathetic characters; in which, indeed, the lead conspirator was female. A decade later, when I found myself in mortal literary struggle with the problem of Pynchonian postmodernism, amid the wreckage of my marriage, the Bloomian laugh was on me.

fangen, umfangen und bis zur Untrennbarkeit, ja bis zur Unkenntlichkeit umschlungen halten, steht über aller szenischen Verständigung und fällt darum in den Souffleurkasten, so nur Shakespeare vergleichbar, von dem auch erst Shakespeare abgezogen werden muß, um die Theaterwirkung zu ergeben. Es wäre denn, daß die Mission einer Bühnenfigur, die ohne Rücksicht auf alles, was hinter ihr vorgeht, zu schnurren und zu schwärmen anhebt, vermöge der Sonderbarkeit dieses Auftretens ihres Beifalls sicher wäre. Noch sonderbarer, daß der in die Dialoge getragene Sprach- und Sprechwitz Nestroys die Gestaltungskraft nicht hemmt, von der genug übrig ist, um ein ganzes Personenverzeichnis auszustatten und neben der Wendung ins Geistige den Schauplatz mit gegenständlicher Laune, Plastik, Spannung und Bewegung zu füllen. Er nimmt fremde Stoffe. Wo aber ist der deutsche Lustspieldichter, der ihm die Kraft abgenommen hätte, aus drei Worten eine Figur zu machen und aus drei Sätzen ein Milieu? Er ist umso schöpferischer, wo er den fremden Stoff zum eigenen Werk erhebt. Er verfährt anders als der bekanntere zeitgenössische Umdichter Hofmannsthal, der ehrwürdigen Kadavern das Fell abzieht, um fragwürdige Leichen darin zu bestatten, und der sich in seinem ernsten Berufe gegen einen Vergleich mit einem Possendichter wohl verwahren würde. Wie alle besseren Leser reduziert Herr v. Hofmannsthal das

capture each other, embrace, and hold each other entwined to the point of inseparability, indeed to the point of indistinguishability, stands removed from anything that a stage scene can communicate and therefore falls into the prompter's box, in a way comparable only to Shakespeare, from whom you likewise have to remove Shakespeare before you can produce a theatrical effect—unless the mission of a stage character who begins to drone and rave without regard to anything going on behind him would be assured of applause by the oddness of such behavior. Odder yet, that the verbal and oral wit that he carries into his dialogue doesn't impede his powers of characterization, of which there's enough left over to outfit an entire dramatis personae and, even as it's causing us to think, to fill the theater with concrete mood, gesture, suspense, and action. He borrows foreign subject matter. Where, though, is the German comedy writer who could borrow from him the power to create a character with three words and a milieu with three sentences? He's all the more creative when he lifts foreign material into his own work. He goes about it differently than the better-known contemporary recaster Hofmannsthal, who strips the hides off honorable cadavers to inter questionable remains in them, and who would no doubt defend his serious professional work against comparison with an author of farces.[27] Like all superior readers, Herr von

27. "In 1904, Hofmannsthal had reinterpreted Sophocles's *Electra*, to much acclaim."—PR

It happens that I studied Hofmannsthal in Berlin. To keep Fulbright funds flowing, I had to present evidence that I'd completed at least one class at the Free University, and after rejecting a course in the modern English novel because the level of critical discourse seemed hopelessly crude by my new standards, I enrolled in a Hofmannsthal seminar; he'd at least written some plays in the period I was supposedly in Berlin to study.

Werk auf den Stoff. Nestroy bezieht den Stoff von dort, wo er kaum mehr als Stoff war, erfindet das Gefundene, und seine Leistung wäre auch dann noch erheblich, wenn sie nur im Neu-

---

Enrollment in the seminar was sparse. Because West Berlin was still controlled by the Allied militaries, its residents were exempt from German military service, which was compulsory elsewhere in the Federal Republic. As a result, the city was a haven for peaceniks and deadbeats, who needed to take some classes to preserve their student status but were none too keen on doing actual schoolwork. The seminar's leader, Professor Wohlleben, required work, and Hofmannsthal was too much an aesthete and too little a politician to interest young leftists.

Every American student of German reads some Hofmannsthal, because his language is elegant and because his habit of raiding literary history for material, which Kraus makes fun of here, lends itself to elementary classroom discussion. He was a prime example of what literature had meant to me (well-wrought texts whose meaning I decoded and abstracted to get good grades in class) before I'd been converted to a more personal and religious experience of literature by his contemporaries Kafka and Rilke.

In my boredom with Hofmannsthal, I became a lit-theory crank turner. I applied doctrinaire structuralism to his famous "Letter of Lord Chandos," which I'd conveniently already studied in college, and then I did a twenty-page Bloomian close-textual reading of his verse play *Death and the Fool*, which he'd written at the age of sixteen. Although I avoided the terminology of "strong" and "weak," the strong poet in my scheme was Goethe, and I was pleased to find an essay in which Hofmannsthal is open about his love/hatred of him and blames him for the suicide of Kleist:

> Yes, who killed the soul of Heinrich von Kleist, who then? Oh, I see him, the old man of Weimar . . .
>
> Oh, I see him, and what a shivering thrill it is to see him. I see him where he lives, where his life is: in the thirty or forty volumes of his work, not in the laundry of his biographers.

Hofmannsthal reduces the work to its material. Nestroy takes his material from where it was barely more than material, invents what he has found, and his achievement would be considerable

---

Hofmannsthal, whose professional specialty was the modern reminting of archaic texts, seemed to me an ephebe who had archetypically struggled and failed to come to terms with Goethe. His play is about an aristocratic aesthete, Claudio, who has looked for life in works of art, rather than having a real life, and then is visited by Death. Hofmannsthal dresses up the text in ways that make it feel *pre*-Goethean, so that instead of sounding like an echo of *Faust* it might read like something that *Faust* echoes, and by comparing lines of the play with lines of *Faust* I was able to argue that this desperate swerve ("clinamen," in the Bloomian parlance that I was carefully avoiding) does Hofmannsthal no good. He loves Goethe's text so much that it kills him as an artist. Unable to resist the still-vital power of Goethe's rhymes and meters, he throws himself metaphorically (and Claudio literally) into the embrace of death. Says Claudio: *Da tot mein Leben war, sei du mein Leben, Tod!* (Even a literal translation, "Since dead my life was, be you my life, Death!" fails to capture the line's suffocatingly palindromic feel, since "dead" and "death" are homonyms in German but not in English.) I concluded by noting that after he wrote this short play, which amounted to his sole, youthful head-to-head confrontation with his major precursor, the only original writing that Hofmannsthal did for the stage was engagement-comedies (including the very elegant and subtle *Der Schwierige*). It seemed to me no coincidence that engagements and comedy writing were two of the very few fields in which Goethe had not excelled: the old man of Weimar drove poor Hofmannsthal into the only scrap of living space still available.

I don't remember feeling as if any of this had personal application to me. I was making a borrowed argument about a play I didn't care about, so that the Fulbright people would fund me for another semester, and meanwhile I was doing my best to construe my own engagement as a happy ending, not an embrace of death, and spending my days much as Claudio does: alone in my room appreciating art rather than plunging into the life of Berlin.

bau der Handlung und im Wirbel der nachgeschaffenen Situationen bestünde, also nur in der willkommenen Gelegenheit, die Welt zu unterhalten, und nicht auch im freiwilligen Zwang, die Welt zu betrachten. Der höhere Nestroy aber, jener, der keiner fremden Idee etws verdankt, ist einer, der nur Kopf hat und nicht Gestalt, dem die Rolle nur eine Ausrede ist, um sich auszureden, und dem jedes Wort zu einer Fülle erwächst, die die Gestalten schlägt und selbst jene, die in der Breite des Scholzischen Humors als Grundtype des Wiener Vorstadttheaters vorbildlich dasteht. Nicht der Schauspieler Nestroy, sondern der kostümierte Anwalt seiner satirischen Berechtigung, der Exekutor seiner Anschläge, der Wortführer seiner eigenen Beredsamkeit, mag

even if it consisted only in the reconstruction of plots and in the whirl of newly created situations—that is, only in the welcome opportunity to entertain the world and not in the voluntary compulsion to observe the world as well. But the higher Nestroy, the one who owes nothing to any foreign idea, is somebody who has only head and no figure, for whom a role is only a pretext for his text,[28] and in whom every word attains a fullness that surpasses character, even the one who stands there in the breadth of Scholzian[29] humor as the model of a basic type in the satellite theaters of Vienna.[30] It wasn't Nestroy the actor but the costumed advocate of his satirical prerogative, the executor of his attacks, the spokesman for his own eloquence, who might have

28. Kraus's quotations from newspapers, too, are a pretext for his texts. He's really pushing the kinship angle here.
29. According to Kehlmann, "Wenzel Scholz was Nestroy's main comic actor-partner, the slow and fat counterpart to quick and thin Nestroy. Nestroy wrote his best parts not for himself but for Scholz."
30. "Kraus liked to contrast the raw force of the offerings in Vienna's less prestigious theaters with what he saw as the stuffy, overly ornate productions of the (imperial) Hofburgtheater. For example, in his essay 'The Last Actors' (1912), he declares that a dialect-speaking troupe of Jewish actors—the Budapester Orpheumgesellschaft—is 'the only real theatrical pleasure' left in Vienna. He goes on to propose that 'the Budapesters' should play on Vienna's most famous stage instead of outside the center of town." —PR

Vienna was and is arguably the most stagestruck city in Europe, and the depth of its attachment to theater is perhaps the main saving grace of its backward-looking culture. When I came to Kraus, I had two preexisting associations with Vienna, both of which probably attracted me to a writer who excoriated the city's supposed charms. One was my reading of John Irving, who'd set some of his fiction there and whose model of literary success I was hoping to emulate and surpass. The other was my mother, who romanticized the city above all others.

jene geheimnisvolle und gewiß nicht in ihrem künstlerischen Ursprung erfaßte Wirkung ausgeübt haben, die uns als der Mittelpunkt einer heroischen Theaterzeit überliefert ist. Mit Nestroys Leib mußte die Theaterform seines Geistes absterben, und die Schablone seiner Beweglichkeit, die wir noch da und dort in virtuoser Haltung auftauchen sehen, ist ein angemaßtes Kostüm. In seinen Possen bleibt die Hauptrolle unbesetzt, solange nicht dem Adepten seiner Schminke auch das Erbe seines satirischen Geistes zufällt. Nur die fruchtbare Komik seiner volleren Nebengestalten hat originale Fortsetzer gefunden, wie etwa den

---

She loved its Sacher torte and its Lipizzaner horses, and when I was in high school she'd somewhat creepily given me a sixth-grade photograph of her friend Ilse's pretty older daughter, which I'd somewhat creepily carried in my wallet through my first two years of college. My mother's mother's people were Catholics from the eastern reaches of the Austro-Hungarian Empire, and her forging of a close friendship with an Austrian, through a business connection of my father's, was intensely meaningful to her.

During both of my years in Germany, I made pilgrimages to Vienna and stayed with Ilse's younger sister, Elisabeth, to please my mother. My father had once helped talk Elisabeth out of her relationship with a good-looking playboy, and she'd now settled down and married a nice businessman who'd been a champion table-tennis player. From my first, Christmastime, visit to them, I remember mainly the many plastic crates of half-liter beer bottles in their basement, the breathless credulity of their young daughter at the visitation of the "Christ child" (not Santa Claus) with presents for her, and the sorrows of my college friend Ekström, who'd come to meet me in Vienna so we could travel on to Spain together. He was so depressed by the city that he left on an earlier train.

On my second visit, from Berlin, in late autumn, Elisabeth and her husband took me out to dinner and to a Schnitzler play, introduced me to people my own age, and were generally gracious hosts, but I needed

exerted that mysterious effect which, while its artistic origins have certainly never been understood, has come down to us as the center of a heroic age of theater. The theatrical form of Nestroy's mind was bound to die out with his body, and the routine of its nimbleness, which we still here and there see popping up with virtuoso poise, is a costume borrowed illegitimately. In his farces, the lead role remains unfilled unless the expert in his greasepaint also happens to come by his satirical spirit. Only the fruitful comedy of his fuller secondary roles has found original successors, such as the actor Oskar Sachs,[31] whose style seems,

---

to tell Elisabeth that my fiancée was cheating on me and that I'd recently suffered a small psychotic break, and I found it strange and damning that Elisabeth wasn't interested in hearing about it; I blamed it on the bourgeois life choices she'd made. Back in Berlin, I sent a letter, ostensibly of apology, in which I continued to attack her with my emotional distress. How horrible it is to be twenty-two. I'd rejected Young Werther as an appalling embarrassment when I'd read the Goethe novel, and now I couldn't help behaving like him.

It was twenty-five years before I returned to Vienna, to give a reading at one of its theaters. After the reading, the city's cultural-affairs councillor hosted a dinner for me and a bunch of local journalists who were there for the free food and drink. The spectacle of their implacable swigging and masticating was Krausian. Thankfully, there was also a goofily friendly, immensely well-read young man who apologized for the journalists and was eager to talk to me about Karl Kraus. His name was unfamiliar, but his novel *Measuring the World* was about to become one of the bestselling fiction titles in German publishing history. This was Kehlmann.

31. "Oskar Sachs (1869–1941) was one of the few Viennese actors who got a kind word from Kraus. In 'The Last Actors' essay, only Sachs and Alexander Girardi are spared Kraus's scorn—more on Girardi below."—PR

Schauspieler Oskar Sachs, dessen Art in ihrer lebendigen Ruhe dem klassischen Carltheater zu enstammen scheint. Aber als Ursprung und Vollendung eines volkstümlichen Typus dürfte ein Girardi, der, ein schauspielerischer Schöpfer, neben der leeren Szene steht, die ihm das Bühnenhandwerk der letzten Jahrzehnte bietet, über den theatralischen Wert der Nestroyschen Kunst hinausragen, welche ihre eigene Geistesfülle nur zu bekleiden hatte. Darum konnte auch ein Bühnenlaie wie Herr Reinhardt

in its vital composure, to descend from the classical Carlthe-ater.[32] But as the origin and perfection of a popular type, an ac-torly creator such as Girardi, who stands on the margins of the empty scene offered by the stagecraft of the past decade, might be allowed to surpass the theatrical value of Nestroy's art, which had only to clothe its own fullness of thought.[33] This is why even a layman of the stage such as Herr Reinhardt could propose a

32. "Christened after a director whose name Nabokov would have loved, Karl Carl, the Carltheater was located in Leopoldstadt and served as a center of Nestroy activity. Nestroy's works were often per-formed there, frequently with him acting in them. And from 1854 until 1860 he held the position of the director of the theater."—PR

33. "Alexander Girardi (1850–1918) was Vienna's most famous oper-etta singer and comic actor at the turn of the century, known particu-larly for his roles in Ferdinand Raimund's farces. So in celebrating Girardi, Kraus wasn't exactly swimming against the current of popular opinion. Indeed, Girardi was a trendsetting celebrity in Vienna. People would imitate how he dressed and talked, even how he walked. But Kraus went much further in his assessment of Girardi than most crit-ics. As Kraus himself emphasized, he had little company in proclaim-ing that Vienna lost its 'cultural heart' when Girardi left for an engagement in Germany. In the same context (the 1908 essay 'Gi-rardi'), Kraus began to develop the idea that Girardi's 'extraordinarily self-asserting' way of using 'scenic possibilities for creative portrayal' didn't lend itself to performing works of great literary value—hence Girardi's lack of compatibility with Nestroy, whom Kraus sees as an author of satirical literature operating as a dramatist. Girardi's own gift for satire thrives precisely where the literary value of what he is per-forming is weak. Kraus observes, about one of his performances, 'if the script was superficial amusement, the accent employed was the deepest mocking of demagogic language,' and goes on to say that Girardi 'ig-nores the literature' in the works he performs. It's the less self-asserting Oskar Sachs who is more 'Nestroy-ready' ('nestroyfähig') in the 'Gi-rardi' essay, just as he is in 'Nestroy and Posterity.'"—PR

einem Girardi einen Nestroy-Zyklus vorschlagen. In Girardi wächst die Gestalt an der Armut der textlichen Unterstützung, bei Nestroy schrumpft sie am Reichtum des Wortes zusammen. In Nestroy ist so viel Literatur, daß sich das Theater sträubt, und er muß für den Schauspieler einspringen. Er kann es, denn es ist

Nestroy cycle to a Girardi.[34] In Girardi, the character thrives on the poverty of its textual support; with Nestroy it shrivels up on the wealth of the words. There's so much literature in Nestroy that the theater balks, and he has to step in for the actor. He can

34. Kehlmann says: "This is a ridiculous insult. Max Reinhardt was arguably the greatest stage director of the twentieth century; calling him 'a layman of the stage' is just pure ressentiment."

Reitter explains: "Max Reinhardt (1873–1943) was a hugely influential director whom Kraus belittled for over thirty years. As so often with Kraus's feuds, things were different—that is, better—in the beginning. Born near Vienna, Reinhardt met Kraus in 1892, when both participated in a student production of Schiller's *The Robbers*. Reinhardt excelled in the role of Spiegelberg while Kraus flopped as Franz Moor; this led him to give up his dreams of becoming an actor. If he envied Reinhardt, he didn't show it at the time. Indeed, he wrote in support of Reinhardt for years, openly acknowledging his 'gifts.' But around 1905, when Reinhardt was achieving celebrity status, Kraus's position changed. A combination of old and new jealousies may have been at work; certainly Reinhardt thought so. But there were also genuine differences of principle and practice. Kraus's drama *The Last Days of Mankind* may have a list of characters that runs to thirteen pages, and it may also call for war propaganda films to be used as a scenic backdrop, but Kraus for the most part was a theatrical minimalist. In his own performances he often sat on a bare stage behind an unremarkable table on which there would be only papers and a glass of water. Reinhardt, by contrast, was known for his big stagings and elaborate sets. In 1911 he produced the Berlin premiere of Hofmannsthal's *Everyman* in a circus arena. Later that year, he turned the Exhibition Centre at Earls Court in London into a cathedral for his staging of Karl Vollmoeller's *The Miracle*. And in 1922 Reinhardt and Hofmannsthal mounted their drama *The Salzburg Great World Theater* in an actual cathedral—prompting Kraus, who had secretly converted to Catholicism in 1911, to proclaim that he was now leaving the church 'out of antisemitism.'

geschriebene Schauspielkunst. In dieser Stellvertretung für den Schauspieler, in dieser Verkörperung dessen, was sich den eigentlichen Ansprüchen des Theaters leicht entzieht, lebt ihm heute eine Verwandtschaft, die schon in den geistigen Umrissen der Persönlichkeit hin und wieder erkennbar wird: Frank Wedekind. Auch hier ist ein Überproduktives, das dem organischen

---

"In an essay written before 'Nestroy and Posterity,' Kraus remarks that Reinhardt's desire to have Girardi perform in a Nestroy cycle is an example of Reinhardt's 'snobbism.' Reinhardt presumably knows that Girardi isn't right for the role, but he wants a big name because he's a snob, and that's what snobs want. 'Nestroy and Posterity' upgrades the insult, in a way. Now Reinhardt, as a 'layman of the stage,' doesn't even seem to recognize how incompatible Girardi and Nestroy are. Now it's ignorance and incompetence that led him to propose a Nestroy cycle."

do it because it's a written art of acting.[35] In this proxyship for the actor, in this embodiment of what easily eludes the actual demands of theater, there lives today a spirit whose affinity with him can now and then be recognized in the very outlines of his personality: Frank Wedekind.[36] Here, too, there's something

35. "One of Kraus's more famous self-descriptions reads: 'I am perhaps the first case of an author who simultaneously experiences his writing as an actor.' Less well known is that the aphorism continues: 'Would I therefore want to entrust another actor with my text? Nestroy's intellectuality is untheatrical. The actor Nestroy was effective because he said what no listener would have understood so quickly that no listener could understand him.' The actual point of the aphorism is to underscore the affinity between Kraus, *the* actorly writer, and Nestroy *the* writerly actor.

"What seems really astonishing now is that before an essay like 'Heine and the Consequences' was read, it was heard. Kraus began giving public lectures in the spring of 1910, and 'Heine and the Consequences,' which wasn't published until the end of that year, was among the first things he brought to the stage. We can only wonder how many of Kraus's allusions and echoes his most educated listeners were able to pick up on as the words flew by." —PR

36. "By 1912 Kraus had been championing Wedekind and his works for nearly a decade. He had even produced—and participated in—a private staging of *Pandora's Box* in 1905, when public performances of it were banned. Kraus played the role of Kungu Poti, Imperial Prince of Uahubee; Wedekind assigned himself the part of Jack the Ripper. This kind of self-casting wasn't unusual for him, and it linked him, as Kraus points out, to the writer-actor Nestroy. Kraus particularly lauded Wedekind's handling of his great theme, which he construed as a version of one of his own themes: gender conflicts reveal both the misogyny and the larger ethical bankruptcy of bourgeois society. Kraus insisted on Lulu's status as a victim, 'a destroyer because she is destroyed from all sides.' The 'world of the poet Frank Wedekind,' he wrote in 1905, is one 'in which woman isn't cursed with taking the cross of ethical re-

Mangel der Figur durch die Identität nachhilft und zwischen Bekenntnis und Glaubhaftigkeit persönlich vermittelt. Der Schauspieler hat eine Rolle für einen Dichter geschrieben, die der Dichter einem Schauspieler nicht anvertrauen würde. In Wedekind stellt sich – wenn ich von einem mir näher liegenden Beispiel sprachsatirischer Nachkommenschaft absehe – ein Monologist vor uns, dem gleichfalls eine scheinbare Herkömmlichkeit und Beiläufigkeit der szenischen Form genügt, um das wahrhaft Neue und Wesentliche an ihr vorbeizusprechen und vorbeizusingen. Auf die Analogie im Tonfall witzig eingestellter Erkenntnisse hat einmal der verstorbene Kritiker Wilheim hingewiesen. Der Tonfall ist jene Äußerlichkeit, auf die es dem Gedanken hauptsächlich ankommt, und es muß irgendwo einen gemeinsamen Standpunkt der Weltbetrachtung geben, wenn Sätze gesprochen werden, die Nestroy so gut gesprochen haben konnte wie Wedekind.

> „Sie steht jetzt im zwanzigsten Jahr, war dreimal verheiratet, hat eine kolossale Menge Liebhaber befriedigt, da melden sich auch schließlich die Herzensbedürfnisse."

Eine solche biographische Anmerkung würde, wie sie ist, auch von einem der Nestroyschen Gedankenträger gemacht werden,

---

sponsibility from man, should she ripen to aesthetic perfection. His deep knowledge, which understands the gap between blooming lips and bourgeois attitudes, is perhaps the only knowledge today worthy of a dramatist.'"—PR

overproductive, in which what's organically lacking in the character is made up for with identification, and which mediates personally between confession and credibility.[37] The actor wrote for a poet a role with which the poet wouldn't trust an actor. In Wedekind—leaving aside an example of linguistic-satirical lineage that means more to me personally—we're presented with a monologuist for whom a seeming conventionality and casualness of scenic form likewise suffices for speaking past us, and singing past us, things that are truly new and essential. The kinship in the cadences of aperçus was pointed out once by the late critic Wilheim.[38] Cadence is that superficiality on which thoughts most rely, and there must somewhere be a common standpoint for observing the world when sentences are spoken that could just as well be Nestroy's as Wedekind's:

> "She's in her twentieth year now, was married three times, satisfied a colossal lot of lovers—sooner or later, the needs of her heart were bound to register."[39]

A biographical comment like this would also be made, just as it is, by a Nestroyan bringer of thought if, with the same vault of

---

37. Kehlmann cuts through some of the fog here: "Kraus is talking about the fact that Wedekind also worked as an actor, playing his own roles, writing roles for himself, and therefore adding an element of personal confession, which is a slightly untheatrical effect but very effective on a different level."

38. "Sigmund Wilheim (1849–1911) was one of the few theater critics in Austria whom Kraus respected. Kraus compared Wilheim's style to that of Ludwig Speidel, the only feuilletonist he admired, and he wrote, in his obituary for Wilheim, 'he truly understood theater, and he was the first in Vienna to comprehend something of Wedekind.'"—PR

39. "From *Pandora's Box* (1904)."—PR

wenn er sich mit dem gleichen Schwung der Antithese über das Vorleben seiner Geliebten hinwegsetzen könnte. Und im „Erdgeist" könnte einer ungefähr wieder den wundervollen Satz sprechen, der bei Nestroy vorkommt:

> „Ich hab' einmal einen alten Isabellenschimmel an ein' Ziegelwagen g'seh'n. Seitdem bring' ich die Zukunft gar nicht mehr aus'm Sinn."

Vielleicht aber ist hier das absolut Shakespearische solch blitzhafter Erhellung einer seelischen Landschaft über jeden modernen Vergleich erhaben. Es ist ein Satz, an dem man dem verirrten Auge des neuen Lesers wieder vorstellen möchte, was Lyrik ist: ein Drinnen von einem Draußen geholt, eine volle Einheit. Die angeschaute Realität ins Gefühl aufgenommen, nicht befühlt, bis sie zum Gefühl passe. Man könnte daran die Methode aller Poeterei, aller Feuilletonlyrik nachweisen, die ein passendes Stück Außenwelt sucht, um eine vorrätige Stimmung

antitheses, he could get himself over his beloved's past. And in *Earth Spirit*[40] somebody could again come close to speaking the wonderful line that occurs in Nestroy:

"I seen an old gray horse once pullin' a brick wagon. The future's been weighin' on my mind ever since."[41]

But here, perhaps, the absolute Shakespearean quality of such a lightning illumination of a mental landscape is sublime beyond any modern comparison. It's a line by which you'd like to reintroduce to the contemporary reader's muddled eye what poetry is: a within fetched from a without, a perfect unity. Observed reality taken up in feeling, not massaged until it fits the feeling. It could be used to reveal the method of all poetastery, all feuilleton poetry, which looks around for a handy piece of the external world

40. Wedekind's play of 1894.
41. "From Nestroy's farce *The Insignificant Man* (*Der Unbedeutende*, 1846)."—PR
    I'm reluctant to add to the already astronomical footnote tally by separately noting the sources of all the Nestroy lines that Kraus will be quoting, but Paul Reitter has done such excellent work in tracking them down that I will list the rest of them here, in order of appearance. 1.) From Nestroy's farce *My Friend* (*Mein Freund*, 1851). 2.) From Nestroy's farce *The Talisman* (*Der Talisman*, 1840). 3.) From Nestroy's farce *The Evil Spirit Lumpazivagabundus* (*Der böse Geist Lumpazivagabundus*, 1833). 4.) From Nestroy's farce *A Man Full of Nothing* (*Der Zerrissene*, 1844). 5.) Also from *A Man Full of Nothing*. 6.) From Nestroy's farce *The Two Night Wanderers* (*Die beiden Nachtwandler*, 1836). 7.) From Nestroy's farce *Earlier Conditions* (*Frühere Verhältnisse*, 1862). 8.) From *The Two Night Wanderers*. 9.) From Nestroy's farce *Earlier Conditions*. 10.) From *My Friend*. 11.) From *The Two Night Wanderers*. 12.) From Nestroy's farce *Terrible Fear* (*Höllenangst*, 1849). 13.) From *Lumpazivagabundus*.

abzugeben. An solchem Satz bricht der Fall Heine auf und zusammen, denn es bietet sich die tote Gewißheit, daß ein alter Isabellenschimmel zu sinnen anfinge: Wie schön war mein Leben früher – Heut' muß ich den Wagen zieh'n – O alter Zeiten Gewieher – Dahin bist du, dahin! – Der Wagen aber sprach munter – Das ist der Welten Lauf – Geht der Weg einmal hinunter – so geht er nicht wieder hinauf . . . Und wir wären über die Stimmung des Dichters inklusive der ironischen Resignation vollständig informiert. Bei Nestroy, der nur holperige Coupletstrophen gemacht hat, lassen sich in jeder Posse Stellen nachweisen, wo die rein dichterische Führung des Gedankens durch den dicksten Stoff, wo mehr als der Geist: die Vergeistigung sichtbar wird. Es ist der Vorzug, den vor der Schönheit jenes Gesicht hat, das veränderlich ist bis zur Schönheit. Je gröber die Materie, umso eindringlicher der Prozeß. An der Satire ist der sprachliche Anspruch unverdächtiger zu erweisen, an ihr ist der Betrug schwerer als an jener Lyrik, die sich die Sterne nicht erst erwirbt und der die Ferne kein Weg ist, sondern ein Reim. Die Satire ist so recht die Lyrik des Hindernisses, reich entschädigt dafür, daß sie das Hindernis der Lyrik ist. Und wie hat sie beides zusammen: vom Ideal das ganze Ideal und dazu die Ferne! Sie ist nie polemisch, immer schöpferisch, während die falsche Lyrik nur Jasagerei ist, schnöde Berufung der schon vorhandenen Welt.

in order to dispose of a stock mood. The case of Heine breaks open and collapses on a sentence like this, for it offers the dead certainty that an old gray horse would start to muse: How good was my life before / This wagon must I pull today / O happy neighs of yore / You've gone, you've gone away! / But the wagon said, Don't frown / It is an old refrain / Once the road starts going down / It never goes up again . . . And we'd be fully informed about the author's mood, including the ironic resignation. With Nestroy, who wrote only rough couplet stanzas, you can detect passages in every farce where his purely poetic piloting of thought through the densest of materials—where more than the mind: the mind's process of assimilation—becomes visible. It's the advantage over beauty possessed by a face that's changeable to the point of beauty. The coarser the material, the more penetrating the process. In satire, the linguistic demands are less easily questioned, and fraudulence more difficult, than in the kind of poetry that doesn't bother earning the stars and for which distance isn't a road but a rhyme. Satire is thus rightly the poetry of impediment, richly compensated for being the impediment of poetry. And how it has both together: of the ideal, the entire ideal, and distance as well! It is never polemical,[42] always creative, while counterfeit poetry is mere yea-saying, a contemptible appeal to the

42. "Kraus was nothing if not polemical, yet he tended not to apply the term 'polemical' to himself or to writers whom he admired. In fact, he often used it to describe attacks against him, with 'polemical' implying, as it still does, a lack of fairness. But Kraus's definition of the category 'polemic' is rather neutral. In an essay that appeared a few months after 'Nestroy and Posterity,' Kraus distinguishes polemic from satire, explaining that the former 'operates within the format of the bad object' and that its specific function is to 'expose the disparity between high standing and insignificance.' The point of polemic is, evidently, to take down what's overrated."—PR

Wie ist sie die wahre Symbolik, die aus den Zeichen einer gefundenen Häßlichkeit auf eine verlorene Schönheit schließt und kleine Sinnbilder für den Begriff der Welt setzt! Die falsche Lyrik, welche die großen Dinge voraussetzt, und die falsche Ironie, welche die großen Dinge negiert, haben nur ein Gesicht, und von der einsamen Träne Heines zum gemeinsamen Lachen des Herrn Shaw führt nur eine Falte. Aber der Witz lästert die Schornsteine, weil er die Sonne bejaht. Und die Säure will den Glanz und der Rost sagt, sie sei nur zersetzend. Die Satire kann eine Religionsstörung begehen, um zur Andacht zu kommen. Sie wird leicht pathetisch. Auch dort, wo sie ein gegebenes Pathos nicht anders einstellt als ein Ding der Außenwelt, damit ihr Widerspruch hindurchspiele. Ja und Nein vermischen sich, vermehren sich, und es entspringt der Gedanke. Ein Spiel, gesinnungslos wie die Liebe. Das Ergebnis dieser vollkommenen Durchdringung, Erhaltung und Verstärkung polarer Strömungen: eine Nestroysche Tirade, eine Offenbachsche Melodie. Hier unterstreicht der Witz, der es auslacht, das Entzücken an einem Schäferspiel; dort schlägt die Verzerrung einer schmachtenden Mondscheinliebe über die Stränge der Parodie ins Transzendente. Das ist der wahre Übermut, dem nichts unheilig ist.

already available world. How satire is true symbolism, inferring a lost beauty from a found ugliness and setting up little images of meaning in place of global concepts! Counterfeit poetry, which takes weighty matters for granted, and counterfeit irony, which rejects weighty matters, have one and the same face, and a single wrinkle separates Heine's lonely tear from Herr Shaw's common laughter. But the joke is nasty to the smokestack because the joke affirms the sun. And acid wants the gleam, and the rust says it's only corrosive.[43] Satire can perpetrate a disruption of religion to arrive at reverence. It inclines toward high emotion. Even in places where a given emotion is deployed like just another object from the outside world, so that satire's contradiction can shimmer through.[44] Yes and No mix and multiply, and thought springs forth. A game, as unprincipled as love. The result of this perfect penetration, preservation, and intensification of polar tendencies: a Nestroyan tirade, a melody by Offenbach. Here someone's rapture at a pastoral play is underscored by the very joke deriding it; there the caricature of someone's pining moonlight love runs riot over parody and into transcendence. This is true high-spiritedness, for which nothing is profane.

43. "A very personal line," says Kehlmann. "Kraus was constantly reproached for being 'only corrosive,' and this is his response to that." I would add that this entire essay—a loving celebration of Nestroy's brilliance—is a response to that.

44. The latter part of this sentence fragment is obstinately opaque. But it may help to compare the "counterfeit irony" of Heine—who doesn't actually credit the emotion of the girl who's moved by a sunset, and who undercuts it with a snarky, conventional-minded reference to the earth's rotation—with the functioning of high emotion in a genuinely satirical work like Joseph Heller's *Catch-22*. The pathos of the mortally wounded Snowden's refrain in that novel ("I'm cold") stands in meaningful aesthetic relation to Heller's acidic satire of the logic preventing Snowden from escaping endless bombing missions.

„Mich hat ein echt praktischer Schwärmer versichert, das
Reizendste is das, wenn von zwei Liebenden eins früher stirbt
und erscheint dem andern als Geist. Ich kann mich in das hin-
eindenken, wenn sie so dasitzet in einer Blumennacht am Gar-
tenfenster, die Tränenperlen vom Mondstrahl überspiegelt, und
es wurd' hinter der Hollerstauden immer weißer und weißer
und das Weiße wär' ich – gänzlich Geist, kein Stückerl Körper,
aber dennoch anstandshalber das Leintuch der Ewigkeit über'n
Kopf – ich strecket die Arme nach ihr aus, zeiget nach oben auf
ein' Stern, Gotigkeit, ‚dort werden wir vereinigt' – sie kriegt a
Schneid' auf das Himmelsrendezvous, hast es net g'sehn streift
die irdischen Bande ab, und wir verschwebeten, verschmelzeten
und verschwingeten uns ins Azurblaue des Nachthimmels . . ."

Gewendetes Pathos setzt Pathos voraus, und Nestroys Witz hat
immer die Gravität, die noch die besseren Zeiten des Pathos
gekannt hat. Er rollt wie der jedes wahren Satirikers die lange
Bahn entlang, dorthin wo die Musen stehen, um alle neun zu
treffen. Der Raisonneur Nestroy ist der raisonnierende Katalog
aller Weltgefühle. Der vertriebene Hanswurst, der im Abschied
von der Bühne noch hinter der tragischen Figur seine Späße
machte, scheint für ein Zeitalter mit ihr verschmolzen, und lebt
sich in einem Stil aus, der sich ins eigene Herz greift und in einem eigentümlichen Schwebeton, fast auf Jean Paulisch, den
Scherz hält, der da mit Entsetzen getrieben wird.

FRAU VON ZYPRESSENBURG: Ist sein Vater auch Jäger? – TITUS:
Nein, er betreibt ein stilles, abgeschiedenes Geschäft, bei dem
die Ruhe seine einzige Arbeit ist; er liegt von höherer Macht
gefesselt, und doch ist er frei und unabhängig, denn er ist Ver-

"A real practical fanatic once told me that the dandiest thing is when there's two lovers and one of them dies first and comes back to the other one as a ghost. I can just see it, when she's sitting there at her garden window some flowery night, with moonlight playing all over her pearly tears, and it would be getting whiter and whiter behind the bushes, and that whiteness would be yours truly—completely spirit, not one speck of body, but with the bedsheet of eternity over my head all the same, on account of decency—I stretches out my arms to her, I points to a star in the sky, 'there shall we be united,' so to speak—she gets the itch for a heavenly rendezvous, and would you believe it, she casts off her earthly shackles and we go amalgamating and waffeting and pendulating into the azure-blue night sky . . ."

Applied emotion presupposes emotion, and Nestroy's wit always has the gravity that knew emotion in its better days. Like the wit of every true satirist, it rolls down the long alley toward where the Muses stand, to strike all nine of them. Nestroy the disputer is the disputatious catalogue of every feeling in the world.[45] The buffoon who was banished from the stage, but went on cracking jokes behind the tragic hero as he was leaving, seems fused with the hero for an epoch, amusing himself in a style that reaches into his own heart and, in a strangely suspended tone, almost like Jean Paul's, sustains the joke that's being perpetrated here with horror.

FRAU VON ZYPRESSENBURG: Is one's father a hunter, too?—
TITUS: No, he runs a quiet, solitary business in which resting is his only work; he lies fettered by a higher power, and yet he's free and independent because he's disposing of himself;—he's

45. Sadly, more untranslatable wordplay here: in the original, "disputatious catalogue" is a play on "catalogue raisonné," which works in German because *Raisonneur* means "disputer" or "person who wrangles."

weser seiner selbst; – er ist *tot*. – FRAU VON ZYPRESSENBURG (*für sich*): Wie verschwenderisch er mit zwanzig erhabenen Worten das sagt, was man mit einer Silbe sagen kann. Der Mensch hat offenbare Anlagen zum Literaten.

Und es ist die erhabenste und noch immer knappste Paraphrase für einen einsilbigen Zustand, wie hier das Wort um den Tod spielt. Dieses verflossene Pathos, das in die unscheinbarste Zwischenbemerkung einer Nestroyschen Person einfließt, hat die Literarhistoriker glauben machen, dieser Witz habe es auf ihre edlen Regungen abgesehen. In Wahrheit hat er es nur auf ihre Phrasen abgesehen. Nestroy ist der erste deutsche Satiriker, in dem sich die Sprache Gedanken macht über die Dinge. Er erlöst die Sprache vom Starrkrampf, und sie wirft ihm für jede Redensart einen Gedanken ab. Bezeichnend dafür sind Wendungen wie:

> „Wann ich mir meinen Verduß net versaufet, ich müßt' mich g'rad aus Verzweiflung dem Trunke ergeben."

Oder:

> „Da g'hören die Ruben her! An keine Ordung g'wöhnt sich das Volk. Kraut und Ruben werfeten s' untereinand', als wie Kraut und Ruben."

Hier lacht sich die Sprache selbst aus. Die Phrase wird bis in die heuchlerische Konvention zurückgetrieben, die sie erschaffen hat:

> „Also heraus mit dem Entschluß, meine Holde!" „Aber Herr v. Lips, ich muß ja dort erst . . ." „Ich versteh', vom Neinsagen

dead.—FRAU VON ZYPRESSENBURG (*aside*): How profligately he uses twenty lofty words to say what can be said with one syllable. The man obviously has the makings of an author.

And it is the loftiest yet tersest paraphrasing of a monosyllabic condition, the way the words here play around death. This blurred emotionality, which Nestroy breathes into the most modest of his characters' asides, has led literary historians to think that his wit is aimed at their noble impulses.[46] In truth, it's aimed only at their phrases. Nestroy is the first German satirist in whom language forms thoughts about things. He liberates language from its lockjaw, and for every cliché it turns him a profit in thought. Indicative are such expressions as:

> "Good thing I drownded my sorrows, or despair woulda driven me straightaway to drink."

Or:

> "The apples go over here! People got no idea how to organdize. They go mixin' up apples and oranges like apples and oranges."

Language is making fun of itself here. The cliché is driven back into the hypocritical convention that created it:

> "All right, out with your decision, my sweet"—"But Herr von Lips, I really must first . . ."—"I understand, there can be no talk

46. "Nestroy's contemporaries Friedrich Theodor Vischer, Heinrich Laube, and Emil Kuh, all of them authors of consequence, charged Nestroy with 'cheapening our ideals through his toxic nastiness.' This sounds a lot like a well-worn criticism of Kraus, and it may be what Kraus is alluding to with the sarcastic line 'noble impulses.'"—PR

keine Rede, aber zum Jasagen finden Sie eine Bedenkzeit schicklich."

Die Phrase dreht sich zur Wahrheit um:

„Ich hab die Not mit Ihnen geteilt, es ist jetzt meine heiligste Pflicht, auch in die guten Tag' Sie nicht zu verlassen!"

Oder entartet zu Neubildungen, durch die im Munde der Ungebildeten die Sprache der höheren Stände karikiert wird:

„Da kommt auf einmal eine verspätete Sternin erster Größe zur Gesellschaft als glanzpunktischer Umundauf der ambulanten Entreprise . . ."

Wie für solche Absicht die bloße Veränderung des Tempus genügt, zeigt ein geniales Beispiel, wo das „sprechen wie einem der Schnabel gewachsen ist" sich selbst berichtigt. Ein Ineinander von Problem und Inhalt:

„Fordere kühn, sprich ohne Scheu, wie dir der Schnabel wuchs!"

Nestroys Leute reden geschwollen, wenn der Witz das Klischee zersetzen oder das demagogische Pathos widerrufen will:

„O, ich will euch ein furchtbarer Hausknecht sein!"

Jeden Domestiken läßt er Schillersätze sprechen, um das Gefühlsleben der Prizipale zu ernüchtern. Oft aber ist es, als wäre einmal die tragische Figur hinter dem Hanswurst gestanden, denn das Pathos scheint dem Witz beizustehen. Echte Herzens-

of refusing, but to say yes, you think some deliberation is in order."

The cliché inverts itself into truth:

> "I've shared adversity with you; it's now my most sacred duty to stick with you in good times, too!"

Or, debased to neologism, the language of the upper classes is caricatured by language from the mouths of the unrefined:

> "All of a sudden, here comes a first-magnitude starlet and makes her societal splash at the pinnacle of the ambulatory *entreprise* . . ."

How merely changing a tense suffices for an intention like this can be seen in an inspired example in which "not mincing one's words" corrects itself. An interpenetration of problem and content:

> "Be bold in your demands, speak openly, without having minced your words!"

Nestroy's people speak bombastically when the joke wants to subvert cliché or counteract demagogic emotionality:

> "Oh, I want to be a dreadful servant for thee!"

He has every domestic speak Schiller sentences, to sober the emotional life of the principals. Often, however, it's as if the tragic hero had been standing behind the buffoon, for the emotion seems to side with the joke. Genuine matters of the heart are

sachen werden abgehandelt, wenn ein Diurnist zu einer Mar-
schandmod' wie in das Zimmer der Eboli tritt:

„Ihr Dienstbot' durchbohrt mich – weiß er um unsere ehema-
lige Liebe?"

Witz und Pathos begleiten sich und wenn sie, von der Zeit noch
nicht gereizt, einander auch nicht erzeugen können, so werden
sie doch nie aneinander hinfällig. Der Dichter hebt zwar nicht
den eigenen Witz unverändert in das eigene Pathos, aber er ver-
stärkt ihn durch das fremde. Sie spielen und entlassen sich
gegenseitig unversehrt. Wenn sich Nestroy über das Gefühl hin-
wegsetzt, so können wir uns darauf verlassen, und wenn sein
Witz eine Liebesszene verkürzt, so erledigt er und ersetzt er
sämtliche Liebesszenen, die sich in ähnlichen Fällen abspielen
könnten. Wo in einer deutschen Posse ist je nach der Verlobung
der Herrschaften das Nötige zwischen der Dienerschaft mit weniger Worten veranlaßt worden:

„Was schaut er mich denn gar so an?" „Sie ist in Diensten
meiner künftigen Gebieterin, ich bin in Diensten ihres künftigen Gebieters, ich werfe das bloß so hin, weil sich daraus ver-
schiedene Entspinnungen gestalten könnten." „Kommt Zeit,
kommt Rat!"

Und wenn es gilt, an Nestroyschen Dialogstellen sein Abkür-
zungsverfahren für Psychologie zu zeigen, wo steht eine Szene
wie diese zwischen einem Schuster und einem Bedienten:

„Ich gratuliere zum heimlichen Terno, oder was es gewesen
und, aber auf Ehr', ich war ganz paff." „Der Wirt gar! Der hat
noch ein dümmeres Gesicht gemacht als Sie. Wetten S' 'was,
daß ich ihm jetzt zehn Frank' schuldig bleib', und er traut sich

being treated when an office clerk approaches a milliner as if on his way to Eboli's room:[47]

> "Your servant's looking daggers at me—does he know about our former love?"

Joke and high emotion go hand in hand, and if the times haven't yet stimulated them to engender each other, they still never cancel each other. To be sure, the poet doesn't elevate his own wit, unaltered, into his own emotion, but he strengthens it with someone else's. The two of them play and release each other mutually unharmed. When Nestroy makes light of feeling, we can trust him, and when his wit cuts short a love scene, he disposes of and replaces every other love scene that could have occurred in a similar situation. Where, in a German farce, after the engagement of master and mistress, have the necessities between manservant and maidservant ever been accomplished in fewer words:

> "Why is he looking at me like that?"—"She's in the service of my future mistress, I'm in the service of her future master, I just toss that out, as various consequentialities could arise from it."—"Time will tell."

And if the aim is to demonstrate, in passages of Nestroyan dialogue, his accelerated method of psychology, where does a scene like this one between a cobbler and a servant stand:

> "Congratulations on the secret jackpot, or whatever it was, but honestly, I was flabbergasted."—"So was the innkeeper, no less! He made an even stupider face than you. I bet you I could be into him for ten francs now and he wouldn't dare say any-

---

47. **The Princess of Eboli is Don Carlos's beloved in the Schiller play.**

nix zu sagen . . . Ja, einen Dukaten wechseln lassen, das erweckt Respekt." „Kurios! (*Beiseite.*) Aber auch Verdacht . . . Unser Herr ist verschwunden. Bei dem Proletarier kommt ein Dukaten zum Vorschein . . . Hm . . . Sie sind Schuster?" „So sagt die Welt." „Haben vermutlich einen unverhofften Engländer gedoppelt?" „Ach, Sie möchten gern wissen, wie ein ehrlicher Schuster zu ei'm Dukaten kommt?" „Na ja . . . auffallend is es . . . Das heißt, interessant nämlich . . ." „Als fremder Mensch geht's Ihnen eigentlich nix an . . . aber nein, ich betrachte jeden, den ich im Wirtshaus find', als eine verwandte Seele. (*Ihm die Hand drückend.*) Sie sollen alles wissen." (*In neugieriger Spannung.*) „Na, also?" „Seh'n Sie, die Sach' ist die. Es liegt hier eine Begebenheit zu Grunde . . . eine im Grunde fürchterliche Begebenheit, die kein Mensch auf Erden je erfahren darf, folglich auch Sie nicht." „Ja, aber . . ." „Drum zeigen Sie sich meines Vertrauens würdig und forschen Sie nicht weiter."

Solche Werte sind versunken und vergessen. Zeitmangel hat wie überall in der Kunst so vor allem im Theater das Publikum zur Umständlichkeit gewöhnt. Nur diese ermöglichte dem von den Geschäften ermüdeten Verstand, sich auch die Genüsse zu verschaffen, deren Vermittlung er so lange für die Aufgabe der höheren Dramatik hielt: die Fortschritte der neueren Seelenkunde kennen zu lernen, einer Psychologie, die nur Psychologie ist, die Lehre, sich auf rationelle Art mit den Geheimnissen

thing . . . Yessiree, to ask for change from a ducat, it arouses respect."—"Strange! (*aside*) But suspicions, too . . . Our master has disappeared. A ducat comes to light among the proletariat . . . Hm . . . You're a cobbler?"—"So they say."—"And I suppose you made good on a long shot?"—"Oh, you're probably wondering how an honest cobbler came by a ducat?"—"Well, it is extra-ordinary . . . I mean, that is to say, interesting . . ."—"As a stranger, it's actually none of your business . . . but, no, to me, anybody I meet in an inn is a kindred soul. (*Shaking his hand*) You shall know everything."—(*In inquisitive suspense*) "Well, so?"—"You see, the thing is, there's an incident at the bottom of this . . . a fundamentally horrible incident that no man on earth may ever learn of, and consequently not you, either."—"Yes, but . . ."—"So show yourself worthy of my trust and probe no further!"

Such values are lost and forgotten. As everywhere in art, and above all in theater, scarcity of time has accustomed audiences to ponderousness.[48] Only this would enable the intellect, weary from business, to procure those further pleasures that it has so long regarded as the task of dramatic high art to provide: getting acquainted with the latest advances in psychology, a psychology that is only psychology,[49] the science of coming to terms with

48. In the world of books nowadays, there's the related paradox of the thousand-page biography. Precisely when the world accelerated technologically and our time for reading began to shrink, the average length of biographies seemed to double. It's as if being bored has become the way to reassure yourself that you're doing serious reading, as opposed to playing Angry Birds.

49. "A neologism that (playfully) expresses Kraus's position on psycho-analysis—the Greek word '*psychros*' means 'fatuous' and 'insignificant.' Kraus was famously critical of psychoanalysis. Indeed, his most widely cited aphorism is a dig at it: 'Psychoanalysis is that disease of the mind

for which it believes itself to be the cure.' Kraus also liked to speak of the 'psychoanals.' He believed that psychoanalysis was driven by psychological pathologies—'you head to the entrance of a stranger's unconscious when your own home is dirty'—but his chief complaint was with the invasiveness and reductionism of its methods. These he even managed to portray as the result of a particularly Jewish striverism: 'They control the press; they control the banks; and now they control the unconscious, too!' Most often, though, Kraus pointed up the intellectual limitations of psychoanalysis: 'A good psychologist can quickly get you inside his head.' Especially appalling to him was the psychoanalytic interpretation of art, which he regarded as a kind of desecration—'muddy boots' in the 'holy place of the artist's dream.'

"It may be that in going after psychoanalysis Kraus was thinking more of Freud's followers than of Freud himself. He tended not to name names in his attacks, though he did occasionally make fun of Freud's name. There was, in any case, some friendly contact between Freud and Kraus. Presenting himself as a devoted reader of *Die Fackel*, Freud solicited Kraus's support in a series of letters written between 1904 and 1906. Kraus, for his part, attended several of Freud's lectures around that time, and in November 1905 he publicly applauded him for trying to debunk the view that homosexuality should be seen as a dangerous form of deviance. Yet despite the common ground between them, the solidarity that Freud hoped for never materialized. The correspondence, never robust, petered out altogether, while Kraus's mocking of psychoanalysis and some of its basic principles (e.g., the Oedipus complex) persisted for decades." —PR

I agree with Kraus that there's a lot to find fault with in Freud: his overemphasis on sex, his brute-force application of the Oedipus story, his fascination with puns (to me, any school of thought or literature that makes too much of puns is a priori suspect), his too-neat contraption of id, ego, and superego, and so on. But the reason he's easy to find fault with is that he was articulating something that had never been articulated—he was grasping at something nearly ineffable; he was trying to be a scientist of things unknowable through science—and if Kraus had been a reader of novels I think he might have acknowledged

this. Freud was developing a theory to account for psychological truths that his beloved Dostoyevsky had noticed and embodied in his novels: that we do things that we're not aware of doing; that we often, and without hypocrisy, say the opposite of what we really mean; that just because a motive is irrational doesn't mean it makes no sense; that we strenuously deny precisely the things that are truest about us; that we fail to see certain obvious, important facts that are right in front of us; that we so often unaccountably sabotage ourselves. Maybe the satirist and the aphorist and even the dramatist can safely ignore Freud's ideas, but the realist novelist cannot.

This may be the place to confess that immersing myself in the letters and the narrative of my year in Berlin makes me feel bad. The particulars are so elusive and fleeting that they're hard to capture in words, but they have to do with my feeling that I'm still the same person I was at twenty-two but also was *never* that person, not even then. As if, by way of writing and introspection and self-consciousness, I had the same kind of distance from myself then that I now have by virtue of being thirty years older. That there's the thinking, planning, self-improving me, and then there's a me that just does what it does—makes mistakes that I know to be mistakes. In 1982 I could feel that my consciousness was riding along on something it couldn't account for. And I went ahead and did a thing that makes no sense to me now: I married somebody I was unlikely to stay married to. Probably I did it because I was trying to control—to over-think—something that ultimately can't be controlled. I wanted to plan out a whole life, because thinking and planning were safer than simply immersing myself in life and seeing what happened. But the controlling, clamping-down self now seems to me not the ego or the superego; it seems, itself, like the id. Freud's schema would suggest that I had an overly dominant superego in Berlin, overriding the impulses of the id and forcing myself to do the "right" thing, but this isn't how it feels. In the letters, the superego always enters late, in a particularly grating tone of optimism, and tries to put the best face on what the fearful, control-seeking id has done. The whole thing makes me very sad.

Freud's psychic architecture of id, ego, superego is more mysterious and suggestive in the original German: the It, the I, and the Over-I.

auseinanderzusetzen, in Spannung gelangweilt von Instruktoren, in Schönheit sterbend vor Langeweile, von der französischen Regel de Tri bis zum nordischen Integral. Kein Theaterbesucher, der es über sich gebracht hätte, ohne die nötige Problemschwere

---

The German word for "id," "*Es*," points toward my objectness—I'm not just good old familiar *me*, I'm also an It, a thing in the world—better than "id" does (at least for us non-Latin-readers). "Id" to me evoked and still evokes the image of some hot, sexual, powerful, toadlike thing inside me that is nonetheless part of "my" self. *It* is more radical, because it suggests that the me I know, my consciousness as I move through the world, is really just a ghost in the machine, a mysterious by-product of a body composed of dumb atoms. Like other great schools of twentieth-century criticism—like structuralism, which posits a self constituted by the language it speaks, and like Marxism, for which the self is the instrument of ideology—Freudianism undermines the notion of an individual with free will and limitless agency. If you look too closely at the self, it disappears.

If I insist that Freud was basically right—that the It does what it does and that my consciousness trails behind it like a yapping little dog, pretending to be in control, inventing motives whose effect is to blind it to what's really going on—I'm susceptible to a structuralist critique: the reason I think that I'm the ghost in the machine of It is that language is separate from its speaker. What I'm describing as a disconnect between self and It is in fact an artifact of the disconnect between me and what I've spoken or written—because pursuit of the elusive It can happen only via language. What haunted me in 1982 and briefly drove me crazy wasn't some chimerical Freudian id but the words that I'd been typing as I hunted for it; it was the words, not the id, that existed independent of me.

And then there's the Marxist critique: psychoanalysis is a bourgeois institution, a diversion for those with the time and money for it. You think you're trying to demystify yourself and better understand the interplay of It and I and Over-I, but in fact all you're doing is developing a new and bigger mystification to obscure your privilege. The real It is

mysteries in a rational way, bored amid excitement by instructors, dying amid beauty of boredom, from the French rule *de tri* to the Nordic integral equation.[50] No theatergoer managing to go to bed without the necessary knotty problem. And meanwhile

---

economic and class relations, which create the ideology that governs you; and so no wonder the It is scary to you. The "Unconscious" is the sex-drenched bogeyman that you invent to avoid the real bogeyman of ideology; and thus, for the hard-line Marxist as for Kraus, psychoanalysis is the disease of the mind for which it believes itself to be the cure.

I definitely had this disease of the mind in Berlin. The cure, for me, was to stop spinning in circles of theory and start living. It was only much later, when I was struggling with my third novel, that I came to appreciate Freud for what he had to teach the fiction writer: that we relate to the world by way of the psychological objects we make of the people closest to us; that a human personality is best understood as a collection of selves in conflict; that we know less than we think we know; that there's no cure for the human condition. Freud, to his credit, became reluctant to speak of cures.

Nowadays such values are, if not lost and forgotten, then certainly embattled. A culture in which people can't sit still for five minutes without pawing their smartphones gets the hopelessly tautological intellectual framework it deserves: "Personality is all just brain chemistry!" If Freud's insights are denied universally enough and vehemently enough, it ceases to matter that vehement denial is a reliable sign that an insight has hit the mark. If the self is just a ghost in the machine anyway, you might as well embrace the machine and, while you're at it, make yourself one. *Id* is what you type on your smartphone when you want it to auto-correct and write "I'd."

50. Another passage where Kraus's sputtering rage makes him all but unintelligible. My guess is that "Nordic integral" is a dig at Ibsen; Reitter points out that "dying amid beauty" is a phrase from the final scene of *Hedda Gabler*. As for "rule *de tri*," Reitter, Kehlmann, and Franzen are collectively stumped. Maybe it has to do with conventional love triangles.

zu Bett zu gehen. Dazwischen der Naturalismus, der außer den psychologischen Vorschriften noch andere Forderungen für den Hausgebrauch erfüllte, indem er die Dinge beim rechten Namen nannte, aber vollzählig, daß ihm auch nicht eines fehle, während das Schicksal als richtig gehende Pendeluhr an der Wand hing. Und all dies so lange und so gründlich, bis sich die Rache der gefesselten Bürgerphantasie ein Ventil schuf in der psychologischen Operette. Im abseitigsten Winkel einer Nestroyschen Posse ist mehr Lebenskennerschaft für die Szene und mehr Ausblick in die Soffitte höherer Welten als im Repertoire eines deutschen Jahrzehnts. Hauptmann und Wedekind stehen wie der vornestroysche Raimund als Dichter über den Erwägungen der theatralischen Nützlichkeit. Anzengrubers und seiner Nachkommen Wirkung ist von der Gnade des Dialekts ohne Gefahr

naturalism, which not only met the psychological requirements but satisfied other demands for home use by calling things by their proper names, exhaustively, with nothing left out, while fate hung on the wall like a pendulum clock keeping perfect time. All of this so thoroughly and at such length, until the vengeance of the fettered bourgeois imagination finally vented itself in the psychological operetta.[51] In the most out-of-the-way corner of a Nestroyan farce there is more expert feeling for a scene and a better view into the stage-flies of higher worlds than in the repertoire of a German decade. Hauptmann and Wedekind stand as poets, like the pre-Nestroyan Raimund, above considerations of theatrical utility.[52] The influence of Anzengruber and his successors is detached at its own risk from the saving grace of

51. "Kraus isn't suggesting that the new 'psychological operetta' provided authentic release. Operetta, in his view, shouldn't make psychological or any other kind of sense: again, its deep realism derives precisely from its nonsensicality. In a later essay on the 'domestication' of operetta, Kraus would write, 'The demand that operetta should hold up before pure reason is the source of pure operetta idiocy.' He added, a few lines later, 'Psychology is the *ultima ratio* of ineptness, and in this way operetta, too, has been flattened.'"—PR

52. "From the 1890s until the First World War, Kraus admired Gerhart Hauptmann (1862–1946), whose naturalist dramas won him much applause. But when the war started, Hauptmann, like so many German artists, made patriotic statements in support of it, and Kraus became critical of him. Later, during the Weimar Republic, Kraus found Hauptmann outright insufferable. He'd been awarded the Nobel Prize for Literature in 1912, and as he became a cultural figurehead in the new Germany he began to style himself as an author of Goethe-like significance. (See the portrayal of Mynheer Peeperkorn, who's loosely based on Hauptmann, in Thomas Mann's *The Magic Mountain*.)

"Ferdinand Raimund (1790–1836) was an actor, writer, and director who gained renown in (and beyond) Vienna for his comedies and

nicht loszulösen. Nestroys Dialekt ist Kunstmittel, nicht Krücke. Man kann seine Sprache nicht übersetzen, aber man könnte die Volksstückdichter auf einen hochdeutschen Kulissenwert reduzieren. Nur Literarhistoriker sind imstande, hier einen Aufstieg über Nestroy zu erkennen. Aber daß dieser, selbst wenn seine Ausbeutung für die niedrigen Zwecke des Theatervergnügens auf Undank stieße, als geistige Persönlichkeit mit allem, was auf der Bühne eben noch Hand und Herz oder Glaube und Heimat hat, auch nur genannt werden darf, wäre doch ein Witz, den die Humorlosigkeit sich nicht ungestraft erlauben sollte. Auf jeder Seite Nestroys stehen Worte, die das Grab sprengen, in das ihn die Kunstfremdheit geworfen hat, und den Totengräbern an die Gurgel fahren. Voller Inaktualität, ein fortwirkender Einspruch gegen die Zeitgemäßen. Wortbarrikaden eines Achtundvierzigers gegen die Herrschaft der Banalität; Gedankengänge, in denen die Tat wortspielend sich dem Ernst des Lebens harmlos macht, um ihm desto besser beizukommen. Ein niedriges Genre, so tief unter der Würde eines Historikers wie ein Erdbeben. Aber wie wenn der Witz spürte, daß ihn die Würde nicht aus-

---

farces. Often seen as Nestroy's immediate forebear in Austro-humor, Raimund got plenty of official recognition after his death—a theater in Vienna was named after him, as was a street—but he wasn't generally taken seriously as a figure in high culture. Kraus thought otherwise. Defending Raimund against Alfred Polgar's less enthusiastic appraisal, Kraus declared him to be 'the greatest Austrian poet.' Granted, for Kraus, this wasn't saying all that much, but he meant it as a major compliment, and Raimund belonged to the small group of authors whose works he read onstage. Nowhere in *Die Fackel* does Kraus offer an appreciation of Raimund anywhere near as thorough as 'Nestroy and Posterity,' but he did make it clear that he prized the beauty of Raimund's language."—PR

dialect.[53] Nestroy's dialect is an artistic tool, not a crutch. You can't translate his language, but you could reduce the authors of folk plays to their scene value in Standard German. Only a literary historian is capable of discerning an advance over Nestroy in this. But the idea that this man, even if his exploitation for the meaner purposes of theatrical pleasure were to meet with ingratitude, can be so much as mentioned as an intellectual personality in the company of those very things that have Hand and Heart or Faith and Home[54] onstage, would be a joke that humorlessness should not permit itself with impunity. There are words on every page of Nestroy that burst open the tomb into which estrangement from art has thrown him, and that go for the throats of the grave-diggers. Full of datedness, an ongoing protest against the people who are up to date. A Forty-Eighter's[55] word-barricades against the reign of banality; trains of thought whose action wordplay renders inoffensive to the seriousness of life, the better to out-wit it. A lowly genre, as far beneath a historian's dignity as an earthquake. But what if the joke sensed that it's intolerable to

53. "Ludwig Anzengruber (1839–1889) was also an Austrian play-wright. Like Raimund and Nestroy, he wrote 'folk' plays, some of them comedies, and the three authors are often grouped together. But only Anzengruber won a larger following outside of Austria. Theodor Fontane and Friedrich Engels, among others, found his portrayal of folk-life to be winningly concerned with social conditions. Kraus, however, was not impressed. Without dwelling on why, he made Anzengruber out to be the lesser author and was irked by his greater acclaim." —PR
54. "A mocking allusion to the titles of Anzengruber's tragedy *Hand and Heart* (1874) and Karl Schönherr's drama *Faith and Home* (1910). Shortly after the latter appeared, Kraus printed in his *Fackel* Berthold Viertel's positive assessment of it. But Kraus later stressed that he hadn't read it himself, and he poked fun at Schönherr's stylistic defi-ciencies and his way of celebrating provincial culture." —PR
55. I.e., somebody from the revolutionary year of 1848.

stehen kann, stellt er sie schon im Voraus so her, daß sie sich mit Recht beleidigt fühlt. Könnte man sich vorstellen, daß die Professionisten des Ideals eine Erscheinung wie Nestroy vorüberziehen ließen, ohne einen sichtbaren Ausdruck ihres Schreckens zu hinterlassen? Die Selbstanzeigen der Theodor Vischer, Laube, Kuh und jener andern besorgten Dignitäre, die sich noch zum hundersten Geburtstag Nestroys gemeldet haben, sind so verständlich, wie die Urteilspolitik Hebbels, der Nestroy ablehnt, nachdem Nestroys Witz ihm an die tragische Wurzel gegriffen hat, Herrn Saphir lobpreist, von dem weniger schmerzliche Angriffe zu erwarten waren, freilich auch Jean Paul haßt und Heine liebt. Speidels mutige Einsicht unterbricht die Reihe jener, die

dignity—that it so fooled dignity in advance that dignity is right to feel insulted. Can you imagine that the professionals of the Ideal would let a phenomenon like Nestroy pass without leaving behind a visible expression of their terror? The self-advertisements of Theodor Vischer, Laube, Kuh, and those other concerned dignitaries[56] who came out for Nestroy's hundredth birthday are as understandable as the judgmental politics of Hebbel, who rejects Nestroy after Nestroy's wit has grabbed him by his tragic roots, extols Herr Saphir, from whom less painful attacks were to be expected, and also, of course, hates Jean Paul and loves Heine.[57] Speidel's courageous insights interrupt the parade of those who,

56. "The eminent Kraus scholar Christian Wagenknecht has (plausibly) speculated that Kraus was thinking, above all, of Theodor Herzl, the dignified (if also somewhat dandified) newspaper editor and founder of political Zionism. In 1901 Kraus wrote a long response to Herzl's critique of Nestroy, charging Herzl not only with not having read and not having understood Nestroy but also with having leaned on (Heinrich) Laube's and (Emil) Kuh's attempt to protect 'dignity' against the eruptive 'wit-genius' on display in Nestroy's dramas." —PR

"By the way, another Kuh, Anton Kuh," says Kehlmann, "was a brilliant writer whose essay 'Zarathustra's Ape' is still the best and funniest attack on Karl Kraus ever. To my knowledge, Kraus, who really did respond to everything that had anything to do with him, never said a word about the essay in *Die Fackel*."

"Kraus's response," says Reitter, "was to take Kuh to court for defamation of character, something he had done before with other people. He won the case, and Kuh, who was unwilling to pay the fines the court imposed, fled Vienna for Berlin."

57. "Friedrich Hebbel (1813–1863) was a much-admired German author—Kafka and Schnitzler were devoted readers of his diaries—who criticized Nestroy in his letters, calling him a 'genius of nastiness' and his farces 'poisonous and amoral.' Earlier, Hebbel had received Nestroy's work more kindly. His tone changed after the appearance (and

Nestroy aus Neigung oder anstandshalber verkennen mußten. Was wäre natürlicher als der Widerstand jener, die das heilige Feuer hüten, gegen den Geist, der es überall entzündet? So einer mußte alle Würde und allen Wind der Zeit gegen sich haben. Er stieß oben an die Bildung an und unten an die Banalität. Ein Schriftsteller, der in hochpolitischer Zeit sich mit menschlichen Niedrigkeiten abgibt, und ein Carltheaterschauspieler mit Reflexionen, die vom Besuch des Concordiaballs ausschließen. Er hat die Katzbalgereien der Geschlechter mit Erkenntnissen und Gebärden begleitet, welche die Güterverwalter des Lebens ihm als Zoten anstreichen mußten, und er hat im sozialen Punkt nie Farbe bekannt, immer nur Persönlichkeit. Ja, er hat den politischen Beruf ergriffen – wie ein Wächter den Taschendieb. Und nicht die Lächerlichkeiten innerhalb der Politik lockten seine Aufmerksamkeit, sondern die Lächerlichkeit der Politik. Er war Denker, und konnte darum weder liberal noch antiliberal denken. Und wohl mag sich dort eher der Verdacht antiliberaler

success) of Nestroy's *Judith and Holofernes* (1849), which parodies Hebbel's breakthrough drama *Judith*. Brief accounts of Moritz Saphir and Jean Paul can be found in the notes to 'Heine and the Consequences.'"—PR

by inclination or for decency's sake, had to misread Nestroy. What could be more natural than the resistance of the keepers of the sacred fire to a spirit who kindles it everywhere? A spirit like this couldn't help having every wind and every worthy of the times against him. He ran into refinement above and banality below. An author who in highly political times busies himself with human lowlinesses, a Carltheater actor whose reflections rule out attending the Concordia Ball.[58] He orchestrated the horseplay of the sexes with perceptions and gestures that the warehouse managers of life had to cast, in revenge, as obscenities, and in social matters he never revealed loyalties, only personality. Yes, he took up the profession of politics—the way a constable takes up a pickpocket. And it wasn't the absurdities within politics that attracted his attention, it was the absurdity of politics. He was a thinker, and so he could think neither liberally nor anti-liberally.[59] And the suspicion of anti-liberal convictions may

58. "The annual ball of Vienna's association of liberal writers and journalists."—PR

59. I was suspicious of politics myself when I started reading Kraus. The sixties had continued well into the seventies, but they were definitely over by '77, the year of my arrival at college, which was also the name of the first Talking Heads album. What David Byrne sang ironically on the band's second record soon came to be straightforwardly true of me and New Wave music and its associated high-strung styles: "I have adopted this and made it my own." I saw Byrne and Joe Strummer and Elvis Costello on small stages in Philadelphia and Munich, and by my senior year I'd managed to become what passed for a hipster at my rather dowdy college. While the music at every big college dance still culminated in Springsteen's "Rosalita," our smaller literary parties were not complete without "Contort Yourself." We needed to feel we represented something new, and what felt new was suggested in the Richard Hell refrain: "I belong to the blank generation and / I can take it or leave it each time."

In Berlin I went further and articulated a principled rejection of politics. I did still like the Marxist theorists, the Frankfurt School especially, because their critique of the "reifications" and "hypostasis" and "one-dimensionality" of consumer capitalism was New Wave in spirit. But the necessary simplifications of political praxis ("I am right and you are wrong") were incompatible with the complexities of literature ("Who's to say who's right?") as I construed it. The particular fervor of my construal was probably rooted in the same privileged-kid psychology as Kraus's—I wanted to be free to play with language, I didn't want to be constricted by political definitions, I wanted to *stand out*, not sign on—and it was heightened in Europe, where culture was more saturated with politics than in America, and heightened further in Berlin, which, when I arrived, was seething with anti-Reaganism and anti-Americanism.

I could understand Berlin's preoccupation with politics: the city was occupied by opposing Cold War military forces, and people were genuinely afraid that Reagan's saber rattling would set off a war of tactical nuclear weapons. But it hurt my feelings that the German students in the Hofmannsthal seminar disliked me simply because I was American. When Reagan visited Berlin that October and a young protester fell under the wheels of a city bus and was killed, I detected something unseemly in the resulting outcry, as if the peaceniks had been looking for their Kent State moment and now they had one. (The poor bus driver: I saw him sobbing on the evening news.) The peaceniks all struck me as hopelessly retro, with their wispy beards and their olive-drab jackets and their No Nukes buttons; Donovan, long since spurned and forgotten in the States, was still a headlining performer in Germany. And the punks, whom I was now encountering on the street, rather than listening to their music in my dorm room, were dirty, violent, and boring. German punks did uglier things with their faces and hair and clothes than punks of any other nation, and their humor consisted of a repeated, dopily ironic embrace of the term "*asozial*" ("antisocial"), which was what their critics called them.

The one thing the peaceniks and the punks and I had in common was that we were competing for low-cost housing. The standard method

for finding something affordable was to go to Zoo Station at six on Saturday night, stand in line at the newsstand that was the first in the city to sell the Sunday paper, and then hurry with the real-estate listings to the nearest pay phone. The third time I did this, I was interviewed by a TV crew reporting on the city's housing crisis, and I was near enough to the head of the line that I managed to be the first person to call a landlady, Frau Keller, who had a furnished room to let. The room was way up in bleak Reinickendorf, far from the university and close to nothing except the airport, which was directly across the street. The furniture was cheap, hideous, and damaged, the communal bathroom was grim, Frau Keller was unfriendly and suspicious of me, one of the neighbors had a loud and gagging cough, and the rent was more than I could afford.

I took the place. Hadn't the eponymous Malte Laurids Brigge, in the Rilke novel that I knew whole chunks of by heart, become a real writer in his depressing furnished room in Paris? To economize, I switched to hand-rolled cigarettes and subsisted on cheap bread and cheese from a nearby Aldi discount market. I set up my typewriter on a small, damaged table and smoked and typed from noon to midnight. I was soon so accustomed to the roar of jets taking off that I perceived it only negatively, as a drop in the audibility of my radio. Outside, the days were getting shorter and the weather worse. The last words of *A Moveable Feast*—"when we were very poor and very happy"—are at once beautiful and untrue to my own experience. I was very poor but not very happy. Except for my host parents, I had no German friends, not even any acquaintances, and the remoteness of Reinickendorf discouraged socializing with the few North Americans I knew. My companions were myself, the flimsy characters in the story I was writing, and my fiancée, whose responses to my letters typically came two weeks after I'd sent them.

V had been offered full scholarships at the country's best English lit graduate programs and had chosen Columbia because living in Manhattan seemed like the literary thing to do; her apartment was across the street from our summer sublet. One afternoon I got a letter from her in which she reported that she'd "broken training"—had slept with

a guy I'd known, and distrusted, at college. I had nothing if not time to respond to this news in writing. I admitted, briefly, to feeling jealous, but I stressed, over and over, that I wasn't angry with her. If anything, I felt proud of her. Her infidelity wasn't nice, but I was in flight from the niceness of the midwestern place I'd come from. Her infidelity made her *interesting*. Not for a second did I imagine breaking off the engagement. But I did immediately set about paying her back.

A week before her bombshell letter arrived, as I was leaving a university building where I'd gone to attend a lecture on Walter Benjamin that turned out to have been canceled, I'd run into two American girls I'd known a little bit during my year in Munich. One was the daughter of the commander of American forces in Berlin; the other, W, was staying with her at the general's palatial house. I'd spent a long evening barhopping with the two of them, fleeing the undanceable music that students in Berlin unaccountably considered dance music; and now, with the implied permission V had given me, I went out on a date with W alone. She had literary ambitions whose vagueness I contrasted unfavorably with the grandiosity of mine, but she was a kind, attractive, warm-blooded twenty-two-year-old and I was desperately lonely. At the end of the evening, we started kissing on the U-Bahn platform. She boarded a train, I remained on the platform, and we kept kissing while the conductor said, as conductors said at every stop, "*Zurückbleiben!*" ("Stay back!"). When the conductor then drily added, for our benefit, "*Aufhören*" ("Stop it"), I felt as if the impersonal German system had melted a little bit, as a gift to me.

A few evenings later, on Halloween, I arrived at the general's with a copy of Fredric Jameson's *The Prison-House of Language*, which I'd been reading on the train. A high wall surrounded the house, and guards were patrolling with assault rifles, which made me feel at once safer and less safe inside. W and I ate and drank and danced with the general's daughter, who then discreetly vanished, leaving us alone in a top-floor guest room. Like V, who'd avowed her love for me before betraying me, I avowed my love for V before going to bed with W. Unlike V, however, I didn't have contraceptives, and so I fell technically short of returning her favor—a failure that haunted me during all the years we were mar-

ried. Early the next morning I slipped out of the house and read about the prison-house of language all the way back to Reinickendorf.

I've had a lot of dumb ideas in my life, but none dumber than the one of combining letters and journals the way V and I did that year. If I hadn't been so ambitious, I might have considered that letters are for the Other and journals for the self, and that the romantic dialogue of letters is at odds with a journal's insistence on honest confession, and that it's dangerous and ultimately impossible to wholly hand over the self to the Other; but since, again, V and I were united in ambition, and since the point of all our writing was to develop our styles and improve our skills, I persisted with the project even after V's bombshell letter had alerted me to the danger. My explicitly stated goal was to save the American novel—from social one-dimensionality, from critical pre-occupation with the prison-house of language, from the off-putting avant-gardism of Pynchon and his kind. Frau Heilgendorff had recently introduced me to a young, aspiring Canadian writer, and after my first dinner with him I'd summarized to V the difference between him and me: "He wants to be part of the non-French-Canadian nationalistic renaissance; I want to be Mohammed." And further:

> I understood that the difference between us is that he is sane and I am not . . . Crazy is not something you "go," it's something you become, gradually, through an accretion in the section of the brain devoted to significance.

I was well aware of the "megalomania" that V and I were fostering in each other, but my life in Berlin was so bizarrely deformed by literary ambition, and my twelve-hour days of smoking and typing so far from a healthy or happy social existence, that I could justify our letter/journal project only by prosecuting it with ever-crazier single-mindedness. It was like kissing in the doorway of a subway car: I managed to steal one night in bed with W before the doors of my existence closed and I returned to my room to wring significance out of it, by writing about it.

After acknowledging to V that it would be painful for her to read any details, I gave her quite a few details. (Good writers used details,

and we were trying to make good writers of each other.) Then I rambled on for a few pages about religion and philosophy—

> It's clear that I haven't read enough marxist lit., because I've never seen a marxist confront what has always struck me as the one problematic term in the entire ideology, namely <u>guilt</u>, the factor that exempts the philosopher from class conflict, since he or she has a privileged position in society yet wants to eliminate the privilege—

before getting to the problem of the prison-house of language, which I was trapped in even as I sat there. The more I tried to write about what I was feeling, the more I seemed simply to be creating language about language, piling up signifiers that referred to themselves and carried me further from, not closer to, the moral and emotional horror of what I'd done to W, which was to use her as a signifier in the hermetic literary world of me and V—

> because dangerous things happen when you spend a night pretending the person you're with is someone else, pretend so vigorously that reality <u>disappears</u> and you're left with this face, these kitten eyes that belong to—whom? WHOM? WHOM WHOM WHOM?

At this point I went literally crazy for about fifteen minutes. Tried to pull my face off with my fingers, tried to rip up the bedsheets with my teeth, ran downstairs and tried to leave the building to call W, but I couldn't unlock the street door, no matter how hard I yanked on it. Some shadow thing in me, some thing that my conscious self could never see clearly but that was no less *me* than my conscious self was, had momentarily got the upper hand.

The thing in control of me made me give the street door a despairing kick, and—it seemed like a miracle, a gift from the world or from God—the lock freed up. Out on the street, liberated from my prison-house, I became halfway sane. I met W for a drink and a proper farewell (she was leaving for Spain the next morning), and she told me it

sounded as if I was spending too much time alone. The next day, alone, I described to V what had happened while I was typing:

It began when I called up the picture of those kitten eyes. That's what made me crumple up and cry. But what made it bad was something else: it was like a self-tightening knot, as I guess I knew it would be, if it ever happened. I'll tell you what my impulses were: to smash the typewriter, to throw it out the window. to smash the mirror with it, smash the window, then smash it. to smash the mirror with the ashtray, to pound the typewriter with the ashtray, to throw the ashtray through the window. to cut my face with a knife. to throw myself out the window. to bloody my fingers trying to rip the typewriter to pieces.

How the knot started tightening. When I began to cry, I knew that I couldn't keep typing. But I wanted to describe what I was feeling. I thought of taking the paper out and writing it longhand. But then the thought, the feeling, of wanting to <u>describe</u> what was <u>happening</u>—this became what was happening. The impulse of wanting to control (through writing) this lack of control turned out to be the real source of the lack of control. So that every time I thought of ceasing to be crazy and going back to the typewriter, I became more crazy and more furious with the typewriter, until I was biting the sheet. It became clear to me that this could go on indefinitely, until the neighbors called the police. So I gave up on the idea of describing this (because IT COULD NOT BE DESCRIBED) and surrendered myself to my self-preservative instinct, went to call [W]. Why the front door nearly did it to me: I was powerless to stop it from being a symbol of the imprisonment I felt not being able to describe what was happening, the schizophrenic fight between the side of me that kept wanting to narrate and the side that refused to be narrated anymore. That the latter side was confronted nonetheless by a symbol nearly drove it into complete control. (One sees in hindsight, of course, how the unconscious tends to the self-tightening: how in all my pulling on the door (which I've had some trouble with before), I didn't once think of pushing.)

Gesinnung einstellen, wo der Gedanke sich über die Region erhebt, in der das Seelenheil von solcher Entscheidung abhängt,
und wo er zum Witz wird, weil er sie passieren mußte. Wie ver-
wirrend gesinnungslos die Kunst ist, zeigte der Satiriker durch
die Fähigkeit, Worte zu setzen, die die scheinbare Tendenz seiner
Handlung sprengen, so daß der Historiker nicht weiß, ob er sich
an die gelobte Revolution halten soll oder an die verhöhnten
Krähwinkler, an die Verspottung der Teufelsfurcht oder an ein
fanatisches Glaubensbekenntnis. Selbst der Historiker aber
spürt den Widerspruch des Satirikers gegen die Behaftung der
Menschlichkeit mit intellektuellen Scheinwerten und hat kein
anderes Schutzmittel der Erklärung als Nestroys Furcht vor der

---

After I finished this letter and put it in the mail, I was too frightened
and disgusted by my typewriter to touch it for several days. I took
W's advice and went out more to see people, including the young
Canadian, James, who turned out to be gay. He was having all manner
of guilt-free sexual adventures and intrigues, and for an apartment five
times the size of mine, in a more accessible neighborhood, he was paying less rent than I was. I still had my literary superiority, but it was all
I had.

V responded to my own bombshell letter with worry and sympathy
but also the news that she was thinking about harming herself; she
mentioned the sharpness of her letter opener and the five-story drop
from her bedroom window. ("Letter" and "story": the section of my
brain devoted to significance continued to find it everywhere. I couldn't
distinguish reality from literary figure, a threat from a trope, which was
the whole trouble with living through letters and stories.) In a different
letter, she reported that she was still "seeing" her guy in New York—it
hadn't been the one-night stand that I'd supposed. I was very confused
by this, but my little psychotic episode had so frightened me that I
smothered my confusion with avowals of love, fidelity, optimism, and
concern for V's well-being.

well be more likely to arise where thought transcends the region in which spiritual salvation depends on this kind of evaluation, and where thought turns into joke because it had to get past it. How bewilderingly unprincipled art is: the satirist revealed it in his ability to set off words that exploded the seeming tendency of his plots, leaving the historian uncertain about what to take more seriously, the praised revolution or the ridiculed yokel, the mockery of someone's fear of the Devil or a fanatical confession of faith. But even the historian can sense that the satirist opposed the affliction of humanity by intellectual sham values, and has no better defense than to explain that Nestroy was afraid of the

---

After my unsatisfactory visit to Vienna, my new Canadian friend offered to let me live with him and split his already low rent. Among the many reasons I said yes was that his place was on Karl-Marx-Straße, which I thought would be a very cool address. I immediately wrote a letter of tortured apology and self-justification to Frau Keller, asking to be excused from my lease and to get my security deposit back, since I was giving her the required thirty-day notice.

A few days before V arrived to spend her winter break with me, Frau Keller came to my room to inspect it for damage. She was a short, stout, sallow, miserable person. I repeated that I'd given her proper notice and was due a refund of 350 marks; she replied that she was about to be hospitalized for a "procedure." As if in a trance, she began to circle the room, pointing out, with heavy sighs of disapproval, the cracked glass top of the coffee table, the broken hinge on the wardrobe, the disgusting stains on the carpeting—all *features* of the room she'd rented me. I said that she knew very well that earlier tenants had done the damage. In reply, she sighed once more, shook her head, unbuttoned the top of her dress, and reached into her enormous bra. I thought she was going to take out a wad of cash, but instead she pulled down the bra and showed me a large bandage on one of her breasts. "*Ist verbrannt, Herr Franzen,*" she said, looking me gravely in the eye. "*Ist verbrannt.*" "It's burned up, Mr. Franzen." I never got my money back.

Polizei. Der Liberale ruft immer nach der Polizei, um den Künstler der Feigheit zu beschuldigen. Der Künstler aber nimmt so wenig Partei, daß er Partei nimmt für die Lüge der Tradition gegen die Wahrheit des Schwindels. Nestroy weiß, wo Gefahr ist. Er erkennt, daß wissen nichts glauben heißt. Er hört bereits die Raben der Freiheit, die schwarz sind von Druckerschwärze. Schon schnarrt ihm die Bildung ihren imponierenden Tonfall ins Gebet. Wie erlauscht er das Rotwelsch, womit die Jurisprudenz das Recht überredet! Wie holt er die terminologische Anmaßung heraus, mit der sich leere Fächer vor der wissensgläubigen Menschheit füllen. Und statt der Religion die Pfaffen, wirft er der Aufklärung lieber die Journalisten vor und dem Fortschritt die Wissenschaftlhuber. Man höre heute den Gallimathias, den der Kometenschuster im Lumpazivagabundus erzeugt. Nach einem unvergleichlichen Aufblick, mit dem er einer skeptischen Tischlerin nachsieht:

"Die glaubt net an den Kometen, die wird Augen machen . . ."

fährt er fort:

"Ich hab' die Sach' schon lang heraus. Das Astralfeuer des Sonnenzirkels ist in der goldenen Zahl des Urions von dem Sternbild des Planetensystems in das Universum der Parallaxe mittelst des Fixstern-Quadranten in die Ellipse der Ekliptik geraten; folglich muß durch die Diagonale der Approximation der perpendikulären Zirkeln der nächste Komet die Welt zusammenstoßen. Diese Berechnung ist so klar wie Schuhwix . . ."

police. Liberals are forever calling in the police to accuse artists of cowardice. So little does the artist take sides, however, that he sides with the lie of tradition against the truth of the swindle. Nestroy knows where the danger is. He recognizes that knowing means believing nothing. He can already hear the ravens of freedom, which are black with printer's ink. The imposing sounds of education have already come clattering into his prayers. How open his ears are to the argot whereby jurisprudence browbeats justice! How well he teases out the terminological pretensions with which empty disciplines fill themselves for a knowledge-trusting human race. And instead of blaming religion for priests, he prefers to blame the Enlightenment for journalists and Progress for the scientific paper pushers.[60] Just listen to the gibberish spouted by the comet-cobbler in *Lumpazivagabundus*. After a matchless glance with which he sizes up a skeptical carpentress:

"She don't believe in the comet, she's in for an eye-opener . . ."

he continues:

"I've had the thing figured out for quite a while now. The astral fire of the solar ring in the golden number of Urion has left the constellation of the planetary system in the universe of parallaxes and landed, by means of fixed-star quadrants, in the ellipse of the ecliptic; in consequence, according to the diagonals of approximation of the perpendicular rings, the next comet will have to smash into the earth. My calculations are as clear as shoe polish . . ."

60. In the original, "scientific paper pushers" is *Wissenschaftlhuber*. Reitter: "Kraus is playing on the Austrianism *Gschaftlhuber*, which means 'someone who makes a lot of his job without being good at it' or, more simply, 'poseur.'"

Und klingt so glaublich, als ob Nestroy das Problem des „Grubenhundes" an der journalistischen Quelle studiert hätte. Der Satz hätte, wie er ist, achtzig Jahre später, als wieder statt eines Kometen die Astronomen sich persönlich bemühten, in der Neuen Freien Presse gedruckt werden können. Ich behalte mir

And sound as plausible as if Nestroy had studied the problem of the "*Grubenhund*" at its journalistic source.[61] The sentence, just as it is, eighty years later, when the astronomers again personally came hither in a comet's stead, could have been printed in the *Neue Freie Presse*.[62] I also reserve the right to send it in sometime.

61. "In February of 1908 Kraus notched one of his most satisfying victories in the eternal struggle against the *Neue Freie Presse*. The occasion was a small earthquake that had rattled Vienna. Posing as a civil engineer and a regular reader of the newspaper, Kraus sent in a pseudoscientific letter full of risible claims—e.g., 'what we have here is telluric earthquake (in the narrow sense),' rather than 'a cosmic earthquake (in the broad sense)'—which the *NFP* nevertheless printed as serious commentary. Three years later, Kraus struck again. He managed to sneak into the *NFP* under another pseudonym (at the time, the paper had a policy of not mentioning him) and again by submitting a report on an earthquake, in which he pretended to be a scientist and offered up a number of absurdities. Among the more over-the-top of these was that 'half an hour before the earthquake, the *Grubenhund* that had been sleeping in the laboratory began to howl.' Despite the *Hund* (dog) in it, the word '*Grubenhund*' doesn't refer to a kind of dog. It's a term for a cart used in mining (the second earthquake was supposed to have taken place in mining country). With the phrase 'the problem of the *Grubenhund*,' Kraus evokes the lazy credulity with which newspapers treated expert scientific testimony. In the essays that revealed the hoaxes, 'The Earthquake' and 'The Grubenhund,' Kraus also suggests that the *NFP*'s Jewish loyalties played a role in the debacle. Kraus gave his first made-up civil engineer a name and address that invited the *NFP* to infer that the engineer was a Jew. If he hadn't done so, Kraus maintains, the *NFP* would have screened the letter more carefully." —PR

62. "The Nestroy line cited by Kraus sends up the would-be scientific talk about the expected appearance, in 1834, of Halley's Comet. Kraus is proposing that the line could have been used, eighty years later, for a prank like his earthquake dispatch: in 1910, the comet's predicted return had attracted a lot of journalistic attention." —PR

auch vor, ihn gelegentlich einzuschicken. Aber noch jenseits solcher Anwendbarkeit in dringenden Fällen will Nestroy nicht veralten. Denn er hat die Hinfälligkeit der Menschennatur so sicher vorgemerkt, daß sich auch die Nachwelt von ihm beobachtet fühlen könnte, wenn ihr nicht eine dicke Haut nachgewachsen wäre. Keine Weisheit dringt bei ihr ein, aber mit der Aufklärung läßt sie sich tätowieren. So hält sie sich für schöner als den Vormärz. Da aber die Aufklärung mit der Seife heruntergeht, so muß die Lüge helfen. Diese Gegenwart geht nie ohne eine Schutztruppe von Historikern aus, die ihr die Erinnerung niederknüppeln. Sie hätte es am liebsten, wenn man ihr sagte, der Vormärz verhalte sich zu ihr wie ein Kerzelweib zu einer Elektrizitätsgesellschaft. Der wissenschaftlichen Wahrheit würde es aber besser anstehen, wenn man ihr sagte, der Vormärz sei das Licht und sie sei die Aufklärung. Zu den Dogmen ihrer Voraussetzungslosigkeit gehört der Glaube, daß zwar früher die Kunst heiter war, aber jetzt das Leben ernst ist. Und auch darauf scheint sich die Zeit etwas einzubilden. Denn in der Spielsaison, die die erste Hälfte des neunzehnten Jahrhunderts ausfüllt, habe man

But even beyond this kind of applicability in urgent cases, Nestroy won't become obsolete. For he took such accurate note of human nature's weakness that posterity could feel observed by him, too, if it hadn't grown a thick skin in the meantime. No wisdom can get through to it, but it has itself tattooed with enlightenment. And thus it considers itself more beautiful than the *Vormärz*.[63] But since enlightenment comes off with soap, lies have to help out. This present day of ours never ventures out without a protective guard of historians to club down memory for it. What it most wants to hear is that the *Vormärz* compares to it like a candle hawker to an electricity company. Scientific truth would be better served, however, if the present day were told that the *Vormärz* is the light and the present day enlightenment. Among the dogmas of its presuppositionlessness is the belief that art indeed used to be gay but life is serious now.[64] And our times manage to be vain about even this. For, supposedly, in the theatrical season that constitutes the first half of the nineteenth

63. The *Vormärz* was the period between 1815 and the revolution of March 1848. Literally "Before March."
64. "The historian Theodor Mommsen (1817–1903), who won the Nobel Prize for Literature back when 'literature' was construed more broadly (1902), had insisted that systematic study of a topic should be embarked on without presuppositions and had thereby prompted a debate about objectivity in the human sciences. Kraus had his doubts about Mommsen's ideal. In 1901 he'd published in his *Fackel* 'The Presuppositionless Mommsen,' a screed against Mommsen by Houston Stewart Chamberlain, and he'd defended Chamberlain when a reader sent in a letter attacking his piece. Kraus's oxymoronic phrase 'dogmas of its presuppositionlessness' suggests that Mommsen's ideal was self-contradictory: the idea that forgoing presuppositions will be productive is itself a (liberal) presupposition.

"The final phrase, about art and life, plays on the last line of the prologue to Schiller's *Wallenstein*." —PR

sich ausschließlich für die Affäre der Demoiselle Palpiti vulgo Tichatschek interessiert, während man jetzt im allgemeinen für die Affäre des Professors Wahrmund schwärmt und nur gelegentlich für die Affäre Treumann. Wenn es sich so verhält, wohl dem Vormärz! Aber der Unterschied ist noch anders zu fassen. Im Zeitalter des Absolutismus war das Theaterinteresse ein Auswuchs des vom politischen Druck aufgetriebenen Kunstgefühls. In der Zeit des allgemeinen Wahlrechts ist der Theatertratsch der Rest der von der politischen Freiheit ausgepoverten Kultur. Unser notorisches Geistesleben mit dem des Vormärz zu vergleichen, ist eine so beispiellose Gemeinheit gegen den Vormärz, daß nur die sittliche Verwahrlosung, die fünfzigtausend Vorstellungen der „Lustigen Witwe" hinterlassen haben, den Exzeß entschuldigen kann. Die große Presse allein hat das Recht, mit Verachtung auf das kleine Kaffeehaus herunterzusehen, das einst mit lächerlich unzulänglichen Mitteln den Personenklatsch verbreitete, ohne den man damals nicht leben konnte, weil die Politik verboten war, während man heute ohne ihn nicht leben kann, weil die Politik erlaubt ist. Ein Jahrzehnt phraseologischer Knechtung hat der Volksphantasie mehr Kulissenmist zugeführt als ein Jahrhundert absolutistischer Herrschaft, und mit dem wichtigen Unterschied, daß die geistige Produktivkraft durch Verbote ebenso gefördert wurde, wie sie durch Leitartikel gelähmt wird. Man darf aber ja nicht glauben, daß sich das Volk so direkt vom Theater in die Politik abführen ließ. Der Weg der erlaubten Spiele geht durchs Tarock. Das müssen die liberalen Erzieher zugeben. Wie sich die Rhetorik des Fortschritts verspricht und

century, people were interested solely in the affair of Demoiselle Palpiti *vulgo* Tichatschek, whereas now they're generally enthusiastic about the affair of Professor Wahrmund and only occasionally about the Treumann affair.[65] If this is how things stand, long live the *Vormärz*! In the age of absolutism, passion for theater was an outgrowth of the artistic feeling aroused by political suppression. In times of universal suffrage, theater gossip is the residue of a culture impoverished by political freedom. Comparing our notorious intellectual life to that of the *Vormärz* is such an unparalleled affront to the *Vormärz* that only the moral degeneracy left behind by fifty thousand performances of *The Merry Widow* can excuse the excess. The grand press alone has the right to look down with contempt on the little coffeehouse that used to spread, by laughably inadequate means, the gossip that people in those days couldn't live without because politics were forbidden, while today people can't live without it because politics are allowed. One decade of phraseological enslavement has supplied people's imaginations with more stage-prop rubbish than a century of absolutist tyranny, with the important difference that intellectual productivity was furthered by prohibitions to the same degree that it's now being crippled by the editorial page. But one shouldn't imagine that people let themselves be marched off from the theater into politics so directly. The path of permissible play leads through pinochle. This the liberal educators must concede. How the rhetoric of Progress slips up and speaks the truth

65. "In Nestroy's *The Evil Spirit Lumpazivagabundus*, there's a character named Signora Palpiti, who turns out to come from Purkersdorf. Ludwig Wahrmund was an Austrian expert on ecclesiastical law whose 'modern' views got him into trouble with the church. Louis Treumann was a Viennese opera singer whose arrest for breach of contract was something of a scandal. Kraus had covered both 'affairs' in 1908 issues of the *Fackel*." —PR

die Wahrheit sagt, ist zum Entzücken in der Darstellung eines Sittenschilderers aus den achtziger Jahren nachzulesen, der die alte Backhendlzeit des Theaterkultus ablehnt und den neugebackenen Lebensernst wie folgt serviert:

> Die Zeit ist eine andere geworden, als wie sie anno Bäuerle, Meisl und Gleich war, und wenn auch die alte Garde des unvermischten Wienertums, die ehrenwerten Familien derer von „Grammerstädter, Biz, Hartriegel und Schwenninger" ihrem ererbten Theaterdrange insoferne Genüge leisten, als sie bei einer Premiere im Fürstschen Musentempel oder bei einer Reprise der „Beiden Grasel" in der Josefstadt nie zu fehlen pflegen, so ist doch das Gros ihrer Kompatrioten durch die mannigfachsten Beweggründe von dem Wege ins Theater längst abgelenkt worden und widmet die freie Zeit einem Tapper, einer Heurigenkost oder den Produktionen einer Volkssängerfirma, die just en vogue ist – Zeit und Menschen sind anders geworden.

can be seen in the delicious comment of a moral historian from the eighties who rejects the roast-chicken era and serves up the fresh-baked seriousness of life as follows:[66]

> Times have changed since the days of Bäuerle, Meisl and Gleich, and although the old guard of unalloyed Viennese, the respectable families, may still scratch the theatrical itch that they inherited from "Grammerstädter, Biz, Hartriegel and Schwenninger" to the extent that they are wont never to miss a premiere at the Royal Temple of the Muses or a revival of *Beiden Grasel* at the Josefstadt, the main force of their compatriots has long since been diverted from the road to the theater by the most various of enticements, and devotes its free time to a game of Tapper, a meal at the local vineyard, or a production by a folksinging company that's currently *en vogue*—times and people have changed.[67]

66. "'Roast-chicken era' is a literal translation of *Backhendlzeit*, which is basically the Austrian equivalent of the term *Vormärz*—it refers to the 1815–1848 period. Kraus is using the conventional meaning while playing on its literal one, with his talk of 'fresh-baked seriousness.' The moral historian in question is Friedrich Schlögl, and the passage Kraus cites comes from Schlögl's book *On Viennese Folk Theater* (1883).

"In the quoted passage itself: *Die beiden Grasel* was a theatrical adaptation of a folksy novel of the same title, published in 1854. The 'Josefstadt' (Theater in der Josefstadt) was already a venerable theater and is now the oldest one continuously performing in Vienna. Tapper was a popular card game, usually played by three people and often involving gambling; it's featured in a number of Schnitzler's works, including *Lieutenant Gustl* (1901)." —PR

67. A front-page article in the *Times* business section on August 9, 2012:

TIME WASTERS, POINTLESS BUT FUN
Times have changed since the best way to pass an idle 10 minutes was
Nokia's famous Snake, or whatever flavor of game was built into your

Später wurde dann das Leben noch ernster, es kamen die Probleme, die Gschnasfeste, die geologischen Entdeckungen, die Amerikareise des Männergesangvereins, und für noch spätere Zeiten wird es wichtig sein, daß sie erfahren: Nicht im Vormärz ist in den Wiener Zeitungen die folgende Kundmachung erschienen:

Die gestrige Preiskonkurrenz beim „Dummen Kerl" brachte Fräulein Luise Kemtner, der Schwester der bekannten Hernalser Gastwirtin Koncel, mit dem kleinsten Fuß (19½) und Herrn Moritz Mayer mit der größten Glatze den ersten Preis. Heute werden die engste Damentaille und die größte Nase prämiiert.

So sieht Wien im Jahre 1912 aus. Die Realität ist eine sinnlose Übertreibung aller Details, welche die Satire vor fünfzig Jahren hinterlassen hat. Aber die Nase ist noch größer, der Kerl ist dümmer, wo er sich fortgeschritten glaubt, und die Preiskonkurrenz für die größte Glatze ist das Abbild einer Gerechtigkeit, die die wahren Verdienste erkennt, neben den Resultaten einer Verteilung des Bauernfeldpreises. Ein Blick in die neue Welt, wie sie ein Tag der Kleinen Chronik offenbart, ein Atemzug in dieser gottlosen Luft von Allwissenheit und Allgegenwart zwingt zur vorwurfsvollen Frage: Was hat Nestroy gegen seine Zeitgenossen? Wahrlich, er übereilt sich. Er geht antizipierend seine kleine Umwelt mit einer Schärfe an, die einer späteren Sache würdig

---

old, dumb cellphone. These basic games were simple entertainment and they were fun—to an extent. But with smartphones, we have thousands of app-enabled ways to pass the time waiting in line at the post office or even when struck with insomnia . . .

Times have changed: the watchword of the ideology of Progress. Aren't we lucky that our phones are so smart now! The only thing that

Later on, life became even more serious, there came the issues, the *Gschnas* parties,[68] the geological discoveries, the American tour of the men's glee club, and it will be important for even later times to learn: it was not in the *Vormärz* that the following announcement appeared in Viennese newspapers:

> Yesterday's competition at the "Dumb Fellow" saw the first prize go to Fräulein Luise Kemtner, sister of the well-known Hernals innkeeper Koncel, for the smallest foot (19½), and to Herr Moritz Mayer for the largest bald spot. Prizes will be awarded today for the narrowest lady's waist and the biggest nose.

This is what Vienna looks like in 1912. Reality is a meaningless exaggeration of all the details that satire left behind fifty years ago.[69] But the nose is even bigger, the fellow is even dumber where he believes that he's progressed, and the contest for the largest bald spot is the image of a justice that recognizes true merit and bestows the Bauernfeld Prize.[70] One glance into the new world as it's manifested in one issue of the local roundup, one breath of this godless air of omniscience and omnipresence, will force the reproachful question: What does Nestroy have against his contemporaries? Truly, he's ahead of himself. As if anticipating, he attacks his small environs with an asperity worthy of a later cause. He's already coming into his satirical inheri-

---

hasn't changed is the tone of writers celebrating how things have changed.

68. "'*Gschnas*' is an Austrian term for a costume ball." —PR

69. I love this line just as it is, but it's also tempting to update it to begin, "Reality *TV shows are* . . ."

70. "A prestigious annual literary prize named after the Austrian writer Eduard Bauernfeld (1802–1890). Kraus often took issue with the prize committee's decision." —PR

wäre. Er tritt bereits seine satirische Erbschaft an. Auf seinen liebenswürdigen Schauplätzen beginnt es da und dort zu tagen, und er wittert die Morgenluft der Verwesung. Er sieht alles das heraufkommen, was nicht heraufkommen wird, um da zu sein, sondern was da sein wird, um heraufzukommen. Mit welcher Inbrunst wäre er sie angesprungen, wenn er sie nach fünfzig Jahren vorgefunden hätte! Wie hätte er die Gemütlichkeit, die solchen Zuwachs duldet, solchen Fremdenverkehr einbürgert, an solcher Mischung erst ihren betrügerischen Inhalt offenbart, wie hätte er die wehrlose Tücke dieses unschuldigen Schielgesichts zu Fratzen geformt! Die Posse, wie sich die falsche Echtheit dem großen Zug bequemt, nicht anpaßt, ist ihm nachgespielt; der Problemdunst allerorten, den die Zeit sich vormacht, um sich die Ewigkeit zu vertreiben, raucht über seinem Grab. Er hat seine Menschheit aus dem Paradeisgartel vertrieben, aber er weiß noch nicht, wie sie sich draußen benehmen wird. Er kehrt um vor einer Nachwelt, die die geistigen Werte leugnet, er erlebt die respektlose Intelligenz nicht, die da weiß, daß die Technik wichtiger sei als die Schönheit, und die nicht weiß, daß die Technik höchstens ein Weg zur Schönheit ist und daß es am Ziel keinen Dank geben darf und daß der Zweck das Mittel ist, das Mittel zu vergessen. Er ahnt noch nicht, daß eine Zeit kommen wird, wo die Weiber ihren Mann stellen und das vertriebene Geschlecht in die Männer flüchtet, um Rache an der Natur zu nehmen. Wo das Talent dem Charakter Schmutzkonkurrenz macht und die

tance. Dawn is already breaking, here and there, on his gentle scenes, and he scents putrefaction in the morning air. He sees all those things coming up that won't come up in order to be present, but will be present in order to climb. With what fervor he would have jumped on them if he'd found them fifty years later! The coziness that tolerates this kind of expansion, accommodates this kind of tourist trade, reveals its inner fraudulence in this kind of blending: what a caricature he would have made of the helpless malice of this innocent, cross-eyed face![71] The farce of counterfeit authenticity cozying up to grand trends, rather than falling in line with them, has followed him like an epilogue; the all-blanketing haze of issues, which the times impose on themselves to while away eternity, smokes above his grave. He turned his mankind out of its little garden of paradise, but he doesn't know yet how it will behave itself outside. He turns back in the face of a posterity that disavows the values of the Spirit, he doesn't live to see the respectless intelligence that knows that technology is more important than beauty and doesn't know that technology is at most a way to beauty, and that there can be no thanks at the destination, and that the ends are the means of forgetting the means. He can't yet see that a time will come where girls take it like a man and their banished sexuality seeks refuge in men to revenge itself on nature.[72] Where talent wages a smear

71. This is a very tough sentence, but I think what Kraus is talking about has a contemporary analogue in cable news: the phony coziness that tolerates the grotesque "expansion" of trivial news, traffics touristically in stories that ought to have no place in public discourse, and makes no tonal distinctions in its blending of serious and meaningless news items.

72. I remember being naive about sex when I was twenty-two, but not a prude, and so it's a disagreeable surprise, when I'm looking through my old letters, to find a horrified and judgmental reference to my Canadian friend's Italian porno magazines. I sound just like my father, at

least regarding the magazines (unlike him, I had no problem with "the fairies," as he called them). Indeed, come to think of it, although I was trying in Berlin to deracinate myself and become a person beyond my parents' ken, I in fact was replicating my father's personality almost point by point. I, too, was solitary, depressive, conventional, prudish, workaholic, given to philosophizing, drawn to pretty women but unshakably loyal, and wary of pleasure lest the pursuit of it consume my whole life. It's true that I was afraid of my father's judgments and frustrated by his inability to understand what I had to say about literature and art, frustrated by his reserve and silences; but I don't think I ever once morally faulted him. I knew that, unlike me, he'd grown up in a hardscrabble town and hadn't had a liberal education.

The person I faulted was my mother. It would be another twenty years before I appreciated the ways in which I'm like her, too. In 1982 she seemed to me a bitch on wheels. (That I had a problem with a morally stringent and boundary-trampling mom and had plunged into a rather insane relationship with a morally stringent and boundary-trampling woman was one of those obvious, important facts that I somehow couldn't see.) By late February, when the semester ended in Berlin, my mother's health had improved enough that I'd been forced to invent a new reason not to break the news of my engagement to her. She was talking about coming to England with my father in April, and (as I explained to V) it would be best for me to meet them there and give them the news in person. (Anything to buy a few more months.) But then, as I was about to leave Berlin for a month in Spain, I learned that the England trip was off. Spain instantly ceased to be a sunny haven where I could relax and work on my novel and became the forbidding Inquisitional place where I would have to write an awful letter to my parents.

I stayed in a small village, in a small house belonging to my friend Ekström's parents. There was no telephone, and my only company was the village cats and two expat British ladies, one a drunk, the other a bigot, both of them very kind to me. I smoked two packs of Ducados a day and consumed little else but coffee, chocolate, bread, and gin, and then wondered why I couldn't sleep; in the sole picture I took of myself

in the village, I look like a fifty-year-old psychiatric patient. But somehow, one night, in the way you might finally dive into a freezing-cold lake, because you're there to swim, I managed to write the necessary letter—making the usual carbon copy, of course, although it's a document I can't bear to read even thirty years later. The lake wasn't so catastrophically cold once I was in it. My parents' letters in reply came two weeks later, my father's reasonable and accommodating, my mother's a scream of pain and anger. At some level I'd imagined their replies would annihilate me. That I survived them amounted to a revelation: however gigantically my parents loomed in my imagination, they had no actual control over what I did with my life.

I still had a month on my two-month rail pass, and after returning to Berlin I went on to Amsterdam and then to Munich for a polite visit with a nerdy and bespectacled girl, a friend of good friends of mine at college, who was working as an au pair for a year. I'd spoken with X once or twice at parties, and "Write to X" had been at the top of my to-do list all year, without my ever writing to her. The first thing I discovered, in Munich, was that without her terrible glasses and her dowdy liberal-college overalls and hairstyle she was breathtakingly beautiful. The next thing I discovered was that "Write to J" had been at the top of *her* to-do list in Munich, without her ever writing; the coincidence seemed highly Significant. Within a day, I'd banished all thought of V, and thirty-six hours later I was in bed with X and trying to decide, quickly, whether to call off my engagement, because X refused to consummate things unless I called it off. She was a midwestern Latina, and her moderate craziness (which was a thing I found irresistible in women at that point in my life) was tempered by a decency and practicality that reminded me of home. I was wildly attracted to her, and we'd been talking nonstop for three days, piecing together a complicated network of college friendships and liaisons whose superstitious upshot was that *we were meant to be*. I wasn't constituted to tell a lie to get the sex I wanted, but why I didn't take the opportunity to shrug off the immense and not particularly joyful complication of me and V, a complication embodied in the half million words we'd typed to each other since the previous summer, is harder to understand. I—or It—must have been bent on

Bildung die gute Erziehung vergißt. Wo überall das allgemeine Niveau gehoben wird und niemand draufsteht. Wo alle Individualität haben, und alle dieselbe, und die Hysterie der Klebstoff ist, der die Gesellschaftsordnung zusammenhält. Aber vor allen ihm nachgebornen Fragen – die der Menschheit unentbehrlich sind, seitdem sie die Sagen verlor – hat er doch die Politik erleben können. Er war dabei, als so laut gelärmt wurde, daß die Geister erwachten, was immer die Ablösung für den Geist bedeutet, sich schlafen zu legen. Das gibt dann eine Nachwelt, die auch in fünfzig Jahren nicht zu bereisen ist. Der Satiriker könnte die große Gelegenheit erfassen, aber sie erfaßt ihn nicht mehr. Was fortlebt, ist das Mißverständnis. Nestroys Nachwelt tut vermöge ihrer künstlerischen Unempfindlichkeit dasselbe, was seine Mitwelt getan hat, die im stofflichen Einverständnis mit ihm war: diese nahm ihn als aktuellen Spaßmacher, jene sagt, er sei veraltet. Er trifft die Nachwelt, also versteht sie ihn nicht. Die Satire lebt zwischen den Irrtümern, zwischen einem, der ihr zu nahe, und einem, dem sie zu fern steht. Kunst ist, was den Stoff überdauert. Aber die Probe der Kunst wird auch zur Probe der Zeit, und wenn es immer den nachrückenden Zeiten geglückt war, in der Entfernung vom Stoff die Kunst zu ergreifen, diese hier erlebt die Entfernung von der Kunst und behält den Stoff in der Hand. Ihr ist alles vergangen, was nicht telegraphiert wird. Die ihr Bericht erstatten, ersetzen ihr die Phantasie. Denn eine Zeit, die die Sprache nicht hört, kann nur den Wert der Information beurteilen. Sie kann noch über Witze lachen, wenn sie selbst dem Anlaß beigewohnt hat. Wie sollte sie, deren Gedächtnis nicht weiter reicht als ihre Verdauung, in irgend etwas hinüberlangen können, was nicht unmittelbar aufgeschlossen vor

---

replicating my father's life of work, of duty, of loyalty; of gratification delayed or even denied altogether. Sex looks like nothing or like everything, depending on when you look at it, and it must have been looking

campaign against character, and education forgets its good up-bringing. Where standards are universally raised and no one meets them. Where everyone has individuality and everyone the same, and hysteria is the glue that holds together the social order. But of all the issues that came after him—issues indispensable to mankind since it lost its legends—he did live to see politics. He was there when the noise got so loud that it raised the dead, which is always a signal that it's time for the Spirit to go home to bed. This then produces a posterity that can't be toured in even fifty years. The satirist could seize the great opportunity, but it no longer grasps him. What lives on is misunderstanding. Thanks to its artistic insensibility, Nestroy's posterity does the same thing as his contemporaries, who were in material agreement with him: the latter took him for a topical jokester, while his posterity says he's obsolete. He hits posterity and so it doesn't recognize him. Satire lives between errors, between the one that's too close to it and the one that it's too far from. Art is what outlasts its subject matter. But the test of art becomes the test of times as well, and if past times in their succession always managed to ex-perience art in their remoteness from its subject matter, these times of ours experience remoteness from art and hold the subject matter in their hands. For them, anything that isn't tele-graphed is over with. Their reporters replace their imagination. Because times that can't hear language can judge only informa-tion value. They can still laugh at jokes, if they were personally party to the occasion. How are they, whose memory extends no further than their digestion, supposed to make the leap into any-thing that isn't explained to them directly? Applying the mind to

---

to me like nothing in Munich, at the predawn hour when you're finally exhausted by unsatisfied desire and only want to sleep a little. Not until I was back in my clothes and standing on a train platform in Hannover, a few hours later, hurling pfennigs, did it look like everything again.

ihr liegt? Vergeistigung dessen, woran man sich nicht mehr erinnert, stört ihre Verdauung. Sie begreift nur mit den Händen. Und Maschinen ersparen auch Hände. Die Organe dieser Zeit widersetzen sich der Bestimmung aller Kunst, in das Verständnis der Nachlebenden einzugehen. Es gibt keine Nachlebenden mehr, es gibt nur noch Lebende, die eine große Genugtuung darüber äußern, daß es sie gibt, daß es eine Gegenwart gibt, die sich ihre Neuigkeiten selbst besorgt und keine Geheimnisse vor der Zukunft hat. Morgenblattfroh krähen sie auf dem zivilisierten Misthaufen, den zur Welt zu formen nicht mehr Sache der Kunst ist. Talent haben sie selbst. Wer ein Lump ist, braucht keine Ehre, wer ein Feigling ist, braucht sich nicht zu fürchten, und wer Geld hat, braucht keine Ehrfurcht zu haben. Nichts darf überleben, Unsterblichkeit ist, was sich überlebt hat. Was liegt, das pickt. Mißgeburten korrigieren das Glück, weil sie behaupten können, daß Heroen Zwitter waren. Herr Bernhard Shaw garantiert für die Überflüssigkeit alles dessen, was sich zwischen Wachen und Schlafen als notwendig herausstellen könnte. Seiner und aller Seichten Ironie ist keine Tiefe unergründlich, seiner und aller Flachen Hochmut keine Höhe unerreichbar. Überall läßt sichs irdisch lachen. Solchem Gelächter aber antwortet die Satire. Denn sie ist die Kunst, die vor allen andern Künsten sich überlebt, aber auch die tote Zeit. Je härter der Stoff, desto größer der Angriff. Je verzweifelter der Kampf, desto stärker die Kunst. Der satirische Künstler steht am Ende einer Entwicklung, die sich der Kunst versagt. Er ist ihr Produkt und ihr hoffnungsloses Gegenteil. Er organisiert die Flucht des Geistes vor der Menschheit,

things that people no longer remember upsets their digestion. They grasp only with their hands. And machines make even hands unnecessary. The organs of these times oppose the calling of all art, which is to enter into the understanding of those who live afterward. There no longer are any people who live afterward, there are only people who live, who express enormous satisfaction that they do, that they live in a present that sees to its own news and conceals nothing from the future. Joyful as the morning paper, they crow upon the civilized dunghill that it's no longer the concern of art to shape into a world. They have their own talent. If you're a villain you don't need honor, if you're a coward you don't need to be afraid, and if you have money you don't need to have respect. Nothing is allowed to survive, immortality is what's outlived itself. Things stick where they lie. Freaks with deformities balance out good fortune, because they can claim that heroes were hermaphrodites.[73] Herr Bernhard Shaw guarantees the superfluity of all that might prove useful between being awake and sleeping. To the irony of his and all shallow minds no depth is unfathomable, to the haughtiness of his and all flat minds no heights are unattainable. There's earthly laughter everywhere. Satire, however, has the answer to such laughter. For it's the art that, more than any other art, outlives itself, and this means the dead times, too. The harder the material, the greater the attack. The more desperate the struggle, the stronger the art. The satiric artist stands at the end of a development that renounces art. He is its product and its hopeless antithesis.[74] He

73. Or that Goethe had Asperger's syndrome, which was one thesis of the long, earnest paper that a German psychologist recently e-mailed me out of the blue.
74. Now that our populace has stopped worrying about the several thousand Russian thermonuclear weapons still aimed at our cities and controlled by a populace that drinks vodka like water, it's difficult to

convey how primary and real and present the atomic danger seemed to many of us in 1982. (Timothy Garton Ash, who was in Berlin around that time, expected nuclear war within ten years.) Every time a clap of thunder awoke me in the night, my first thought was that the apocalypse had come. At any moment of any day, some person or machine in Nebraska or Siberia could make a mistake, I would be killed an hour later, and within a year or two no vertebrate animal on the planet would be alive. And Berlin aggravated my fears, not only because it was a Cold War hot spot but because it still bore grim scars of past apocalypses and near apocalypses. My host family lived near the site of the infamous Wannsee Conference; the wasteland where the Nazi central command bunker had been located was now AUTODROM, a closed track where student drivers could practice; and the West Berlin U-Bahn and the S-Bahn both had lines running underneath East Berlin, passing stations whose entrances had been bricked up twenty or thirty years earlier. In the older S-Bahn trains you could open the windows and practically reach out and touch advertising posters that had been put up in the 1950s. The very quaintness of these yellowed ads for cigarettes and chewing gum was ominous; I imagined our own contemporary billboards persisting in forever-deserted stations after all human life had been expunged.

When I remember how oppressed I was by fears and premonitions of thermonuclear war, and how unlikely it seemed that the world would last long enough for me to have a normal life span, it makes more sense to me that I stuck with V and our engagement. Young people are said to have no conception of their mortality, but I had the opposite problem: I thought I'd be lucky to live another ten years. And so I needed to accomplish a whole life *now*. V and I needed to save the world (or at least the American novel) *now*. If I was still alive at thirty-two, I'd be so happy not to be dead that I could deal with any bad consequences of having married young. The apocalyptic and the megalomaniacal were so intertwined in me that they almost amounted to the same thing. After my narrow escape from Munich, I was also *angry*, angry at the world for having denied me the pleasure of sex with X; and when I then

came to the angry, apocalyptic, and arguably megalomaniacal Karl Kraus, I found the paternal example I'd been looking for.

I didn't strictly have to take a course in the spring semester—the Fulbright people weren't likely to ask for a refund if they learned that I'd blown off further schoolwork—but a seminar on *The Last Days of Mankind* was being offered at the Free University, and I was attracted by the title and by the word "apocalypse" in the course description. The seminar was led by Herr Professor Hindemith, who was wry and soft-spoken, wore his hair long, and dressed like a student. Unlike the Hofmannsthal seminar, Hindemith's class was wildly overenrolled, because Kraus's play was about war, and war was bad, and Kraus hadn't liked it, and students in Berlin didn't like it either, and what could be more agreeable than spending a semester talking about how bad war was? At the class's first meeting, every seat at the U of tables was filled. Students in olive-drab jackets lined the walls and sat on the window-sills and crowded at the door, most of them puffing on hand-rolled cigarettes. A student at the tables, a young woman with flaming cheeks, raised her hand to say that she was allergic to smoke and to ask Hindemith to ban smoking in the classroom.

"But our fellow student is surely in the minority," an older male student immediately objected.

"Protect minority rights," Hindemith countered with an ambiguous grin.

The young woman pressed her case, the pitch and volume of her voice rising as she detailed the health risks of first- and secondhand smoke and declared that it was *torture* for her to be in this classroom. Finally, to quiet her, Hindemith suggested that the matter be put to a vote. Though I believe he was a smoker himself, he voted for the ban, as did five or six others of us. The smoke really was unbelievably thick. But a forest of olive-drab-clad arms were raised against the ban, there was cheering and jeering and laughter, and the young woman fled the classroom, never to be seen again.

The Last Days of Mankind is extremely long (Kraus, in his foreword to it, suggests that ten evenings would be needed to produce it properly)

but no longer than some novels. Hindemith, however, knew that this was still way too much reading to ask of Free University students of the day. Instead, we'd be spending the entire semester discussing only the two-hand scenes between the characters of the Grumbler and the Optimist, about 130 pages altogether. Hindemith did assign two Kraus essays as supplementary reading—"Heine and the Consequences" and "Nestroy and Posterity"—and because Kraus was so difficult, he suggested that we form small groups to study the essays outside of class.

My group consisted of two other people my own age—a nice, lost boy named Stefan, a tart-tongued and relatively conscientious girl named Ursula—and Axel, a classic, burly, beer-faced leftist ten years older than we were. At our first meeting I confessed that it took me half an hour to read one page of Kraus's prose, and that I hadn't quite finished reading the Heine essay. Ursula and Stefan were eager to sympathize—they didn't do better than five pages an hour themselves. Axel sat shaking his head, lamely leafing through his pages, which he obviously hadn't even looked at, and tentatively muttering random phrases of Marxist jargon, hoping to hear from us that maybe one of them applied to Kraus. Like a big bear, he was sort of adorably puzzled and grizzled to look at, but ferally selfish underneath. I loved Ursula for being unable not to laugh at him. ("He's in his twentieth semester," she remarked to me later, "and there's not a trace of the first nineteen.") She and Stefan were the first and last German students I became even halfway friends with in two years in Germany; I actually went out drinking with them once or twice before I returned to the States. And the study group was a success. Ursula and I managed to work out some of what Kraus meant by satire, with Stefan neither helping nor hindering us, his eyes always soulful.

Axel disappeared after our second meeting, but I continued to see him at the seminar, because absolutely nothing got done in the seminar; he felt more comfortable there. The sessions went like this: Hindemith began by calling our attention to a pregnant line in one of the Grumbler-Optimist dialogues; somebody raised a point of procedure; the point of procedure was furiously debated for twenty minutes; Hindemith redirected us to the text; somebody else asked a totally wrong-

headed and irrelevant question (e.g., "Was Kraus in contact with Rosa Luxemburg?"); and the remainder of the class was spent discussing politics. Halfway through the semester, I stopped bothering to attend. I'd already signed up to present a paper on the last day of class, and I could work on the paper at home.

The Last Days of Mankind is the strangest great play ever written. At first glance, it can be mistaken for postmodern, since the bulk of its 793 pages consists of *quotation*; it's unabashedly a play about language. Kraus maintained that, with the exception of the Grumbler-Optimist scenes and the verse fantasias, every line spoken by its several hundred characters was something he had personally heard or read during the First World War, and many of the characters bear the names of real-life personalities: Hofmannsthal appears in it, unflatteringly, as does the jingoistic war correspondent Alice Schalek, who was sort of the Judith Miller of her day. But what makes the play modern, rather than postmodern, is the figure of the Grumbler, who in most respects is indistinguishable from Kraus himself. His friend the Optimist keeps coming to him with fresh phrases of propaganda and journalism, trying to persuade him that the war is a glorious thing and is going well, and the Grumbler aphoristically demolishes every one of them. He calls the Optimist his "cue bringer," and indeed the Optimist is scarcely less subordinated to war-perverted language than Hofmannsthal and Schalek and the myriad other figures. Only the Grumbler comes across as fully human. His coordinating subjectivity is too central to be postmodern.

In my paper I tried to make sense of two strange moments late in the play. In the first, the Optimist asks the Grumbler what "heroic renown" might mean, and the Grumbler shows him a pair of clippings. One is a newspaper account of some veterans of a battle on the Eastern Front being paraded around a Viennese theater and applauded as a prelude to "a production of Eysler's *The Woman-Eater*, with Fritz Werner and Betty Myra in their familiar starring roles." The other clipping is a description of a product for peddlers to sell to families of soldiers killed in action, a grotesquely kitschy framed poster in which a photo of the dead man can be inserted, "so elegant and moving that it will be

desired by rich and poor alike," with a list of "prices for distributors." The Optimist, aghast, says the clippings can't be real. He begs the Grumbler to say that he's invented them, and the Grumbler *shakes his hand* and says, "I thank you. They are by me."

The other moment, related in theme, is the conclusion of the Grumbler's final monologue, delivered from his writing desk, where he's reading from a manuscript:

> If the voice of this age had been preserved in a phonograph recording, the inner lies would have suffered for the outward fidelity, and the ear wouldn't have distinguished the one from the other. In this way, time renders the essence unrecognizable and would grant amnesty to the greatest crime ever committed under the sun, under the stars. I've rescued the essence, and my ear has discovered the sound of deeds and my eye the gesture of speeches, and my voice, simply by repeating, has quoted in such a way that the fundamental tone remained recorded for all time.
>
> > And let me speak to the yet unknowing world
> > How these things came about: so shall you hear
> > Of carnal, bloody, and unnatural acts,
> > Of accidental judgments, casual slaughters;
> > Of deaths put on by cunning and forc'd cause,
> > And, in this upshot, purposes mistook
> > Fall'n on the inventors' heads; all this can I
> > Truly deliver.
>
> And if the times could no longer hear, a Being above them would still hear! I've done nothing more than abbreviate this deadly quantity which, in its unmeasurability, is counting on the imbalance between times and *Times*. All of its blood really was just ink—now the writing will be done in blood! This is the world war. This is my manifesto. *I have considered everything carefully.* I have taken upon myself the tragedy that disintegrates into scenes of disintegrating mankind, so that the Spirit that takes pity on sacrifice may hear, even if it has renounced for

all future its connection with human hearing. May it receive the fundamental tone of these times, the echo of my bloody insanity, through which I share in the guilt for these noises. May it let this stand as a redemption!

This is the last we see of the Grumbler, and he's clearly quite out of his mind. Throughout the play, he's been the only character to imagine the horror of mechanized death in the trenches, the only character to see through the lies and propaganda. This would be less notable if there were only ten characters, but there are hundreds; the numerical imbalance casts the Grumbler as a profoundly solitary prophet. Nothing can save Austrian humanity, but he will be the one person to record its downfall for whoever and whatever comes after. With "*I have considered everything carefully,*" he is quoting from the Austrian emperor's proclamation of war, laying claim to a kind of imperial power. His megalomania in this final scene is reminiscent of King Lear in his scenes on the heath; also of my own psychotic moment in the fall. It didn't occur to me when I was writing my paper, but I must have been drawn to the scene because I'd experienced something like it: alone at my writing desk, racked by guilt, awaiting apocalypse, reading my own words, convinced that I could see what no one else could see, and getting so lost in figuration that reality dissolved. Blood as ink, ink as blood: figuration has driven the Grumbler crazy, too, making the outside world indistinguishable from the inside of his head. His thoughts aren't the echo of his times, his times are the echo of his thoughts! Which is why, in the earlier scene, he thanks the Optimist and accepts credit as the author of monstrosities he didn't write, merely quoted.

In my paper, I applied "Nestroy and Posterity" to the figure of the Grumbler. I called particular attention to the satirist's relationship with an age that has lost all connection to the Spirit: "He is its product and its hopeless antithesis." Kraus had certainly been nearly alone in his early opposition to the war; Hauptmann, Rilke, Mann, and Musil all wrote in patriotic support of it, and, as Edward Timms notes in his big Kraus study, "Every socialist party in Europe voted unanimously with its own government in favour of war, with the exception of two

er ist die Rückwärtskonzentrierung. Nach ihm die Sintflut. In den fünfzig Jahren nach seinem Tode hat der Geist Nestroy Dinge erlebt, die ihn zum Weiterleben ermutigen. Er steht eingekeilt zwischen den Dickwänsten aller Berufe, hält Monologe und lacht metaphysisch.

Serbian socialists and the Bolshevik caucus in the Russian Duma." But Hermann Hesse, too, was against the war from the beginning. As it proceeded, Kraus found a growing number of sympathizers in Vienna, including some within the government who provided him with documents that he worked into his play, and by 1917 the Austrian Socialists were calling for an armistice. Kraus may have felt alone, but he had to know that he was not alone. And so I argued that the Grumbler, in his total isolation and its attendant megalomania, should be seen as another of Kraus's satiric exaggerations. What would the product and hopeless antithesis of an insane war look like? It would look like the Grumbler. The abstracted, ideal satirist.

I remember reading in a liner note that after Stravinsky finished writing *Petruchka* he was laid low for weeks with "acute intracostal neuralgia due to nicotine poisoning." Although my Kraus paper was as rough and ploddingly written as *Petruchka* is perfect, I combusted what

organizes the Spirit's flight from mankind, he is the rear guard. After him, the deluge. In the fifty years since Nestroy's death, his spirit has experienced things that encourage it to go on living. It stands wedged in between the paunches of every profession, delivers monologues, and laughs metaphysically.

---

even for me was an enormous number of cigarettes while writing it. I was trying to be the one person in the seminar to actually read and understand the text, I was wrestling on my own with one of the most difficult German-language authors, and I was doing it while V brooded on a sofa and my Canadian friend waltzed in and out, humming opera. By the time I took the U-Bahn out to the last class of the semester, I had a bad cold and a Dickensian cough. With burning eyes, and in stumbling German, I read my paper aloud and let Professor Hindemith bat aside the one question with which a leftist interrupted me: "You use the word 'positivistic'—are you defending Karl Popper?" When I was finished, I had my proudest moment in two years in Germany—one of the proudest in my life, in fact. Hindemith smiled at me, looked around the smoke-filled room, and said, "Here's a lesson for us all. It took an *American* to explain what we've spent a whole semester trying to understand." Then we discussed Karl Popper.

NACHWORT ZU „HEINE UND DIE FOLGEN"

Afterword to "Heine and the Consequences"

Die tiefste Bestätigung dessen, was in dieser Schrift gedacht und mit ihr getan ist, wurde ihr: sie fand keine Leser. Ein Gedrucktes, das zugleich ein Geschriebenes ist, findet keine. Und mag es sich durch alle äußeren Vorzüge: den bequemen, noch in feindlicher Betrachtung genehmen Stoff, ein gefälliges Format und selbst durch den billigsten Preis empfehlen – das Publikum läßt sich nicht täuschen, es hat die feinste Nase gegen die Kunst, und sicherer als es den Kitsch zu finden weiß, geht es dem Wert aus dem Wege. Nur der Roman, das Sprachwerk außer der Sprache, das in vollkommenster Gestalt noch dem gemeinen Verstande irgend Halt und Hoffnung läßt, nährt heute seinen Mann. Sonst haben vor dem Leser jene, die ihm mit dem Gedanken im Wort bleiben, einen unendlich schweren Stand neben denen, welche

The deepest confirmation of what was thought in this essay and accomplished by it is what happened to it: it found no readers. A printed thing that's simultaneously a written thing finds none. Though it may have every outward merit in its favor—content that's accessible and remains agreeable even under hostile scrutiny, a pleasing format, and even the lowest price[1]—the public isn't fooled, it has the keenest nose against art, and even more surely than it knows its way to kitsch, it steers clear of value. Today only the novel, the work of language outside of language, which even in its most perfect form grants common sense some kind of hold and hope, can earn its author a living. Otherwise the people whose words to the reader abide with thought are in an endlessly difficult position compared with those who deceive

---

1. "'Heine and the Consequences' first appeared, in 1910, as a small stand-alone publication, a pamphlet for which Kraus obviously had high hopes. Priced at eighty pfennigs in Germany, it didn't cost much more than an equally long issue of *Die Fackel*. The following year, Kraus reprinted the essay in *Die Fackel*, with this afterword as a foreword. Foreword became afterword a decade later, when Kraus reprinted the essay once again, in his collection *The Destruction of the World Through Black Magic* (1922)."—PR

ihn mit dem Wort betrügen. Diesen glaubt er sofort, den andern erst nach hundert Jahren. Und keine irdische Träne aus den Augen, die das Leben vom Tod begraben sehen, verkürzt die Wartezeit. Nichts hilft. Die Zeit muß erst verstinken, um jene, die das sind, was sie können, so beliebt zu machen, wie diese da, welche können, was sie nicht sind. Nur daß dieses Heute noch den besondern Fluch des Zweifels trägt: ob der Kopf, der die Maschine überlebt, auch ihre Folgen überstehen wird. Nie war der Weg von der Kunst zum Publikum so weit; aber nie auch hat es ein so künstliches Mittelding gegeben, eins, das sich von selbst schreibt und von selbst liest, so zwar, daß sie alle schreiben und alle verstehen können und bloß der soziale Zufall entscheidet, wer aus dieser gegen den Geist fortschreitenden Hunnenhorde der Bildung jeweils als Schreiber oder als Leser hervorgeht. Die einzige Fähigkeit, die sie als Erbteil der Natur in Ehren halten: von sich zu geben, was sie gegessen haben, scheint ihnen auf geistigem Gebiet als ein Trick willkommen, durch den es gelingen mag, zwei Verrichtungen in einer Person zu vereinigen, und nur weil es noch einträglichere Geschäfte gibt als das Schreiben, haben sich bisher so viele unter ihnen Zurückhaltung auferlegt und begnügen sich damit, zu essen, was die andern von sich gegeben haben. Wie derselbe Mensch sich in einer Stammtischrunde vervielfacht hat, in der ein Cellist, ein Advokat, ein Philosoph, ein Pferdehändler und ein Maler sitzen, durch den Geist verbunden und nur vom Kellner nach den Fächern unterschieden: so ist zwischen Autor und Leser kein Unterschied. Es gibt bloß noch Einen, und das ist der Feuilletonist. Die Kunst weicht vor ihm zurück wie der Gletscher vor dem Bewohner des Alpenhotels. Einst konnte man den, so rühmten die Führer, mit Händen greifen. Wenn der Leser heute ein Werk mit Händen greifen kann,

him with words. He believes the latter immediately, the former only after a hundred years. And no earthly tear from eyes that see life buried by death will shorten the waiting period. Nothing helps. An age first has to rot past stinking to make the people who are what they can do as beloved as these people here, who can do what they are not. Except that this Today carries the particular curse of doubt: whether the head that survives the machine will also survive its consequences. Never before was the road from art to audience so long; but there has also never existed such an artificial hybrid,[2] a thing that writes of its own accord and reads of its own accord, so that, indeed, they all can write and all can understand, and purely social accident determines who, among this horde of educated Huns who progress against the Spirit, emerges as writer and who as reader. The sole ability that they hold in honor as a trait inherited from nature: regurgitating what they've eaten seems welcome to them in the intellectual realm, as a trick through which it might be possible to unite two functions in one person, and it's only because there are businesses more profitable than writing that so many of them have restrained themselves so far and satisfy themselves with eating what the others have regurgitated. Just as the same person is duplicated at a table of tavern regulars, a cellist, a lawyer, a philosopher, a horse trader, and a painter who are all of one mind and distinguishable to the waiter only by their trades: there's no difference between author and reader. There's only one person now, and that's the feuilletonist. Art backs away from him like a glacier from an alpine hotel guest. There was a time, the guide boasts, when you could put your hands on it. If a reader today can

2. I.e., the newspaper, specifically the feuilleton. The riff that follows—on the interchangeability of reader and writer, the self-sufficing loop of eating and regurgitation—further points to the kinship between feuilletons then and the blogosphere now.

dann muß das Werk eine üble Seite haben. Der Herausgeber dieser Zeitschrift ist sich durchaus bewußt, daß sie ihr Ansehen großenteils jener Empfänglichkeit verdankt, die sich etwa dem vorzüglichen Romanautor nicht gleich darum entzieht, weil sie vom Hörensagen weiß, daß er auch ein Künstler ist. Er darf sich die Nachsicht getrost zunutze machen. Der Herausgeber der Fackel hat nicht selten das Gefühl, daß er an jener schmarotzt. Sie würde ihm unwiderruflich verweigert, wenn die Leser gar erführen, in welchem Stadium der Unzurechnungsfähigkeit solch witzige Anläßlichkeiten entstehen, von welcher Kraft der Selbstvernichtung diese Treffsicherheit lebt und wie viel Zentner Leid eine leichte Feder tragen kann. Und wie düster das ist, was den Tagdieb erheitert. Das Lachen, das an meinen Witz nicht heranreicht, würde ihnen vergehen! Sähen sie, daß der kleine Stoff, der ihnen zu Gesicht steht, nur ein schäbiger Rest ist von etwas, das sie nicht betasten können, sie gingen endlich davon. Ich bin bei denen, die sich einbilden, meine Opfer zu sein, nicht beliebt; aber bei den Schadenfrohen noch immer weit über Verdienst.

put his hands on a work, the work must have a bad side. The publisher of this magazine is well aware that it owes its reputation mainly to a sensibility that doesn't shrink from some excellent novelist merely because he's also rumored to be an artist. He can confidently exploit the indulgence. The publisher of *Die Fackel* not infrequently has the feeling that he's freeloading on it. It would be retracted irrevocably should his readers ever discover in what a state of insanity such witty happenstances came to be written, on what powers of self-annihilation such self-assurance lives, and how many hundredweight of suffering the lightest pen can carry. And how gloomy the thing that brightens the idler's day.[3] Their laughter, which doesn't reach as far as my wit, would die in their mouths. If they could see that the petty material directly in front of them is just a shabby remnant of a thing they cannot touch, they would finally go away. Among those who flatter themselves that they're my victims, I am not loved; but the people who look on with schadenfreude still give me far more credit than I deserve.[4]

3. Indeed, nobody is funnier than depressives. Not only that, but the more depressive they are, the funnier they are—up to a point. My friend who committed suicide was the funniest friend I ever had.
4. This paragraph particularly interests me because it's shadowed by Kraus's envy of fiction—which, after my immersion in his work, I began in earnest to try to write.

As a wedding present, three months after I returned from Berlin, my college German professor George Avery gave me a hardcover edition of Kraus's *The Third Walpurgis Night*. George, who had opened my eyes to the connection between literature and the living of life, was becoming something of a second father to me, a father who read novels and cared about them deeply; an alternate father who, in his Greek-American way, embraced every pleasure and preferred beauty to engineering. I'd been a good student of his, and it must have been a wish to

become his best ex-student *ever*—to prove myself worthy, to demonstrate my love—that led me, in the months following my wedding, to try to translate the two difficult Kraus essays I'd brought home from Berlin.

I did the work late in the afternoon, after six or seven hours of writing short stories, in the bedroom of the little Somerville, Massachusetts, apartment that V and I were renting for $300 a month, while our elderly landlords, Mr. and Mrs. Frongillo, shouted at each other upstairs and watched television at high volumes. I was so bent on proving to my parents that I could succeed as a writer, and on proving to George that I still cared about the writers he loved, that I could work seventy hours a week for months at a stretch.

When I'd finished drafts of the two translations, I sent them to George. He returned them a few weeks later, with marginal notations in his microscopic handwriting, and with a letter in which he applauded my effort but said that he could also see how "devilishly difficult" it was to translate Kraus. Taking his hint, I looked at the drafts with a fresh eye and was discouraged to find them stilted and nearly unreadable. Almost every sentence needed further work, and I was so worn out by the work I'd already done that I buried the pages in a file folder.

But Kraus had changed me. When I gave up on short stories and returned to my novel, I was mindful of his moral fervor, his satirical rage, his hatred of the media, his preoccupation with apocalypse, and his boldness as a sentence writer. I wanted to expose America's contradictions the way he'd exposed Austria's, and I wanted to do it via the novel, the popular genre that he'd disdained but I did not. I still hoped to finish my Kraus project, too, after my novel had made me famous and a millionaire. To honor these hopes, I collected clippings from the Sunday *Times* and the daily *Boston Globe*, which V and I subscribed to. For some reason—perhaps to reassure myself that other people, too, were getting married—I read the nuptials pages of the *Times* religiously, clipping headlines like

CYNTHIA PIGOTT MARRIED TO LOUIS BACON

and, my favorite,

MISS LEBOURGEOIS TO MARRY WRITER

I read the *Globe* with an especially cold Krausian eye, and it obligingly enraged me with its triviality and its shoddy proofreading and its dopily punning weather headlines. I was so disturbed by the rootless, meaningless "wit" of HEAD-ON SPLASH, which I imagined would not amuse the family of someone killed in a car crash, and of AUTUMNIC BALM, which offended my sense of the seriousness of the nuclear peril, that I finally wrote a slashingly Krausian letter to the editor. The *Globe* actually printed the letter, but it managed, with characteristic carelessness, to mangle my punch line as "Automatic Balm," thereby rendering my point incomprehensible. Although Kraus was no Freudian, he had a Freud-like belief in the significance of journalistic parapraxis—he saw an unconscious compulsion to truth-telling in mistakes like "King Lehar" for "King Lear" (Franz Lehár being an operetta composer whom Kraus couldn't stand)—and I, who was both Krausian and Freudian, believed it was no accident that some typesetter at the *Globe* had "inadvertently" protected the paper from recognizing its own linguistic culpability. I was so enraged that I later devoted many pages of my second novel to making fun of what a shitty paper the *Globe* was. (In a tacit abandonment of my Kraus project, following the failure of my first novel to make me rich or famous, I also deployed the best clippings I'd saved from the *Times* in a chapter of the second novel, as examples of the rhetoric of Progress.) My rage back then—directed not just at the media but at Boston, Boston drivers, the people at the lab where I worked, the computer at the lab, my family, V's family, Ronald Reagan, George H. W. Bush, literary theorists, the minimalist fiction writers then in vogue, and men who divorced their wives—is foreign to me now. It must have had to do with the profound isolation of my married life with V (those were the only substantially friendless years of my life) and with the ruthlessness with which, in my ambition and poverty, I was denying myself pleasure.

There was probably also, as I've argued, an element of the privileged person's anger at the world for disappointing him. If I turned out not to have enough of this anger to make me a junior Kraus, it was because of the genre I'd chosen. Kraus twice, in his "Afterword," makes envious reference to the novelist, first as the one kind of linguistic artist who can actually earn a living, and then, more snidely, as the kind of writer whose audience isn't frightened away if "he's rumored to be an artist." When a hard-core satirist like Kraus manages to achieve some popularity, it can only mean that his audience doesn't understand him. But when novelists start taking this position, you get the dead end of mid-century American art fiction; you get late Gaddis. (I'll pass over in silence the attitudes of art-fiction writers in much of contemporary Europe.) But it's actually a reasonable and defensible position for an aphorist and densely allusive satirical glosser like Kraus. The lack of an audience whom he could respect was a foregone conclusion, and so he never had to stop being angry: he could be the Great Hater at his writing desk, be his society's hopeless antithesis, and then he could put down his pen and have a cozy personal life with whatever friends he hadn't made into enemies with his writing. It was an arrangement that worked throughout his life. Whereas, when a novelist finds an audience, even a small one, he or she is in a different relation to it, for the reason Kraus suggests: the relation is based on recognition, not misunderstanding. With a relation like that, with an audience like that, it becomes simply dishonest to remain so angry. And the mental work that fiction fundamentally requires, which is to imagine what it's like to be somebody you are not, further undermines anger in the long run. The more I wrote novels, the less I trusted my own righteousness, and the more prone I was to sympathizing with people like the typesetters at the *Globe*. Maybe it was a sneering jerk who'd written "Automatic," but maybe it was some soul who'd simply been asked to do too much too quickly. Plus, as the Internet rose to power, disseminating information that could be trusted as little as it cost to read it, I became so grateful to papers like the *Times* and the *Globe* for still existing, and for continuing to pay halfway responsible reporters to report, that I lost all interest in tearing them down.

And so, sometime in the nineties, I took my bad Kraus translations out of my active file cabinet and put them into deeper storage. Kraus's sentences never stopped running through my head—*And they all have a tone of discovery, as if the world had only just now been created . . . Reality is a meaningless exaggeration of all the details satire left behind fifty years ago*—but I didn't think about my project again until I met Daniel Kehlmann. I felt that I'd outgrown Kraus, felt that he was an angry young man's kind of writer, ultimately not a novelist's kind of writer. What's drawn me back to him now is partly my affection for Kehlmann and my susceptibility to his enthusiasm; partly the opportunity to understand better, thanks to Paul Reitter, what the hell Kraus was talking about; and partly the beauty of Kraus's language and humor, to which I've attempted to do more justice here than I did at twenty-three; but also, and maybe most important, a nagging sense that apocalypse, after seeming to recede for a while, is still in the picture.

In my own little corner of the world, which is to say American fiction, Jeff Bezos of Amazon may not be the Antichrist, but he surely looks like one of the Four Horsemen. Amazon wants a world in which books are either self-published or published by Amazon itself, with readers dependent on Amazon reviews in choosing books, and with authors responsible for their own promotion. The work of yakkers and tweeters and braggers, and of people with the money to pay somebody to churn out hundreds of five-star reviews for them, will flourish in that world. (Kraus's dictate "Sing, bird, or die" could now read "Tweet, bird, or die.") But what happens to the people who became writers *because* yakking and tweeting and bragging felt to them like intolerably shallow forms of social engagement? What happens to the people who want to communicate in depth, individual to individual, in the quiet and permanence of the printed word, and who were shaped by their love of writers who wrote when publication still assured some kind of quality control and literary reputations were more than a matter of self-promotional decibel levels? As fewer and fewer readers are able to find their way, amid all the noise and disappointing books and phony reviews, to the work produced by the new generation of this kind of writer—I'm thinking of Rachel Kushner's *The Flamethrowers*, Adam

Haslett's *You Are Not a Stranger Here*, Sarah Shun-lien Bynum's *Ms. Hempel Chronicles*, Clancy Martin's *How to Sell*—Amazon is well on its way to making writers into the kind of prospectless workers whom its contractors employ in its warehouses, laboring harder for less and less, with no job security, because the warehouses are situated in places where they're the only business hiring. And the more of the population that lives like those workers, the greater the downward pressure on book prices and the greater the squeeze on conventional booksellers, because when you're not making much money you want your entertainment for free, and when your life is hard you want instant gratification ("Overnight free shipping!").

But so the physical book goes on the endangered-species list, so responsible book reviewers go extinct, so literary novelists are conscripted into Jennifer Weinerish self-promotion, so the Big Six publishers get killed and devoured by Amazon, so independent bookstores disappear: this looks like an apocalypse only if most of your friends are writers, editors, or booksellers (as most of mine are). Plus it's possible that the story isn't over. Maybe the Internet experiment in consumer reviewing will result in such flagrant corruption (already one-third of all online product reviews are said to be bogus) that people will clamor for the return of professional reviewers. Maybe an economically significant number of readers will come to recognize the human and cultural costs of Amazonian hegemony and go back to local bookstores or at least to barnesandnoble.com, which offers the same books and a superior e-reader, and whose owners have more progressive politics. Maybe people will get as sick of Twitter as they once got sick of cigarettes. Twitter's and Facebook's latest models for making money still seem to me like one part pyramid scheme, one part wishful thinking, and one part repugnant panoptical surveillance.

I could, it's true, make a larger apocalyptic argument about the logic of the machine, which in Kraus's day was still localized in Europe and America but has now gone global and is accelerating the denaturization of the planet and sterilization of its oceans. I could point to the transformation of Canada's boreal forest into a toxic lake of tar-sand

by-products, the leveling of Asia's remaining forests for Chinese-made ultra-low-cost porch furniture at Home Depot, the damming of the Amazon and the endgame clear-cutting of its forests for beef and mineral production, the whole mind-set of "Screw the consequences, we want to buy a lot of crap and we want to buy it cheap, with overnight free shipping," and the direct connection between this American mind-set and a new Chinese prosperity that—in a classic Krausian collision of old values with new valuables—funds the slaughter of millions of Pacific sharks for the luxury of their fins and tens of thousands of African elephants for their ivory. And meanwhile the overheating of the atmosphere, meanwhile the calamitous overuse of antibiotics by agribusiness, meanwhile the widespread tinkering with cell nucleii, which may well prove to be as disastrous as tinkering with atomic nucleii. And, yes, the thermonuclear warheads are still in their silos and subs.

But apocalypse isn't necessarily the physical end of the world. Indeed, the word more directly implies an element of final cosmic judgment. In Kraus's invocation of the Deluge at the end of "Nestroy," as in his talk of a "fully dehumanized zone" in his "Final Word" (my translation of which will follow this long dilation) and his endless chronicling of crimes against truth and the German language in *The Last Days of Mankind*, he's referring not merely to physical destruction. In fact, the great title of his play would be better rendered in English as *The Last Days of Humanity*: "dehumanized" doesn't mean "depopulated," and if the First World War spelled the end of humanity in Austria, it wasn't because there were no longer any people there. Kraus was appalled by the carnage, but he saw it as the result, not the cause, of a loss of humanity by people who were still living. Living but damned, cosmically damned.

But a judgment like this obviously depends on what you mean by "humanity." Whether I like it or not, the world being created by the infernal machine of techno-consumerism is still a world made by human beings. As I write this, in the fall of 2012, it seems as if half the advertisements on network television are featuring people bending

over smartphones; there's a particularly noxious/great one in which all the twenty-somethings at a wedding reception are doing nothing but taking smartphone photos and instantly texting them to one another. To describe this dismal spectacle in apocalyptic terms, as a "dehumanization" of a wedding, is to advance a particular moral conception of humanity; and if you follow Nietzsche and reject the moral judgment in favor of an aesthetic one, you're immediately confronted by Bourdieu's persuasive connection of aesthetics with class and privilege; and the next thing you know, you're translating *The Last Days of Mankind* as *The Last Days of Privileging the Things I Personally Find Beautiful*.

And maybe this is not such a bad thing. Maybe—I already had intimations of this in Berlin, at twenty-two, alone at my desk—apocalypse is, paradoxically, always individual, always personal. (Think of the Grumbler, alone at his desk, sinking into the psychotic solipsism that's the end point of his apocalyptic thinking.) I have a brief tenure on earth, bracketed by infinities of nothingness, and during the first part of this tenure I form an attachment to a particular set of human values that are shaped inevitably by my social circumstances. If I'd been born in 1159, when the world was steadier, I might well have felt, at fifty-three, that the next generation would share my values and appreciate the same things I appreciated; no apocalypse pending. But I was born in 1959, when TV was something you watched only during prime time and on weekends, and people wrote letters and put them in the mail, and every magazine and newspaper had a robust Books section, and venerable publishers made long-term investments in young writers, and New Criticism reigned in English departments, and the Amazon Basin was intact, and antibiotics were used only to treat serious infections, not pumped into healthy cows. It wasn't necessarily a better world (we had bomb shelters and segregated swimming pools), but it was the only world I knew to try to find my place in as a writer. And so today, fifty-three years later, Kraus's signal complaint in the Nestroy essay—that the new world has lost the capacity even to *be* a posterity—can't help ringing true to me. Kraus was the first great instance of a writer fully experiencing how modernity, whose essence is the acceler-

ating rate of change, *in itself* creates the conditions for personal apocalypse. Naturally, because he was the first, the changes felt particular and unique to him, but in fact he was registering something that has become a fixture of modernity. The experience of each succeeding generation is so different from that of the previous one that there will always be people to whom it seems that key values have been lost and there can be no more posterity. As long as modernity lasts, *all* days will feel to someone like the last days of humanity. Kraus's rage and his sense of doom and apocalypse may be the antithesis of the upbeat rhetoric of Progress, but, like that rhetoric, they remain an unchanging modality of modernity.

Paul Reitter offers this very astute refinement: "For Kraus, it did matter what the particular changes were, though we certainly might be able to appropriate his apocalypticism in such a way that it doesn't. In Kraus's day, and even before it, there was a lot of theorizing about the destabilizing effects of modernity—'all that is solid melts into air,' etc.—which led to intense crises of the self, maybe even to something like personal apocalypses. What Kraus contributed to the conversation, I think, is the insight that the rise of the mass media machine is an absolutely central part of this process (it's one of its enabling conditions as much as it's one of its consequences), not least because of the inherent antagonisms between the ascendant mass media and the (privileged) kind of spirituality/imaginativeness that, as Kraus saw it, makes us human. And my sense is that the key point of continuity, in terms of Kraus's relevance, is this dynamic, rather than the persistence of a general culture of rapid change. Today there are people who embrace the radicalized culture of media as something that will finally enable us to actualize our full potential as social beings, and then there are those—a lot of them, I think—who have brooded over books like Sherry Turkle's *Alone Together* and are wrestling with apocalyptic doubts and wondering whether our even more insane media moment will spell the end of an essential part of us (even if their notion of what's essential differs from the Krausian notion of an essential imaginative Spirit, and even as they themselves screw around on their iPads). For

Mag nun die Fackel sich in so vielen unrechten Händen befinden: wenn sich das, was von mir geschrieben ist, in einen andern Druck wagt, so langen wenige darnach. Für eine Sammlung von Satiren oder Aphorismen soll das nicht beklagt sein. Eine solche ist mit den seltenen Lesern zufrieden, denen die textliche Veränderung ein neues Werk bedeutet. Aber an der Schrift „Heine und die Folgen", die als Manuskript in den Buchverlag kam, hat es sich gezeigt, daß es nicht mehr Leser gibt, als jene wenigen. Und diese Erfahrung kann gerade sie nicht schmerzlos hinnehmen. Denn ihr Wille ist, Leser zu schaffen, und das könnte ihr nur gelingen, wenn sie Leser findet. Sie trägt den Jammer des deutschen Schrifttums aus, und sie ist nicht zufrieden damit, daß ihre Wahrheit sich an ihr selbst erfülle. Darum betritt sie den Weg der Reue, der aus dem Buch zurück in die Zeitschrift führt, und auch diese Notwendigkeit sei ihr gefällig, die Perversität des geistigen Betriebs unserer Tage zu erweisen. Hier, im vertrauten Kreis, wird sie wenigstens den Versuch machen, zu mehr tauben Ohren zu sprechen, als in der großen deutschen Öffentlichkeit zu haben sind.

Denn es ist nicht zu denken, daß sie just für den Gegenstand taub waren, von dem zu ihnen die Rede ging. Von Heine hören sie noch immer gern und wenn sie auch nicht wissen, was soll es bedeuten. Sicherlich würde die Schrift, wenn sie bloß den Lebenswert seiner Kunst verneinte, jenem Zeitgefühl nichts Neues

---

the latter group, Kraus should be an inspired voice from the past, because even if the human imagination proved more durable than he thought it would, he was the first to size up the apocalyptic-seeming confrontation between mind and modern media machine, and he expressed it more forcefully and memorably than anyone else ever has."

Given that *Die Fackel* finds itself in so many wrong hands: if something I've written proceeds to venture into other print, few people will reach for it. With a collection of satires or aphorisms, this would be nothing to complain about.[5] Things of that sort are content to find the rare reader for whom textual alteration signifies new work. But the essay "Heine and the Consequences," which came to the book publisher as a manuscript, has made it clear that there no longer are any readers besides these few.[6] And it, of all texts, can't help feeling pained by this discovery. For its wish is to create readers, and it can't succeed at this unless it finds readers. It enacts the misery of German-language letters, and it isn't content to make itself the demonstration of its own truth. And so it treads the path of remorse, which leads from the book back into the magazine; and would that even this exigency might please it, as proof of the perversity of the business of the Spirit in our times. Here, in familiar environs, it will at least make the attempt to speak to more deaf ears than are to be had in the greater German public.

Because it's not to be thought that they were simply deaf to the subject about which they were being addressed. They're still happy to hear about Heine, even if they know not what it means.[7] If the essay merely rejected the living value of his art, it would surely say

5. "Kraus is referring to *The Great Wall of China*, a collection of his essays, and *Dicta and Contradicta*, a book of his aphorisms. Both had recently been published by the same press that put out 'Heine and the Consequences'—namely, the Albert Langen Verlag."—PR
6. "If the pamphlet's readership wasn't what Kraus wanted it to be, neither was it as bad as he's making it out to have been. Readers quickly went through the first two editions; in 1911, Langen released a third edition, even though 'Heine and the Consequences' had been reprinted in *Die Fackel*."—PR
7. "A play on a line from Goethe's poem 'Ballad,' 'Die Kinder, sie hören es gerne' ('The children, they're happy to hear it'). And yet another play

sagen, das sich selbst durch die Verabredungen der Intelligenz nicht betrügen läßt. Sicherlich läßt es sich eher zur Bettelei für ein Heine-Denkmal als zur Lektüre seiner Bücher herumkriegen. Und dem Haß, der dort ansetzte, wo nicht Liebe, nur intellektuelle Heuchelei die Grabeswacht hält, würde zwar einige Erbitterung, aber kein allgemeines Interesse antworten. Diese Schrift indes, so weit entfernt von dem Verdacht, gegen Heine ungerecht zu sein, wie von dem Anspruch, ihm gerecht zu werden, ist kein literarischer Essay. Sie erschöpft das Problem Heine nicht, aber mehr als dieses. Der törichteste Vorwurf: daß sie Heine als individuellen Täter für seine Folgen verantwortlich mache, kann sie nicht treffen. Die ihn zu schützen vorgeben, schützen sich selbst und zeigen die wahre Richtung des Angriffs. Sie sollen für ihre Existenz verantwortlich gemacht werden, und der Auswurf der deutschen Intelligenz, der sich sogleich geregt hat, bewies, daß er sich als die verantwortliche Folge fühle. Es

on Heine's line, from the 'Lorelei' poem, 'Ich weiß nicht, was soll es bedeuten' ('I know not what it means').” —PR

nothing new to that contemporary sensibility that doesn't even let itself be fooled by the collusions of the commentariat. It would surely sooner be brought around to begging for a Heine monument than to a reading of his books. And the hate that developed there, where not love but mere intellectual hypocrisy stands watch over the grave, would be greeted with some bitterness, to be sure, but not with any general interest. This text, meanwhile, as far removed from suspicion of being unfair to Heine as from pretension of being fair to him, is not a literary essay. It doesn't exhaust the problem of Heine, but it does more than this.[8] The most ridiculous reproach—that it holds Heine responsible as an individual culprit for his consequences—can't touch it. The people who pretend to defend him are defending themselves and revealing the true direction of the attack. They should be held responsible for their existence, and the sputum that German intellectuals immediately coughed up is evidence that they feel themselves to be the respon-

8. "Which brings us back to the question of what Kraus hoped to accomplish with 'Heine and the Consequences.' Here's a story I've been telling myself about the essay. Kraus composed it at the moment when his skepticism toward psychoanalysis was intensifying, maybe even peaking, in the aftermath of his bitter falling-out with a member of Freud's circle, Fritz Wittels. After the split, Wittels had proceeded to analyze Kraus in a most unflattering way. In a paper titled 'The *Fackel* Neurosis,' delivered to the Vienna Psychoanalytic Society in January 1910, Wittels proposed that Kraus's hatred of Moriz Benedikt be seen as a neurotic symptom, stemming from an unresolved oedipal tension with his own father. It isn't clear whether Kraus knew exactly what Wittels said about him, but Kraus published some of his harshest aphorisms about psychoanalysis only a few months later. And it's very tempting, therefore, to read 'Heine and the Consequences' as Kraus's response to the psychoanalytic talk about him. The message being: If you want to know how to stage a conflict with a literary father figure, read and learn.

waren Individuen, die durch ihre eigene Lyrik schwer genug gestraft sind oder durch ihre eigene Polemik zu sehr insultiert waren, als daß sie einer besondern Abfertigung bedurft hätten.

"And here's another story I tell myself. 1909 marked the tenth anniversary of the founding of *Die Fackel*. German literary culture made (still makes) a big deal of anniversaries, and the date occasioned fawning tributes to Kraus, several of which he printed. He also published some unsatisfying retrospective thoughts of his own. What feels off about them is that they don't address how his orientation had changed. Kraus presented, as the compliment of which he was 'proudest,' a congratulatory note from a reader who described himself as a 'simple worker'; and yet *Die Fackel* had recently taken a more literary turn and lost some of its following among Vienna's working class. Similarly, Kraus's anniversary aphorisms gesture at continuity—'upon being told that there's someone who hasn't slept for ten years, this snoring present rolled onto its other side'—but his aphorisms, which would play a key role in *Die Fackel*, had begun to appear in mature form only around 1907. They were, indeed, part of the paper's literary turn.

"It may seem odd to speak of such a shift. Kraus had always been known as an excellent stylist and satirical wit, and his literary judgments really mattered to people. Before he started feuding with Franz Werfel, he was enthusiastic about him, and when Kraus published one of Werfel's early poems in *Die Fackel* it was, for Werfel, like a dream come true. *Die Fackel* was literary from the start, in the sense both of having literary qualities and of being concerned with literature. What changed was the degree of literariness. During the early years, Kraus simply didn't deliver rhetorical performances like 'Heine and the Consequences.' This is why so few of his most quotable lines derive from that decade.

"But the turn itself: what caused it? It may have had something to do with the restlessness of midlife—Kraus certainly became restless in many ways around this time. It was in 1910 that he began to hold public readings, which no doubt encouraged him to pay even more attention to the

sible consequence. There were individuals severely enough pun-
ished by their own poetry or too gravely insulted by their own
polemics to have needed to respond in detail. The few who were

---

sound of his sentences and to fully unleash his dazzling capacity for verbal mimicry. A year later, Kraus made himself *Die Fackel*'s sole author; he
also converted, secretly, to Catholicism. But I think a better explanation
for the turn is that, as Kraus's critique of the effects of literary journalism
became more apocalyptic and more central to his mission, he felt moved
to oppose those effects more concertedly on the level of form as well. He
did this by cultivating an even more difficult, even more literary style,
hoping to jump-start the imaginations that the feuilleton was deaden-
ing. In essence, Kraus went from being a journalist against journalism to
being a literary journalist against literary journalism.

"In 1909, Kraus had missed a good opportunity to give an account
of this new paradox. But he soon made up for it with 'Heine and the
Consequences.' Using Heine as a foil, the essay responds to the need for
an updated self-explanation and delivers it resoundingly, albeit by way
of a radicalized paradoxicality. It's here that Kraus expresses his mature
critique of the feuilleton most thoroughly; it's also here that he spells
out the differences between the feuilleton and his own artistic journalism most explicitly ('It was veiled so that the inquisitive day couldn't get
at it. Now the veils are rising . . .'). And if you wanted to draw attention
to your self-explanation, what better foil could there be than Heine, the
ardently beloved and badly embattled ur-feuilletonist in German culture? 'Heine and the Consequences' didn't get the kind of initial notice
that Kraus had hoped for. But how would he have fared with a self-
justifying takedown of one of the later literary journalists whom he went
after just as fiercely—and with as much moral opprobrium—and whom
he actually devoted a lot more space to savaging? Kraus reckoning with
Heine in sensationalistic, spectacularly paradoxical ways, leveling
antisemitic-sounding criticisms against Heine only to undermine some
of the basic principles of antisemitic discourse (e.g., the originality-
imitation hierarchy): this was something new."—PR

Die wenigen, die sich geärgert, und die vielen, die nicht gelesen hatten, haben bestätigt, was geschrieben war. Nicht die Gefahr, eine Entweihung Heines zu erleben, wohl aber die Furcht, das Feindlichste zu hören, was diesem Zeitalter der Talente gesagt werden kann, hat dem Ruf ein stärkeres Echo ferngehalten. Nicht eine Wertung Heine'scher Poesie, aber die Kritik einer Lebensform, in der ein für allemal alles Unschöpferische seinen Platz und sein glänzend elendes Auskommen gefunden hat, wurde hier gewagt. Nicht die Erfindung der Pest, nicht einmal ihre Einschleppung wurde getadelt, aber ein geistiger Zustand beschrieben, an dem die Ornamente eitern. Das hat den Stolz der Bazillenträger beleidigt. Hier ist irgendwie die Sprache von

annoyed and the many who didn't read have confirmed what was written.[9] It wasn't the danger of experiencing a desecration of Heine, but surely the fear of hearing the most hostile thing that can be said to this age of talents, that prevented the shout from having a stronger echo. It wasn't an evaluation of Heinean poesy, but a critique of a form of life in which everything uncreative has once and for all found its place and its brilliantly wretched accommodation, that was essayed here. Not a denunciation of the invention of a pestilence, nor even of its importation, but a description of a spiritual condition on which ornaments fester. This offended the pride of the bacteria carriers. Here language is somehow re-

9. "Here, too, Kraus is accentuating the negative to the point of stretching the truth. Yes, some early reviewers of 'Heine and the Consequences' expressed annoyance. But there were also favorable responses. Readers of *Die Fackel* would have known this because Kraus, who liked to catalogue and comment on reactions to his work, publicly kept track of how his Heine essay went over with the critics. In two separate discussions he complains of being misunderstood—no surprise there. Yet the impression that emerges isn't that Kraus's (uncomprehending) reviewers were for the most part hostile. To the contrary, the initial reception of 'Heine and the Consequences' seems to have been, on balance, admiring. Consider how Kraus begins the first of his two discussions. He writes, 'Thoroughly in agreement with 'Heine and the Consequences' are the accounts in: the *Zeit am Montag* (Berlin, December 5); the *Freisinnige Zeitung* (Berlin, December 11); the *Londoner General-Anzeiger* (December 24); the *Hamburger Nachrichten* (December 25); and, further, *Die Wage* (Vienna, December 25).' Kraus goes on to quote Franz Pfemfert, a well-known cultural critic, taking him to task in the magazine *Der Demokrat*. But Pfemfert didn't so much question Kraus's arguments as charge him with being irresponsible. According to Pfemfert, Adolf Bartels and Heine's other antisemitic detractors would find plenty of new ammunition in 'Heine and the Consequences.' So what if Kraus had attempted to distance his position on Heine from Bartels's?

allem, was sie einzuwickeln verpflichtet wurde, gelöst, und ihr die Kraft, sich einen bessern Inhalt zu schaffen, zuerkannt. Hier ist in dieser Sprache selbst gesagt, daß ihr der kalligraphische Betrug fremd sein, der das Schönheitsgesindel zwischen Paris und Palermo um den Schwung beneidet, mit dem man in der Kunst und in der Hotelrechnung aus dem Fünfer einen Neuner macht. Das haben sie nicht verstanden, oder als bedenklich genug erkannt, um es nicht hören zu wollen.

Um aber die Unfähigkeit, die eine redliche Wirkung des begabten Zeitgeistes ist, nicht schwerer zu belasten als die Bosheit, die in allen Zeiten die sozialen Möglichkeiten gegen den Gedanken mobilisiert hat, muß gesagt werden, daß noch ein besonderer Verdacht den Autor dazu bestimmt hat, vom Verlag Albert Langen das Recht des Wiederabdruckes dieser Schrift zu erbitten. Sein bekannter Verfolgungswahn, der ihm sogar zugeflüstert hat, daß es ihm in zwölf Jahrgängen nicht gelungen sei, sich beliebt zu machen, ließ ihn an eine absichtliche Unterdrückung der Broschüre glauben. Stellte ihm vor, daß die aufgestöberten

---

Did he really think that a screamer like Bartels would care about such disclaimers? Having brushed off Pfemfert's accusation, Kraus proceeds to cite and mock a review that presents 'Heine and the Consequences' as a rare misstep by a great author. And that's it for the disapproval. Kraus's next move is to quote a passage from a letter by the esteemed, recently deceased critic Samuel Lublinski, in which Lublinski says about Kraus's essay: it is 'the most formidable attack' on Heine 'and also the most compelling one.' In the final excerpt Kraus provides, his reviewer gushes, 'I rank his Heine book above all previous books about Heine.' Kraus's second discussion, published just one month later, isn't much different. The review on which it focuses ends with the lines: 'Heine and the Consequences' is 'an achievement one cannot ignore. All in all, it comes across as a timely verdict.'

"For the next few decades, 'Heine and the Consequences' continued to elicit mixed responses. Perhaps most notable is the resonance it

leased from everything it was obligated to outwit, and the power to acquire better content is celebrated. Here this very language declares itself a stranger to the calligraphic fraud that admires the beauty mongers from Paris to Palermo for the verve with which, in art and in the hotel bill, a five-note is made into a niner. This they didn't understand, or recognized as dangerous enough that they didn't want to hear it.

But so as not to chastise lack of ability, which is an honest effect of the gifted zeitgeist, more severely than the malice that social possibilities of every age have mobilized against thought, it must be said that a particular suspicion has compelled the author to ask the publisher Albert Langen for the reprint rights to this document. The author's well-known persecution mania, which has gone so far as to whisper to him that he hasn't managed to make himself loved in twelve years' time, led him to believe that the pamphlet was intentionally suppressed.[10] He imagined that

---

found among the Frankfurt School thinkers, who, like Kraus, were concerned about the commodification of literature. In 1931 Walter Benjamin called the essay the best thing ever written about Heine. And in 1956, on the hundredth anniversary of Heine's death, Theodor Adorno described Kraus's 'judgment' of Heine as ineradicable. Eventually, though, the debate about 'Heine and the Consequences' was taken over by critics who hadn't come of age in Kraus's world, and who as a group had a harder time getting past the antisemitic stereotypes in his text. When this happened, 'Heine and the Consequences' fell into disfavor. Hence the fact that Edward Timms mentions it only *twice* in his landmark Kraus study of 1986."—PR

10. "Kraus is being self-ironic here, but he isn't joking: in June of 1911 he wrote a letter to the Langen Verlag in which he speculates that his enemies were using their influence to undermine the marketing of 'Heine and the Consequences.'"—PR

"Twelve years' time" refers to how long Kraus had been publishing *Die Fackel*.

Wanzen aus der Matratzengruft sich in Bewegung gesetzt und just dort angesiedelt hätten, wo der ihnen bekannte Weg vom Gedanken in den Handel führt. Die Furcht vor der Presse kann Berge versetzen und Säle verweigern: vielleicht bedarf es nicht einmal der Anregung, um einen Wiener Buchhändler im Vertrieb einer gefährlichen Broschüre, von der nur ein kleiner Gewinn abfällt, lau zu machen. Zumal einen von jenen, die noch heute der Fackel einen autorrechtlichen Prozeß verübeln, den ihr erster Drucker geführt hat. Ist es denn nicht eine Wiener Tatsache eigenster Art, daß nicht nur den Blicken der spazierenden City das Ärgernis meiner Bücher entzogen wird, sondern daß die Hefte der Fackel, die in einer Zeile mehr Literatur enthalten als die Schaufenster sämtlicher Buchhandlungen der Inneren Stadt, und an deren letztes Komma mehr Qual und Liebe gewendet ist als an eine Bibliothek von Luxusdrucken eines Insel-Verlags – gezwungen sind, zwischen Zigarren, Losen und Revolverblättern ihre Aufwartung zu machen, um die Kosten zu decken, die eine nie belohnte und nie bedankte Mühe verursacht, während im Chor das Ungeziefer des Humors die Sache für lukrativ hält und sich an dem Begriff der „Doppelnummer" weidet! Eine Zeitschrift, welche die legitimsten administrativen

bugs flushed from Heine's mattress-grave had sprung into action and settled in precisely on the road they know so well, the one that leads from thinking to commerce. Fear of the press can move mountains and shutter halls; a hint is perhaps not even needed to make a Viennese bookseller tepid in marketing a dangerous pamphlet that generates only paltry profit.[11] Especially not one of the ones who are even now still sore with *Die Fackel* about a civil action that its first printer brought against it. Is it not, then, a most indicative Viennese circumstance that not only will the glances of the strolling city be spared the irritation of my books, but that copies of *Die Fackel*—one line of which contains more literature than the collective show windows of every downtown bookstore, and on whose least comma more torment and love are expended than on a library of luxury editions by Insel— are compelled to offer themselves amid cigars, lottery tickets, and tabloids to cover the costs of a never-rewarded and never-appreciated labor, while an entire chorus of humor-loving vermin considers the thing lucrative and gloats over the idea of the "double issue."[12] A magazine that avoids like leprosy the most

11. "Kraus had good reason to think that people were trying to get between him and his audience. In December of 1910, for example, a 'shuttering of the hall' caused one of his lecture evenings to be canceled. What happened was that the owner of the hall suddenly backed out of his arrangement with Kraus without giving a meaningful explanation. Kraus surmised that the owner's friends in the press had prevailed upon him to shut the performance down."—PR
12. "In Vienna, *Die Fackel* was sold mostly on the magazine racks of tobacco shops. Kraus began putting out 'double issues' of *Die Fackel* in 1905. These weren't quite twice as long as a single issue, but they cost twice as much, and they soon went from being something new and dif-

Hilfen wie den Aussatz flieht, so aus sich selbst leben möchte, um so gegen sich selbst zu leben, buchgeboren wie kaum ein Buch im heutigen Deutschland, muß die Stütze des zuständigen Handels, die ihm Pflicht wäre, entbehren und in der österreichischen Verbannung jene Schmach verkosten, die den wegen eines politischen Delikts Verurteilten in die Zelle der Taschendiebe wirft. Ahnt die freigesinnte Bagage, deren kosmisches Gefühl die Gewinnsucht ist und von der man die Gnade erbetteln muß, für irrsinnig gehalten zu werden, wenn man keinen Profit macht, ahnt sie, wie viel Genüsse sie sich mit dem Geld erkaufen könnte, das mein Werk des Hasses verschlingt, bis es die Gestalt hat, mit der ein Selbstverherrlicher nie zufrieden ist – weil es erst dann ihm die Fehler enthüllt, die die andern nicht merken! Aber hier, in sein Archiv, nimmt er, was ihm beliebt, und zieht er ein, was andernorts nicht beliebt hat. Hier kann ihn nichts enttäuschen. Eine Arbeit, die statt zwanzig Auflagen nicht die zweite erlangt hat: hier kann ihr nichts mehr geschehn. Ihr Verfasser, dessen Lust es ist, in die Speichen seines eigenen Rads zu greifen, sich selbst und die Maschine aufzuhalten, wenn ihm ein Pünktchen mißfällt, wird nie mehr einem fremden publizistischen Betrieb seine Hilfe gewähren. Er wirbt nicht um neues

ferent to being the norm. What Kraus is making fun of here is the (gloating, gleeful) suspicion that the profit motive was behind this practice."—PR

legitimate sponsorship,[13] that in its desire to earn its own living makes life harder for itself, and that is book-born like hardly a book in contemporary Germany, has to do without the support of its own industry, which ought to have an obligation to it, and to get a taste, in Austrian exile, of the sort of ignomiy that throws the person condemned for a political offense into jail with the pickpockets. The pack of liberals whose cosmic feeling is avarice, and whom you have to beg for the mercy of excusing you as crazy if you fail to make a profit: Does it have any idea how many pleasures it could buy with the money that my work of hate devours before it achieves the form with which a self-glorifier is never satisfied—because only then does it reveal to him the errors that the others don't notice? But here, in his archive, he takes what he likes and collects what is liked nowhere else. Here nothing can disappoint him. A work that instead of twenty editions didn't see a second one: here nothing more can happen to it. Its author, whose pleasure it is to reach into the spokes of his own wheel to shut down both himself and the machine when the tiniest point displeases him, will never again lend his assistance to an alien publishing concern.[14] He will never again try to win a new audience. For him, *Die Fackel* is not a

13. "There was, for example, minimal advertising in *Die Fackel*, whose production never depended on advertising revenues." —PR
14. "Kraus published just one more book with the Langen Verlag, a collection of aphorisms that appeared in 1912. In the same year, he managed to establish his own imprint within Kurt Wolff's publishing house—the Press of Karl Kraus's Writings (Verlag der Schriften von Karl Kraus). He eventually went over to a freestanding operation with a much better name: *Die Fackel* Press (Verlag *Die Fackel*)." —PR

Publikum. Die Fackel ist ihm nicht Tribüne, sondern Zuflucht. Hier kann ihn das Schicksal einer Arbeit nur bis zur Vollendung aufregen, nicht bis zur Verbreitung. Was hier gelebt wird, mag im Buche wiedererstehn. Aber es ist Lohn genug, unter dem eigenen Rade zu liegen.

platform but a haven. Here the destiny of a work can move him only through the point of its completion, not through its dissemination. What's being lived here may be resurrected in a book. But it's recompense enough to be bound to one's own wheel.[15]

15. Indeed. To write a sentence like "Art backs away from him like a glacier from an alpine hotel guest," to find the perfect metaphor and to set it in the most elegant possible sentence, and then to publish it in a magazine whose every issue you personally proofread with a gimlet eye, does amount to recompense. But maybe not a sufficient one, not a permanent one; because writing is the strangest social/antisocial art. When you finally become good enough at it to participate in the community of past writers to which you were drawn as a solitary reader, the pleasure is a weirdly *social* one; and yet the kind of person who is so keen to engage with that community that he or she submits to years of grueling apprenticeship is liable to be hungry for engagement with a community of the living, too. Kraus may say that he doesn't care about reaching non-deaf ears. But all he's doing is defending himself against further disappointment, not eradicating its cause. He still wants readers. All writers do.

ZWISCHEN DEN LEBENSRICHTUNGEN

SCHLUSSWORT

BETWEEN TWO STRAINS OF LIFE

FINAL WORD
[TO "HEINE AND THE CONSEQUENCES"]

Nicht die Feststellung der unerheblichen Tatsache, daß die Schrift „Heine und die Folgen" neben der Verbreitung durch die Fackel nun doch im siebenten Jahr bei der dritten Auflage hält, erfordert die Ergänzung. Ein anderes sei nachgetragen, das gleichfalls, indem es scheinbar etwas berichtigt, einer tieferen Betrachtung erst dessen Richtigkeit zu erkennen gibt. Alles, was hier und in allen Kapiteln über den Lebensverlust des heutigen Lebens und den Sprachverrat deutscher Menschheit gesagt ist, hat die gedankliche Spur, die bis zum Rand dieses Krieges führt, der meine Wahrheit auch zur Offenbarheit gemacht hat. Nur dort bedarfs einer Darlegung, wo ich gerade in dem Drang, der Maschine zu entrinnen, einer schon völlig entmenschten Zone den Vorzug vor jenem Schönheitswesen gab, das dem unaufhaltsamen Fortschritt noch weglagernde Trümmer von Menschen-

To report the insignificant fact that "Heine and the Consequences" is in its third edition in seven years, after having been
circulated in *Die Fackel* as well, is not the motive for this supple-
ment.[1] The wish is to append something else, which likewise, in
the guise of a correction, allows the correctness of a deeper observation to be recognized for the first time.[2] Everything that's
said here, and in every chapter about the loss of life in contemporary life and the linguistic betrayal of German humanity, has a
train of thought leading to the brink of this war, thanks to which
my truths now also have the quality of self-evidence. An explanation is needed only at the point where, in my desperation to
escape the machine, I said that I preferred an already fully
dehumanized zone to that beauty-smitten thing that resisted
the relentless march of progress with the leftover wreckage of

1. "The funny thing here is that Kraus has gone from understating his
readership (in the first Afterword) to overstating it—this third edition he's talking about appeared six years earlier!" —PR
2. In other words: "I seem to be taking back what I said, but I'm not
really taking it back, because I was even more right than you knew!" To
read Kraus's foregoing "Afterword," you wouldn't imagine it "insignificant" that "Heine and the Consequences" has sold well in the interven-

tum entgegenstellte. In den später geschriebenen Aphorismen ist
die zum Krieg aufgebrochene Antithese zugunsten eben jener
Lebensform entschieden, als einer, welche die Sehnsucht nach
Leben und Form hatte und eben um solcher Sehnsucht, um
eines selbstretterischen Instinktes willen, die Notwehr gegen
die Tyrannei einer wertlosen Zweckhaftigkeit auf sich nehmen

---

ing six years. The imperiousness with which Kraus dismisses the fact
that he's found a lot of readers—after having insulted his audience and
drawn all manner of conclusions from the failure of his pamphlet to
find readers—is surely intended as a provocation. And yet this fact
really is insignificant compared with the two major self-contradictions
he's addressing in this "Final Word." In "Heine and the Consequences"
he declared his allegiance with German culture and his rejection of Romance culture, and he inveighed against politics, particularly liberal
politics; but now, as a result of the First World War, he's publicly rejecting Germany and aligning himself with its enemies, and he's coming to
side with the Socialists in their opposition to the war. He's got some
'splainin' to do.

Kehlmann adds: "Kraus's most alienating quality, for me at least,
was his absolute refusal ever to admit that he'd changed his mind. There
are lots of subjects on which he has completely different views before
the war and after, or in the late 1920s. But he can never admit it. Instead he heaps mockery and scorn on anybody who talks about his
changing opinions. The saddest case, for the Kraus admirer, was his attacks on the defenders of Dreyfus—and, worst of all, the downright
insane fact that he remained unwilling, even decades later, to admit
that Dreyfus was innocent and he'd been wrong."

I agree that this does not speak well of Kraus. His never-apologizing
moral certitude was one of the reasons I lost my taste for his work as
I moved out of my morally certain twenties and into my morally confused thirties. And the fact that he had more money than many of his
detractors, and used his inherited wealth to pursue expensive lawsuits
against them, darkens the picture even further.

humankind.[3] This antithesis, now broken open by the war, was resolved in later aphorisms in favor of precisely the latter life-form, as the one with a yearning for life and for form, which, on account of just such a yearning, and of a self-preservative instinct as well, was obliged to undertake emergency defense against the tyranny of a valueless utility, according to which life is finished

---

Reitter weighs in: "I'm of several minds about Kraus's no-apologies policy. Moral certitude is so much a part of his voice that it's hard even to imagine an apology-issuing Kraus—he'd be a fundamentally different writer. Or you could say that apologizing was inconsistent with Kraus's brand. For all his wisecracking and wordplay, Kraus fashioned himself, to no small degree, as a modern-day wrathful prophet. Amid all the moral rot, he was the eloquent, fulminating, incorruptible seer who gave his works titles like 'Apocalypse' and *Judgment Day*. And what kind of wrathful prophet figure goes around retracting his statements and expressing remorse?

"Kraus's policy was also a product of his off-the-charts competitiveness, and it no doubt functioned as a means of intimidation. All the literati in Kraus's orbit had been put on notice. If they went after Kraus, they would be getting into it with someone who would never back off or back down or take back anything. Ever. Feuding with Kraus was like stepping into the ring with Tyson in his prime. There was glory to be won, but would you survive?

"If you did survive, Kraus might have his (busy) lawyer Oskar Samek try to force an apology out of you in court. Kraus himself didn't have too much legal trouble, because he took care to play within the rules, meting out personal but permissible insults (like '*Geist* smeared on *Brod* is schmaltz,' in a squabble with Max Brod, whose last name is pronounced just like the German word for 'bread') and defending his weaker positions as passionately as his best ones. Maybe, then, the saddest thing about Kraus's refusal to retreat is the energy it cost him."

3. This refers to the opening paragraphs of "Heine and the Consequences," in which Kraus was plain about his preference for the "roaring of the German workday" to the beauty of life in Latin countries.

sollte, gemäß der das Leben Fertigware ist und die Kultur die Aufmachung. Denn es mußte die Frage, „in welcher Hölle *der Künstler* gebraten sein will", abdanken vor der zwingenden Entscheidung, daß *der Mensch* in dieser Hölle nicht gebraten sein will, durch die richtende Erkenntnis des Künstlers selbst, der nun nicht mehr das Recht und nicht mehr die Möglichkeit hat, die sichere Abschließung seines Innern zu suchen, sondern nur noch die Pflicht, zu sehen, welche Partie der Menschheit gleich ihm um die Erhaltung solchen Glückes kämpft und gegen den Zwang einer Lebensanschauung, die aus dem Leben alle Triebe gepreßt hat, um es einzig dem Betrieb zu erhalten. Daß es aber jene Regionen sind, von deren Wesensart in ruhiger Zeit die Störung kam, darüber sich einem Zweifel hinzugeben, wäre Kriegsverrat an der Natur, die sich der Maschine erwehrt. Sie tut's, und tue sie's auch mit Hilfe der Maschine, dem Künstler gleich, der die Betriebsmittel der Zeit nicht verschmäht hat, um ihr zu sich zu entfliehen. Er bejaht vor der Unvollkommenheit des Lebens den Lebensersatz und vor den halben Individualitäten das System des ganzen patentierten Persönlichkeitssparers. Der sich der Maschine bedient, gewinnt in dem

products and culture the trappings. The question "in which hell would *the artist* prefer to fry" gave way to the urgent verdict that *humanity* preferred not to fry in this hell, as a result of the corrective insight of the artist himself, who now no longer has the right and no longer the possibility of seeking to securely lock away his inner self, but only the duty of seeing which parties of mankind are struggling, like him, for the preservation of this kind of happiness and against the coercions of a philosophy of life that has squeezed all the motivations out of life, so as to save it solely for the profit motive. But the fact that those were the regions from whose character the disturbance came in peaceful times: to succumb to doubt about this would be wartime treason against the nature that is warding off the machine.[4] It does it; and it does it, if need be, with the help of the machine itself, like the artist who isn't above using the industrial methods of his times to preserve himself from them.[5] Faced with the imperfection of life, he affirms the substitute for life; faced with half individuals, he affirms the patented system for avoiding personalities entirely. The person who helps himself to the machine is rewarded to the

4. Our best guess about the word "nature" here is that it refers not to Nature but to Romance nature, Romance character—specifically, France and Italy. This helps make sense of the next sentence: France and Italy didn't invent the war machine, but to defend themselves against the inventor of it (Germany) they've resorted to war machines of their own. This also picks up on the sentence above it, the one about Romance culture undertaking "emergency defense" against Germany's mechanistic functionality.

5. Artists are still doing this. I know writers who use that computer software—I believe it's called Freedom—that denies them access to the Internet during working hours. I use noise-canceling headphones when it's loud at my office, and, for me, e-mail and digital voice mail are vital tools in restricting and managing the flood of communication that modern technology has unleashed.

Maße, als sie alle verlieren, die die Maschine bedienen. Denn diese macht den Menschen nicht frei, sondern zu ihrem Knecht, sie bringt ihn nicht zu ihm selbst, sondern unter die Kanone. Der Gedanke aber, der nicht wie die Macht eine „Neuorientierung" braucht, um sich am Ruder wieder zu finden, weiß: Er schuf sich nur den Notausgang aus dem Chaos des Friedens, und was an der Wertverteilung „deutsch-romanisch" widerspruchsvoll schien, war nur der Widerspruch des neuen Daseins gegen sich selbst, der heute ereignishaft seine Lösung erfährt. Die Auffassung, die den „Lazzaroni als Kulturideal neben dem deutschen Schutzmann" scheinbar nicht gelten lassen wollte, sie bestätigte ihn darin mehr als jene, die es – im Sinne des „Malerischen" – wollten und die die eigentlichen Deutschen sind. Das Wort vom „Schönheitsgesindel zwischen Paris und Palermo" mag nun auf jene Hunnenhorde der Bildung reflektieren, die an der Verwandlung von Lebenswerten in Sehenswürdigkeiten schuld ist. Was hier von der Sprache und dem

same extent that the people who help the machine are impoverished. Because the latter doesn't liberate a person but makes him its slave, it brings him not to himself but under artillery fire. However, the kind of thinking that, unlike power, doesn't need a "New Orientation"[6] to reestablish its command knows that it was merely creating an emergency exit from the chaos of peace, and that what seemed contradictory about the division of values into "German-Romance" was merely the internal contradiction of modern life, which is today being resolved by way of events.[7] The frame of reference that seemed unwilling to accept the "*lazzarone* as a cultural ideal alongside the German constable" thereby affirmed him more than the ones who were willing to accept the ideal—because it promised "picturesqueness"—and who are the real Germans. The phrase "beauty mongers from Paris to Palermo" may now apply to that horde of educated Huns who bear the blame for transforming the values of life into tourist attractions.[8] The thinking here about language and human

6. "'New Orientation' (*Neuorientierung*) was a slogan used by the Austrian government after Franz Joseph died, in 1916: Austria would be going in a new direction, though where it was headed wasn't clear."—PR
7. I.e., by the First World War, then in progress. This is also the "collapse" to which Kraus refers in the very difficult sentence below.
8. If I may very freely paraphrase: "Yes, you have to inspect your hotel bill carefully in Italy, but I've always rather liked the country, and if I got carried away with saying nasty things about Paris it was only because Heine was a celebrity there; I'm not a Romance philologist, the language I love is German, and if you thought my essay was an attack on Romance culture you completely misunderstood it; my real target was a modern Germanic culture that is founded on utility and greed and literal-mindedness and is therefore all the more grotesque in its smittenness with Romance culture, as evidenced especially in the language of German feuilletons. Now that we're seeing how much more

Menschen gedacht war, ist dem Typus, der tieferer Zwecklosigkeit nachhangend in der Sonne lungern kann, blutsverwandter als dem unerträglichen Eroberer eines Platzes an der Sonne, dessen Geistesart es freilich entsprochen hat, ein bunteres Dasein ornamental zu entehren und damit den Untergang zu beschönigen. In jenem geweihten Sinn, der die „basaltfreie" Ordnung und Zweckhaftigkeit wahrlich nur zu dem höheren Zwecke will, um ungestört die Schlösser und Wunder der Seele zu betreuen, mußte ich die Umgebung solches Warenpacks vorziehen, weil es die besten Instrumente abgab, um mir Ruhe vor einer lärmvollen Welt zu verschaffen, in der sie, nur weil sie keine Menschen mehr waren, selbst nicht mehr stören konnten. Aber die andern taten es, weil sie's halb waren. Es war mir einst zu wenig, und jetzt ist es doch so viel geworden. Und an dieses Problem, in welchem ganz ähnlich auch die Antithese Berlin-Wien zu Gunsten Wiens bereinigt wird, wirft der Zusammenbruch noch die Erkenntnis, daß gerade in der Sphäre der

---

horrific the German war machine is than its Latin counterparts, I'm asking you to believe that I showed more respect for the Romance cultural ideal by denouncing it than the Germans did by embracing it for their greedy, utilitarian purposes."

Kraus was at least attempting here to walk back the nationalistic implications of the Heine essay, to disavow its applicability to a repugnant wartime cult of Germanic purity and superiority. In *The Third Walpurgis Night*, fifteen years later, he wouldn't even mention that he himself, as a Jew, had once employed some of the antisemitic tropes with which the Nazis were justifying their violent program of purification. Maybe his longstanding indifference to history had come back to haunt him, or maybe, at some level too deep to be acknowledged, he was ashamed.

beings is more akin to the type who can laze around in the sun, wallowing in deeper aimlessness, than to the insufferable conqueror of a place in the sun, with whose way of thinking it was of course in keeping to ornamentally dishonor a more colorful existence and thereby beautify its own downfall. In that consecrated state of mind, which desires "basalt-free"[9] orderliness and utility truly only for the higher purpose of tending to the castles and marvels of the soul without being disturbed, I had no choice but to prefer the company of commercial scum like that, because they provided the best instruments for securing respite from a noisy world in which, only because they were no longer human beings, they themselves could no longer disturb me. The others did, however, because they were half human.[10] This used to be too little for me, and now it has ended up being so much. And this problem—in which, very similarly, the antithesis Berlin-Vienna is settled in favor of Vienna—is further illuminated by the collapse, which reveals that the entire contradiction was

9. "The 'consecrated' referent here is Goethe's 'America' poem, which begins: *'Amerika, du hast es besser / Als unser Kontinent, das alte / Hast keine verfallene Schlösser / Und keine Basalte'* ('America, you have it better / Than our continent, the old one / You have no decrepit castles / And no basalt'). Goethe regarded Europe's basalt deposits as scars, the marks of violent volcanic episodes, and for him they were symbols of instability, both past and present. America, which Goethe became enthusiastic about as an old man, seemed to have it, well, 'better.' His poem goes on to suggest that unlike Europeans, Americans aren't 'inwardly disturbed' by 'futile conflict' and 'unproductive memories.' With his talk of wanting 'basalt-free orderliness,' Kraus is invoking Goethe's outlook to clarify his own prewar priorities and preferences: he wanted external orderliness and functionality not for their own sake, but for the same higher reason Goethe did: because they allow one 'to tend to the castles and marvels of the soul.'"—PR
10. I.e., the French, the Italians.

Lebensmechanik der ganze Widerspruch selbst enthalten war. Daß es nicht allein um „deutsch-romanisch", sondern um „deutsch-weltlich" geht, zeigt sich, indem die bunte Welt auf Farbe dringt. Amerika, das es besser hat, und die Welt der alten Formen vereinigen sich, um mit einem Kunterbunt fertig zu werden, das von dort die Sachlichkeit, von da die Schönheit zusammenrafft und immerzu in der tödlichen Verbindung von Ware und Wert, in der furchtbaren Verwendung der alten Embleme für die neuen Realien durchzuhalten hofft. Der Angelsachse schützt seinen Zweck, der Romane seine Form gegen den Mischmasch, der das Mittel zum Zweck macht und die Form zum Vorwand. Da hier die Kunst nur Aufmachung ist; da diese Sachlichkeit, diese Ordnung, diese elende Fähigkeit zum Instrument einem auf Schritt und Tritt den Verlust an Menschentum offenbart, den es gekostet hat, um ein so entleertes Leben dem Volkstum zu erringen; da es selbst die Oberflächenwerte, für die alle Seelentiefe und alle Heiligkeit deutschen Sprachwerts preisgegeben wurde, im Zusammenstoß der Lebensrichtungen nicht mehr gibt; da der Deutsche eben doch kein Amerikaner war, sondern nur ein Amerikaner mit Basalten – so taugt der Zustand nicht mehr zum Ausgangspunkt der Phantasie. Weil sie Geist und Gott und Gift benützen, um das Geld zu erraffen, so wendet sie sich von den Entmenschten einem Schönheitswesen zu, das

situated squarely in the sphere of life's mechanization. That it's not a matter simply of "German/Romance" but of "Germany/world" is shown by the colorful world's insistence on its color.[11] America, where things are better, joins forces with the world of antique forms to finish off a higgledy-piggledy that scrapes together functionality from here and beauty from there and keeps hoping to muddle through with its deadly conflation of valuables and values, the frightful application of old emblems to new realities. The Anglo-Saxon defends his ends and the Latin his form against a mishmash that turns means into an end and form into a pretext. Since art here is merely trappings; since, everywhere you look, this literal-mindedness, this orderliness, this miserable facility with instruments reveals the loss of humanity it has cost to win for the populace a life so emptied out; since there are no longer even the superficial values for which all depth of soul and all the sacred value of the German language were sacrificed in the collision of two strains of life; since the German really wasn't an American at all, but merely an American with basalts— conditions here can no longer serve as a starting point for the imagination. Because they use Mind and God and gas[12] to gather gold, the imagination turns away from a dehumanized people and toward a beauty-smitten one, which defends its wreckage

11. A couple of very tough sentences here. What "colorful world" (a common colloquial phrase in German) is Kraus talking about? "My sense," Reitter says, "is that the world is the world outside Germany, which is defending its diversity (or color) against the onslaught of the great gray German war machine. With 'life's mechanization' (*Lebens-mechanik*), Kraus is underscoring what he saw as the mechanical or machinelike nature of Germans, something he often did during the First World War."

12. I.e., poison gas, in the trenches. The word "gold," which follows, is "money" (*Geld*) in the equally alliterative original.

gegen die unerbittliche Wut der Zeit seine Trümmer verteidigt. Auf der Flucht aus ihr habe ich Unrecht tun müssen. Die Partei der Menschenwürde habe ich nie verleugnet und jetzt, wo, ach, der Standpunkt erreicht ist, sie nehmen zu können, habe ich dem Weltgeist nichts abzubitten als die Schuld, in solcher Zeit geboren zu sein, und den Zwang, sichs auf der Flucht häuslich einzurichten.

against the inexorable fury of the times. In my flight from it, I was compelled to commit an injustice. I've never rejected the party of humane values, and now, when, oh, the standpoint has been reached where I'm able to side with it, I owe the world's Spirit an apology for nothing but the guilt of having been born in times like these, and for the necessity of making my home in the escape from them.

MAN FRAGE NICHT...

LET
NO ONE
ASK...

Man frage nicht, was all die Zeit ich machte.
Ich bleibe stumm;
und sage nicht, warum.
Und Stille gibt es, da die Erde krachte.
Kein Wort, das traf;
man spricht nur aus dem Schlaf.
Und träumt von einer Sonne, welche lachte.
Es geht vorbei;
nachher war's einerlei.
Das Wort entschlief, als jene Welt erwachte.

Let no one ask what I've been doing since I spoke.
I have nothing to say
and won't say why.
And there's stillness since the earth broke.
No word was right;
a man speaks only from his sleep at night.
And dreams of a sun that joked.
It passes; and later
it didn't matter.
The Word went under when that world awoke.[1]

---

1. I'm grateful to the gifted translators Damion Searls and Jonathan Galassi for their help in rendering this poem, and to Daniel Kehlmann for this short essay about it:

"'Let no one ask...' is a poem about appropriateness, the right word for the right occasion. For decades, Kraus had hounded stupid journalists, incorrect usage, bad usage, and everything else wrong with a late-feudal-bourgeois society stultified by the media. But now, suddenly, he was confronted with a phenomenon of an entirely different order, a thing more evil and horrifying than perhaps any the world had ever seen. In contrast to many of his contemporaries, Kraus recognized this circumstance immediately. He saw what was new about National

Socialism, he understood what Hitler was trying to do, and he was under no illusions that this all could end in anything but an epochal catastrophe.

"And so at first he wrote—nothing. There was no reaction from Karl Kraus to Hitler's seizure of power; month after month went by, and *Die Fackel* failed to appear. Kraus's admirers expected that he would eloquently attack Hitler, criticize him, condemn him, mock him, but instead: not a word. From today's standpoint, it seems easy to understand this silence as precisely the commentary whose failure to appear so appalled Kraus's readers. And yet it was simply not appropriate to take the same words and the same raging tone in which the *Neue Freie Presse*, Franz Lehár, and Max Reinhardt had been attacked and apply them to Goebbels, Göring, and Hitler, as if there were ultimately no difference between them. So Kraus remained silent, unshakably so, even as many of his followers turned away from him.

"All the while, as we now know, he was writing a lengthy book from which he would much later, in July 1934, print excerpts under the title 'Why *Die Fackel* Isn't Coming Out,' and which appeared in its entirety, as *The Third Walpurgis Night*, only posthumously (which also, by the way, ought to forever put to rest the idea that 'nobody could have known' from the outset how dangerous the Nazis were). But finally, in 1933, the year of the putsch—in late October, to be precise, nine months after Hitler became chancellor—one solitary issue of *Die Fackel* came out. It was four pages long, and it contained Kraus's obituary of his architect friend Adolf Loos (the great rationalist and enemy of baroque ornament), an advertisement for Kraus's own translation of Shakespeare's sonnets, and the poem 'Let no one ask...'

"The poem is about the powerlessness of words in the face of a development so dark as to have gone beyond the reach of satire. Kraus was never one of the great German lyric poets, except in this one moment. 'Let no one ask...' is far and away his best poem, a masterpiece of brevity and despair, its pathos immanent in its very laconicism. In a way, it remains Kraus's most important statement about National Socialism, artistically superior even to *The Third Walpurgis Night*, because it is so short. And we shouldn't forget that this isn't a matter of political

theory: Kraus fully expected that Austria wouldn't hold out for long (for this very reason, he supported the clerical-reactionary regime of the Austrian dictator Engelbert Dollfuß, whom he saw as the only politician fighting full-force against this danger), he had no illusions about the cruelty of the Nazis, he had to assume that as soon as they came to power in Austria they would either drive him into exile or kill him—which, if he hadn't been lucky enough to die of natural causes shortly before then, is exactly what would have happened. (Try to imagine how Kraus would have fared in exile, and it can't be done, even as theater of the absurd, it's just unthinkable.) 'Let no one ask...,' which was admired by Bertolt Brecht and Walter Benjamin, among others, is perhaps not the best but certainly one of the most important short poems of the twentieth century, a chilly masterpiece that gives voice to its own muteness. 'The Word went under when that world awoke': if it's even possible for silence to be rendered in words, Kraus succeeds in doing it here."

ACKNOWLEDGMENTS

Without the persistent encouragement of Paul Reitter and Daniel Kehlmann, I never would have embarked on this project. (They have no one but themselves to blame for how much work it turned out to be.) Paul is a model of the scholar dedicated to thought and careful research, and I'm indebted to him for sharing his deep knowledge of Kraus and his times, for patiently helping me solve many translation puzzles, for plunging whole-heartedly into the footnoting game, and for devoting a huge amount of energy to a book that doesn't even have his name on the front cover. I'm scarcely less indebted to Daniel for reading multiple drafts of the translations, for offering dozens of good suggestions and line edits, for saving both Paul and me from several embarrassing mistakes, and for bringing bold opinions to his footnotes and boundless enthusiasm to the project as a whole.

The copy editors Maxine Bartow and Mareike Grover did heroic work on what must have been a nightmare manuscript; Jonathan Galassi caught many infelicities in the translation and gently brought me to my senses at certain points where I'd lost

them; Henry Finder protectively argued me out of some rhetorical excesses and faulty analogies in the footnotes. Kathy Chetkovich, who knew nothing of Kraus, gave the manuscript a lay reading and reported on her characteristic effort to understand every sentence in it. In the early 1980s, my wife read the wretched first drafts of the translations and made suggestions that proved valuable nearly thirty years later. And George Avery not only introduced me to Kraus and commented minutely on the early drafts, he started me down the road of literature, from which everything has followed, including this book.